LIKELY TO SUCCEED

Most Likely To Succeed

Six Women from Harvard and What Became of Them

Fran Shumer

RANDOM HOUSE
NEW YORK

TO, FOR, AND OCCASIONALLY BY
KEVIN

ACKNOWLEDGMENTS

I would like to thank my editor, Jonathan Galassi, my family and my friends.

The individuals depicted in the following pages are composite figures, based on my observation of many friends and acquaintances, in college and elsewhere, across a number of years. Names, characteristics, locations and other significant details have been changed. My aim is not to offer a journalistic account of the period, but to tell a series of stories whose heart and soul are true.

Library of Congress Cataloging-in-Publication Data

Schumer, Fran.
Most likely to succeed.

1. Women college graduates—United States—Biography.
2. Harvard University—Alumni—Biography. I. Title.
HQ1412.S34 1987 378.744'4'0922 86-10129
ISBN 0-394-54324-6

Manufactured in the United States of America
23456789
First Edition

Typography and binding design
by Barbara M. Bachman

CONTENTS

PART ONE

Girls

1970–1974

In your dorm you meet many nice people. Some are smarter than you. And some, you notice, are dumber than you. You will continue, unfortunately, to view the world in exactly these terms for the rest of your life.

—LORRIE MOORE, *Self-Help*

CHAPTER 1

Freshmen

Smash Separate But Equal
—SIGN ABOVE GIRLS' BATHROOM

It was a small room, two beds and a desk, with a lamp for either girl. There was a trunk and an abundance of tartan plaid skirts on the bed. It was apparent that someone had moved in but she was gone, so I had yet to discover who my roommate would be. I knew two things about her, from a letter the college had mailed to me during the summer: her name (Kate Mallarkin) and where she was from (Northbrook, Illinois); and from those two facts I had spun the most incredible tales. Kate Mallarkin had blond hair and had grown up in Paris. Kate Mallarkin was a deep and pensive brunette who was fluent in ancient Greek. Kate Mallarkin had short, curly red hair that some people said was as fiery as her soul.

In truth, Kate Mallarkin was short and wan and her hair was as nondescript as the rest of her, except for her broad, flat Chicago accent that determined the way she said my name. "Free-an." I thought it was the most disgusting sound I had ever heard. "Do you like science fiction?" she asked. "No," I said in a way that indicated I disapproved of it as well. We would not be friends, that much was clear.

Before she left the room, her mother took my mother aside and asked if I would mind taking Kate under my wing as I appeared to be a sociable girl. My mother conveyed this to me, but as there was a fairly flawless system of communication between us she added, "Try not to be disappointed. You'll meet other girls."

I met them all, en masse, at a tea that afternoon. I was verging on anorexia, so I noticed only the food—tiny finger sandwiches filled with unidentifiable paste, expensive bakery butter cookies and tiny iced cakes. The women interested me less. One was engaged in conversation with a professor whose name, according to the red-rimmed tag stuck to his lapel, was David Riesman. "You worked in a bakery?" Professor Riesman asked. "No, I didn't 'work' in a bakery," said the woman, who had white-blond hair and wore tasseled golf shoes. "I 'opened' one, on a little island off the coast of Maine." "How enterprising of you." "Not really," she said, and went on, as if she had lived her whole life knowing that one day it would all appear on her résumé.

It was one of a hundred conversations I heard that day about teaching children in Africa, living in a Mongolian yurt or working for a candidate in whom one truly believed. No one at the tea had lain on the beach that summer and perfected her tan.

"DON'T you want to be a pioneer and go to Princeton?" my father asked the day the admissions notices arrived in the mail. Princeton and Yale were admitting their second class of female freshmen and my father thought it would be exciting to send his daughter there. I had no interest in making history. New Haven had seemed dull the weekend I visited it, even with the Black Panthers staging their May Day rally, and Princeton was too much like a country club. But my older brother had gone to Harvard and I endowed everything he did with a certain mystique. I had visited Cambridge and liked what I had seen. It was electric—so many young people concentrated in one place.

My father stopped my mother on the street: not only was the woman we had just passed wearing no bra but her nipples stuck through the weave of her loosely crocheted shirt. "Abe." My mother grabbed my father's arm. "For that you'd send your daughter to Radcliffe?"

"Radcliffe": even the name had a curious and jagged edge, not gentle and flowing on the tongue like Wellesley, or prim and businesslike like Smith. Radcliffe sounded dark and sardonic, brooding, like Heathcliff or some other romantic "difficult" soul. Radcliffe had a reputation for attracting brooding difficult girls, a stereotype partially encouraged by the college itself. Other catalogues pictured women dressing up for mixers or picking flowers by a lake; Radcliffe's brochure featured a somber woman looking somewhat aloof as she lugged her book bag up the steps of Widener Library. She seemed to symbolize the credo we would hold there: "A pox on happiness," a friend of mine put it. "Intelligence matters more."

THE rumor was that we were smarter than the boys. Harvard men were chosen by the Harvard Admissions Committee, which supposedly sought a "diverse student body." (In practice, that translated into better football teams and more sons of alumni.) But the Radcliffe classes, still chosen by the Radcliffe Admissions Committee, even after coeducation, were depressingly "pure," a conglomeration of women whose grades were too high and aptitude scores too good; at sixteen or eighteen, they were already so accomplished that you knew something was wrong.

They showed up accomplished but left Radcliffe disabled. It was a well-known paradox that Radcliffe women, ten, fifteen or twenty years after graduation, did not achieve as much as one might expect. There were famous exceptions, like Gertrude Stein and Adrienne Rich, but by and large Radcliffe women had performed less well than women from other colleges, particularly

Wellesley, Smith and other all-female schools.* Some people blamed Harvard: Radcliffe women shared classes with Harvard men and very likely were intimidated by them. Or, as eighty percent of Radcliffe women eventually married Harvard men, perhaps "distracted" was the more appropriate term. But these explanations seemed only partially true. There was such a thing as a tyranny of intelligence and it seemed to affect women more than men. The first week someone pointed out the daughter of a famous novelist in one of my classes who looked older than we did, twenty-eight, perhaps. It was whispered that she had had two nervous breakdowns and was now back at Radcliffe for a third time.

The stories of those who cracked were matched by tales of those who had escaped. (And these excited us, with their hint of rebellion, for which of us very studious girls was not secretly dying to rebel?) My favorite was the one about the Radcliffe student who was now a topless dancer at the Metropole Cafe in Times Square. She couldn't take the pressure, people said. Yet the pressure was not generated by the college; it was self-imposed. "Womanitis," my older brother called it, a curious malady that seemed to afflict women in inverse proportion to their gifts: "The brighter they are, the dumber they feel." Orientation week one of the deans reminded us that every year a few students inevitably prove to be Admissions Committee "mistakes"—students who just can't keep pace with all the work. The men made a big joke of it, clowning around and calling each other "the mistake." But none of the very bright women sitting around me could even conceive of this as a joke. Secretly, each of us feared she was it.

ORIENTATION week, they called those first days that dragged on interminably as we waited for the upperclassmen to arrive. Actu-

*Vivian Gornick, "Why Radcliffe Women Are Afraid of Success," *The New York Times Magazine*, January 14, 1973, p. 10.

ally, it was disorienting to have all that time on your hands and nothing to do. You were given a little map in your packet of orientation week materials and a guide through Harvard Square. Other roommates skipped merrily to the Sears Roebuck in Porter Square, and like newlyweds, began cultivating a relationship based on the careful selection of dormitory furnishings. Kate and I did not venture so far. She sat on her bed and watched me, while I tried to spend as little time as possible in the room.

It was necessary to make curtains. I did not know how to sew and neither did Kate. It would have been simpler to buy ready-made ones, but the possibility did not occur to me, and Kate wasn't accustomed to taking the lead. Instead, we bought a few yards of blue felt. It looked pretty enough on the bolt in the fabric store, but when held up to light its effect was grim: the material looked mottled and blotchy and hardly let in any light. Even the sunniest mornings looked like four o'clock on a winter afternoon.

With some urgency I set out to find a friend, but I did not like the women on my floor. They struck me as silly, the way they galloped in a herd, always checking their watches, arranging when and where to meet for their little outings in Harvard Square. If my choice was to trot about with them or stay home alone, I preferred to stay alone. But Kate's mother was right: I was sociable and could not last long without a friend.

Who's to say why a certain woman appeals to you? Is it a shared sensibility conveyed in a glance? Kate's blank face conveyed nothing. But by the end of the week I had met Daisy. A silly name for such an intelligent girl, although it was appropriate in some ways because she was so sunny, always flashing an insouciant smile that was just the slightest bit wry. She was not like the flower so much as a weed, joyful and irrepressible, who appeared to have just sprung up in someone's otherwise carefully tended garden. But what a pretty weed Daisy was, tall and slightly gawky (but many of us were then; even at eighteen our knobby parts hadn't yet rounded into curves). She had hair the color of strongly brewed tea and a nose that was the slightest bit wide (there was something Russian about the way it flattened out). Still, it was the eyes that made her face, smiling blue eyes with tiny hen's feet even then, because Daisy laughed so much. She always looked as if someone had just told a joke, and only she had caught its humor. As I said, there was something wry about her smile.

We met early one morning because we were both so nervous that neither of us could sleep. Daisy didn't get along with her roommate either, so we shared a little joke about them. Mine was The Fish and hers was The Pig. We were nasty, but then her roommate, a graduate of the Bronx High School of Science, did bear an astonishing resemblance to that animal and, besides, we disliked her so much we didn't care. The Pig was the parody of the female genius every woman hopes not to be. If her opening line to Daisy was not, "I got eight hundred on my college boards, what were your scores?" it was something close.

Since it was unthinkable for either of us to form an alliance with her roommate, we formed one of our own, dubbing ourselves a couplet of "bubbies." *Bubbie* is the Yiddish word for grandmother, but we used it to mean "friend," though even "friend" could hardly convey the depths of loyalty the term came to imply for us.

I'll never forget the stories Daisy told me then. They concerned her family. She was everything to them and if they erred, it was in loving her too much. Perhaps this was because she was an only child. Perhaps it was part of a more general frustration. The hunger in Harvard students for high grades, for prestige, for success was very often the unexpressed talent or energy or desire of a parent, usually a mother. Daisy's mother had stayed home and raised her only child. Her husband earned enough money as an executive for a prominent manufacturing firm so that there was no need for her to work. Her main interests were Daisy and her garden, and since the gardening season in Minnesota is short, she occupied herself mostly with Daisy's accomplishments, which, by age sixteen, were already vast.

Unlike most of the rest of us, Daisy had not wanted to go to Radcliffe. Though she was a star in high school (voted "Most Likely to Succeed" by her class), she was afraid that at Radcliffe she would be overwhelmed. She wanted to go to the University of Minnesota but her parents discouraged her. They said it was a question of character and that Daisy would feel better about herself for making the harder choice. Daisy finally convinced them to let her have it her way, but just as she was about to send off her apologies to Radcliffe she changed her mind and checked off the box marked "Yes." So here we were, sitting in our Lanz nightgowns, hugging our knees in the corridors of Holmes Hall in the middle of the night.

I would have liked to spend more time with Daisy but we had different tastes. She liked to troop around with the herd of women I disdained. I'd say to her, "Daisy, come take a walk with me to find some books in Harvard Square," and she'd answer "Okay," but two minutes later, with a combination of distress and enthusiasm on her face, she'd return to say, "Bubbie, guess what! Sally and Ann are going down to the Coop. Why don't we join them?" "Let's go ourselves," I would retort. "Well, I already told them I'd be coming," she'd reply and gallop off. I don't think she liked me any the less; it was just that, during that year, for security's sake, she wanted to adhere to the group. And she had befriended its leader, a tall pretty redhead named Maureen, whom I did not like.

Not that I was unimpressed with Maureen. That first week she seemed to emerge quite naturally as the leader of the women on our floor, with her black patent-leather boots and nubby gray suit, bucking at the head of the galloping herd. She told me the first week, when all of us admitted to sky-high ambitions, that she was interested in going into politics, and one could easily imagine her in that arena—one smile worth a thousand votes.

Her family lived in a small town in southern New Hampshire, and during our first weekend at school she invited everyone out to their large white colonial house set against a backdrop of hills. I was prepared not to like her or her family, with their American flag on the lawn and diplomas on the walls, but they were charming hosts. Maureen's father showed us his rock collection and her mother fed us hot dogs and Cokes. Before we left, Maureen's two brothers, big burly youths, each of whom had been president of his high school class and captain of a varsity team, sat down at the piano and played Broadway tunes. They were hard to resist.

Like them, Maureen had been president of her high school class, but she had surpassed her brothers in sports. She was superior in almost every athletic pursuit, and when I saw a picture of her clipped from the local paper, her face burning with sweat, her hockey stick cocked for a swing, even I had to admit she was beautiful. Not that her features were perfect in the classical sense: the eyes tended to narrow and the nose was a little too long. But she had the confident looks of a winner.

And losers be damned. She was not cynical except about people who were. Once I heard her make a disparaging remark about demonstrators. She said that if people were unhappy it was probably their own fault. "How can you like her?" I asked Daisy later that week. Daisy had observed the same little flaws in Maureen but somehow that did not prevent the two of them from being friends. So if I saw Daisy with Maureen, I learned to walk the other way.

HARVARD College instituted coeducational dormitories in the spring of 1970. The women were welcomed heartily down at Harvard, but the first batch of male recruits enlisted to live in the Radcliffe dorms were made fun of. People called them wimps and worse, accusing them of moving up to Radcliffe because down in the more competitive atmosphere of Harvard they couldn't get dates. By the time we arrived at Radcliffe, the experiment had already entered its second phase, but we were freshmen and the men who had trouble getting dates turned their attentions on us.

The first day I saw him, riding the elevator alone. By the next day, it seemed, she was constantly at his side. He was tall and pimply, slovenly in his T-shirt and jeans. She was sweet and pretty, with a kittenlike nose. A freshman, she had not yet made the transition from skirts to jeans, from hometown comeliness to Cambridge sloth. I never got to know their names, but that wasn't the point; I viewed them as a symbol of what coeducation meant —a raw deal for women and a gold mine for men.

Practically overnight the rules had changed. Five years earlier men had been required to wear jackets and ties in the dining halls, and women weren't allowed in the undergraduate library in Harvard Yard. Now mattresses were pushed together on the floors and even the toilets were co-ed. I was going to the bathroom down the hall from my room when I noticed the person in the stall next to mine had her feet facing the wrong way. It took me a minute to realize "she" was a "he." "Smash Separate But Equal," a sign above the "ladies' " room said in the telegraphic language of the "Movement." What an anachronism the Radcliffe dorms now seemed, with their genteel "sitting rooms" and satin settees. Now the parlors lay idle, like period rooms cordoned off in a museum. Some women were indifferent to the presence of men; most were not. Many, liberated from four years at an all-girls boarding school, embraced the idea of living with men and quickly coupled off. You saw pairs lumber into the dining hall in their bathrobes with hair that was ostentatiously wet, a sign that they had just taken a shower and probably just made love. Was everyone making love all the time? Probably not, but if you were not, you were suspicious that everyone else might be.

A study in one of the psychology courses of the early days of cohabitation found that rather than increase sexual activity in the dormitories, the presence of men actually had a dampening effect, what they called the "incest taboo": You slept with men you dated, but were friends with the ones in your dormitory. But this research must have been done in other dormitories, for in ours there was considerable carrying-on, and the walls weren't very thick. A girl who lived downstairs from me was going with the president of a staunchly anti-Soviet group, who, in the height of passion, would let out a piercing Hungarian Freedom Fighters' cry.

Vladimir sounded like a more interesting roommate than Kate, but the housing office had reserved one all-female corridor for women who did not feel comfortable living with men. I did not know that I would be living on the all-female floor until I arrived at school and then I had to plumb my memory for the explanation. During the summer the housing office had mailed us detailed questionnaires in which we were asked if we minded a roommate who: smoked, smoked dope, had men in her room, had men in her bed, drank. I thought "No" but marked off "Yes." It would be more prudent to err on the conservative side, my mother advised. My reward was the nunnery and now I understood why my roommate was Kate.

Not that I languished without male attention freshman year. I was struggling with my trunk when a man with an irritatingly nasal voice asked, "Can I help?" "No," I snapped. He wrested one end of the trunk away from me anyway and directed his roommates to pick up the other. It bothered me that he had ignored my "no," but it was more infuriating that he seemed to feel this was my way of being coy, which it wasn't: I simply didn't want his help. He introduced himself as David Benson, from the South Side of Chicago. His heroes were Ho Chi Minh and Mayor Richard Daley, facts he seemed to feel important that I know. That he was very handsome, tall and blond did not lodge itself in my consciousness then. I noticed only a certain wildness about the eyes.

It is not so much that he befriended me as that he imposed

himself on me, from the first day. He had seen my picture in the "pig book," officially the *Radcliffe Freshman Register.* Every year the men at Harvard would comb through the book and, on the basis of the pictures the women had sent in, rate their looks; hence the name "pig." (It too became a casualty of the women's movement. In later years the pictures of the freshman men and women were displayed in the same book, so the practice became less offensive.) My picture was a flattering one, but then I had been forewarned. My older brother said this would very likely be the key to my social life, so my mother and I, not so liberated as we were eager for me to meet men, took his warning as valuable information and set about to create the prettiest picture we could. I spent two hours working on my hair the night before, sleeping on painfully large rollers fashioned out of Campbell's soup cans (straight hair was very fashionable just then), and applied the tiniest bit of eyeliner the next morning, as I didn't want to appear too made up. Then we drove to Avalon Studios on Kings Highway and there, in a roomful of pictures of brides and bar mitzvah boys, I sat for my portrait. My brother approved, and I mailed the picture off to the registrar.

The disadvantage of having a flattering portrait in the "pig" book was that you were besieged by callers from Harvard. Although that had been the original idea, you envisioned handsome callers like Ryan O'Neal (*Love Story* had come out the previous year). What you had in reality was a collection of bold, impolite, vulgar, shy and sometimes boorish men—boys, in other words. But then we were girls.

"Where'd you get your picture taken, at a professional photography studio?" David sneered.

"No," I replied, wanting to appear nonchalant. "My Uncle Shelly took it."

He laughed because it was so obvious a fib. I was willing to talk to him then, for there is something appealing about a man you cannot lie to.

Why did he love me, or persuade himself that he did, when the only things he knew about me were that I was from Brooklyn and belligerent? It never made sense, which is why I always felt he was in love with the image of a woman I was not. It may have been that he was lonely; a lot of freshmen were. Or that he was disoriented. He was on scholarship and most of his classmates were not, although with David this always seemed to be a matter of pride. He boasted of his proletarian origins (such as they were; his father taught school). It may even have been that he really loved me. But this crazed pursuit did not feel like love.

What were his reasons? First, he liked that I was from Brooklyn. "Too many rich kids at this school anyway," he'd say. "I'm from a neighborhood not so different from yours, South Side Chicago." It was considered a handicap to be rich or middle class in those days, so that often when you asked people where they were from, first they would say "Chicago" or "Detroit," and only upon further interrogation admit that they were from the outlying suburbs, like Winnetka or Bloomfield Hills. It was status to be poor, and David believed I was. This game of proletarian one-upmanship was partly my fault. My classmates seemed so impressed that I was from Brooklyn, my father was an exterminator and I had gone to a large, urban public high school that I did not try to elaborate that I had grown up in a comfortable section of Flatbush, my father owned his exterminating business, and although I had graduated from James Madison High School, I was isolated in an honors track as exclusive as many private schools. I played the game but then everyone did. We were still under the spell of the sixties, which we had missed by only a year, and believed it was important to be "political," synonymous with being "left," and it was honorable to be poor. A professor in my radical economics course ("Contradictions of Capitalism") spent an entire lecture justifying the fact that he had a summer house in Maine. (It enabled him to endure the stresses of the capitalist system, he said.)

David's second reason was that I was indifferent to him and he loved fighting injustice, which he believed my indifference toward him to be. I did not like the way he made such a fetish of his—or my—being poor. My reaction to his sweeping generalizations was to rebut them, but David liked a woman who answered back. Once I met him with two of his roommates—Henry Wong, who was Chinese, and Marcus Tebbitts, who was black. David had told me so often about his fraternal ties to people of all different backgrounds that I was provoked to make some terrifically obnoxious comment like, "Well what have we here, a poster for National Brotherhood Week?" He smacked his forehead with his hand and said, "Oh God," a gesture that suggested both pleasure and pain. He was in for trouble and he relished the thought. I asked him to leave and when he did not I made a great commotion, all of which my roommate Kate observed from her sentinel post by the bed. She had not turned a page of her science fiction book since the moment David walked into the room; at least Kate, for a change, seemed to be having fun.

THIS was only the beginning of David's campaign, which lasted through the fall. As he had a way of making a great stir about things, his quest soon became legend in Harvard Yard. Often I would introduce myself to strangers, and just as I said my name a look of recognition would brighten their faces and they would say, "So you're the famous Fran," which was flattering in a way. From their various accounts, I learned that each night, when enough beer had been drunk, my name was bellowed out into the eventide of Harvard Yard: "Fran, why are you doing this to me? Why won't you go out with me?" And other freshmen in the dormitories surrounding Holworthy Hall would open their windows and join in one long commiserative howl—for which of these boys had not known the experience of being spurned?

The campaign escalated as Christmas approached. He called me all the time. "Is Fran home?" "No," my roommate would answer. Kate was enough of a sport to lie even when I had not asked her to. "She's away with friends for the weekend," she would say while I lay cringing on my bed. Phone messages would greet me whenever I returned to the room, and when they did not provoke a response, he resorted to verbal assaults. "Fran, David is looking for you," his friends would call out to me on the street. I wondered if the grin on their faces didn't suggest a little complicity, as if they too knew he was just a little mad. But they divulged nothing. "He said he'll see you at eight," as if his getting the message to me implied my tacit consent. Then there were the major onslaughts (more calls, more notes, accidental "meetings" in Harvard Square) and these multiplied throughout the fall until they reached a peak during the Thanksgiving break. He hitchhiked, on a blustery winter night, to my parents' house in Brooklyn just so he could return and describe its exterior to me. When I failed to be impressed (I was only annoyed, as at that point I truly wished he would leave me alone), he grew enraged.

"You don't live in any poor 'hood," he told me. (He spoke a kind of improvised black dialect: "hood" for neighborhood, "lid" for hat, "square" for cigarette.)

"I never said I did," I answered, but I had, and so for the second time was caught in a lie and for the second time felt a glimmer of affection for him.

BUT I was too distracted for David or for anyone else that term. It was not what I had expected, not David, not the men, not the college, not any of it. Had I been asked to say exactly what was wrong, I might have pointed to my roommate (The Fish) or my room (it was barren and dark, thanks to those hideous blue curtains), but the problem was all of this and more. Cruelly, my mother's refrain about her college years played in my head. She was so happy, a young girl having a first taste of independence.

She had walked twenty blocks from her house to college, not so far that she couldn't come home for lunch; I took an Eastern Airlines shuttle that transported me into another world in which I watched myself acting absurd. "You mean it passes?" I asked a friend of my older brother's, a senior with whom he had fixed me up. "It passes," he said. The first week of his freshman year he had bought and returned a coat to the Harvard Coop, "six times," he admitted, because the pressure of making a decision was too great.

I knew what he meant. Even by the second month of school, I had had fantasies of being in the army just so someone would tell me what to do. There were no rules at Harvard, which was drifting through an era of academic laissez-faire. Virtually nothing was required of us except that we learn how to swim, a condition of the legacy bequeathed to Harvard on behalf of Harry Elkins Widener, who had drowned aboard the *Titanic* because he could not. And that we did nude. Perhaps students from private schools were used to more freedom. At James Madison, I had been handed a schedule that dictated what I would do from the moment I entered its ironclad doors (whose outer handles had been removed to prevent students from leaving or entering at will) until evening, when, after piano practice and homework, I collapsed into bed.

"Are you at least having a decent social life?" my mother asked. "Not really," I answered. "Selma, tell her to 'put out,' " my father chimed in. "Abe!" my mother screamed and quickly hung up.

During Christmas vacation my mother drove me to knitting stores. A few women in my dormitory crocheted and my mother thought it might calm my frazzled nerves. I produced six lumpy squares for the black shawl I was going to make, but it didn't help. Schoolwork wasn't the problem. The joke was that the only thing harder than getting into Harvard and Radcliffe was flunking out. It was possible to take a complete semester of "guts" (easy courses) and emerge with passable grades. Among the more popular ones: Natural Sciences 8 ("Physics for Poets"); Geology 10 ("Rocks for Jocks"); Abnormal Psychology ("Nuts and Sluts"); The Psychology of Small Groups ("Patty Cake") and Moral Dilemmas in Nazi Germany ("Krauts and Doubts"). The easy Fine Arts course that featured a slide show every day was called "Darkness at Noon." Very quickly one detected the many holes in the teaching system, in which graduate students carried most of the workload. I received an A on one of my earliest exams, which made me and the graduate student who graded it even. I hadn't read the book and he obviously hadn't read my exam. More work, or more challenging work, might have filled the hours but would not have helped my emotional state. I had trouble with papers, which I wrote in a nervous frenzy, one messy draft that I could not bear to reread. My habit of pulling out my hair became so extreme that one evening I left an entire set of eyebrows on my desk. During Thanksgiving my eighty-five-year-old grandfather asked me what I thought about the book I was carrying under my arm, *Suicide,* by the French sociologist Emile Durkheim. "Ah, Durkheim," he sighed. My grandfather had not completed the eighth grade but had taught himself English by attending the free lectures at The Cooper Union at night. "So what do you think of Durkheim?" he asked. I muttered something and stumbled embarrassed out of the room. I had read the book only the previous week but could not remember anything that it said.

IT was in this state that I entered the Harvard *Crimson*'s quaint Georgian brick headquarters at 14 Plimpton Street. I walked into its messy paper-littered offices, redolent of cigarettes and printer's ink, not because I wanted to write but because I was eager for something to do. The *Crimson* was among the few college papers that were financially independent of their affiliated institutions. Perhaps that was why it was able to get away with its politics, which were often somewhere to the left of Peking. (In 1969 the *Crimson* made headlines in Paris for supporting Ho Chi Minh's National Liberation Front.) That the *Crimson* was more professional than other student dailies was the opinion of its staff, but university officials, whose comments were quoted (or "misquoted") or who were the frequent target of its barbs, felt differently. In later years Daniel Steiner, the university's legal counsel, once asked what I was doing with my life. "Writing fiction," I said. "You must have gotten plenty of practice for that at the *Crimson*," he replied.

Anyone could write for the *Crimson,* provided he survived a grueling seven-week tryout known as the "comp" (short for "competition"). Candidates were given a "news lead" and seven hours to pursue it. The atmosphere was tense. There was an "open" book (that is, open to public view), in which one's work was appraised (from "v-v-strong," which, in *Crimson* jargon, meant "very very strong," to "v-v-poor"), and a "closed" book, whose comments took into consideration more than just a candidate's prose: "Nice legs but no tits. Too bad." In later years the closed book was banished to a scrap heap upstairs, but certain remnants of the attitude prevailed. When I was a junior I worked for a cool, blond editor who did not like my articles. "She's not so great, she speaks with a phony Southern accent" (I had just returned from a summer down South and had picked up a little twang) and furthermore, "she doesn't even have nice legs."

Neither my legs nor I made it past the third week of freshman comp. Strange-looking men in World War II aviator jackets handed me assignments and I froze. I often worked through dinner and had to grab a bite at Bartley's Burger Cottage around the block, but my stomach was a mess and the combination of all that acid and Bartley's grease gave me a terrible case of the runs. I spent most of my freshman comp in the *Crimson* ladies' room, where even the graffiti intimidated me, they were so wickedly good.

It was a relief then to get out into the frosty night air and make the ten-block journey back to Radcliffe. My route cut through the Brattle Street area, one of the prettiest neighborhoods in Cambridge, where many of the Harvard professors live. The houses were so lovely and I was so homesick. Their cozy interiors —the sliver of life I caught between window ledge and shade— called to me. Often I imagined myself knocking on the door of one of them and inviting myself inside. But first I had to cross the Cambridge Common, a habitat of lost souls. These were not the healthy faces of my Harvard classmates, the brisk night air painting color on their cheeks, but the faces of hippies and flower children left over from the sixties who haunted the premises at night, hollow-cheeked and toothless wraiths, their stringy hair alive with nits, their eyes burned out by drugs. I felt then more strongly than I had ever felt in my life the desire to go home. I walked hastily to the other end of the cold barren common, which, in spring, sprouts not grass but mud. Even cheerless Radcliffe seemed to beckon.

RADCLIFFE took one other girl from my high school freshman year. Her name was Miranda Fine and she had golden curly hair and crystalline blue eyes. I deserted her after only five months, but if Miranda were telling this story she would insist it was she who deserted me.

Radcliffe did not take many girls from James Madison. It drew its New York contingent mainly from private schools in Manhattan, like Brearley and Dalton. The headmistress at Brearley once asked all the girls in the school who were applying to Radcliffe to walk to one side of the gym. Half the room shifted over. At

Madison, only a few women applied to Radcliffe every year and fewer got in.

The private school women were learned, worldly and gloriously bored. They were veterans of extensive therapy and discussed their psychic selves as if they were analyzing characters in a play. What was most astounding was the matter-of-fact way in which they discussed their own malaise. "Fucked up? Of course I'm fucked up. My father's been in analysis for years." One girl said she had been seeing a psychiatrist since she was eight. It only dawned on me, when I shared a lift home with her during Christmas vacation and saw that she lived on Central Park West, how backward I was. To be in analysis and live on Central Park West: that was class.

Women from Brooklyn were a different breed; there were fewer of us, and we were mainly products of the public schools, which meant we were geniuses in such *Sputnik*-generation staples as science and math and ignorant of almost everything else. "Grade grubbers," they called us. But then it took high grades to draw the attention of the Admissions Committee to the public schools. My year was exceptional, for both Miranda and I were tapped.

Our mothers had been roommates at college. They were placed together by accident and lived together for less than a year, but still my mother talked about Ruth. "I'm just a housewife," she would say, "but Ruth, now there's an interesting girl." I thought it was odd. My mother made such a fuss about my wearing nice clothes and keeping a neat house, and yet the women she admired did none of these things. Ruth was indifferent about clothing and her house was not the decorator's showcase that ours was. Unlike most of my mother's friends, she had not gotten married immediately after college but had worked for a time as an economist in Washington. But it was not her accomplishments that caused her name to be praised so often in our house. I believe my mother loved Ruth for her character. She was noble, self-effacing, and her intelligence was softened and lent depth by compassion.

As I later learned from Miranda, a reciprocal admiration was expressed in her house. Ruth felt inadequate when she compared herself to my mother, who was envied or admired for the cheerful efficiency with which she ran a house. "Selma always looks so lovely, and is so good at making people feel at home," Ruth would say. I can just hear my mother laughing, deflecting Ruth's praise. And so Miranda and I acquired not merely our mothers' talents—Miranda's scholarly abilities and my more social skills—but the habit of admiring in one another what we ourselves did not have.

We were in the same honors track in high school but, as Miranda took Spanish and I took French, our schedules rarely overlapped. People said she was very smart, and when they found out we were both applying to Radcliffe they took bets as to which of us would get in. It was to Miranda's credit that we did not compete with each other during that year. On the one occasion when the subject arose, she walked up to me, warmly shook my hand and said, "It will be so nice if Radcliffe takes both of us. Then we'll each start college with a friend."

We had our first real chance to talk two weeks before we were due to arrive up at school, at the freshman tea organized by the Radcliffe Club of New York. I was delighted to meet my prospective classmates, all of whom I thought were beautiful, especially the ones my mother regarded as strange. "Did you see that one with the big ugly glasses [this was before tortoiseshell rims were in style] and the wild bushy hair?" But Miranda told me she had felt forebodings even then. She felt immature and more graceless than the other women we met. There had been signs, she said, in high school. Other girls seemed to have a poise that she lacked. She could never dress right or fix her hair. I hardly knew her, but even looking at her I saw it wasn't true. She had deep blue eyes and a mass of frizzy blond curls that settled easily about her like a billowing cloud.

At first I was bent upon the notion of making new friends and did not look her up. But after those first few difficult weeks at Radcliffe, when I saw I was not as happy as I had expected to be, I went to find her. She lived in a dormitory across a road from mine, the most modern of the Radcliffe houses, made of brick and glass. It had an enchanting mound of greenery in the center of its dining room, and through the trees I used to look out over the tables for her. We were uneasy friends because we did not know each other that well, but she presumed with me a familiarity that drew me to her room. "Franny," she said, and I liked people who called me by that name. "How could *you* be upset?"

We dispensed with the civilities quickly. "You're not happy here?" I asked her. "Neither am I."

Miranda's problems were different from mine. I blamed Radcliffe; for me the problem was "out there," but Miranda viewed her surroundings with a much more tolerant eye. She took easily to the work and had much more evenhanded opinions of the people we met. Even David, whom she knew through his repeated assaults on me, did not appear to her so hateful but only "crazy" and "a little immature." Her moods, then, seemed influenced by other things and I did not understand them. She said she had been depressed before and that she knew sooner or later she would have to face up to the problems she had. At first I thought it was so much talk.

But even I could see, after those first difficult months at Radcliffe, that she was right, that she had problems other women did not have. She would get "upset" and when she was "upset," her eyes would tear and she could not eat. What I admired then was her persistence. I would rationalize: "Everyone has difficulty adjusting freshman year," I would tell her. "You'll see. You'll feel better soon enough." But Miranda insisted there was something wrong. In this, as in everything, she was honest and stubborn, to a self-defeating extent. She analyzed everything she did and in the process of observing her own demise, hastened it.

Miranda had frequent upsetting attacks of nerves; she would cry and shake. These stopped as inexplicably as they began. Someone would broach a totally unrelated topic and Miranda, who might have just been weeping to me, would suddenly talk as if nothing was wrong. She spoke then in the soft and compelling manner that had originally drawn me to her. As long as she was not talking about herself, she was intelligent, confident and calm.

When my words did not help (perhaps they were part of the problem) she went to talk to one of the deans. The dean kept interrupting the conversation to talk to her French poodle, who was stationed in the room. She was of the older generation of Radcliffe administrators, eccentric and somewhat difficult to reach, but she was also wise. "The trouble with a school like Radcliffe," she noted, "is that it attracts so many bright introspective women, who all go around talking about their problems and this has an amplifying effect." But this did not help Miranda, who sat in the dining room and pulled at her hair, which, when she was feeling poorly, she did not wash.

Her attacks of anxiety worsened as winter approached. For longer periods she did not eat. Slowly, I began to abrogate our friendship. By now both of us saw that we weren't helping but rather dragging each other down. We vowed not to run to each other so often and not to spend so much time in each other's room. But when, after a particularly bad day, I felt my confidence give way and nothing could offer solace—not Daisy, who was busy with her other friends, or Kate, who only stared at the walls—I would race through the brightly lit corridors, fly out the double set of doors marked Exit, and cross the roadway that separated our dorms. When I arrived at her room it was always the same: "Are you any better?" "No." "How about you?" "I'm afraid not very good."

Miranda's moods kept worsening, until I grew to dread seeing her. My confessions elicited sympathy and support from

Miranda but hers aroused more complex emotions in me. Once she called me into her room because she had a terrible confession to make. "What is it?" I asked. She looked at me and then lowered her dark lovely blue eyes, made even more lovely by their heavy fringe of lash. She mentioned a succession of things, none of which seemed very serious to me. But the intensity of her self-loathing had a force of its own. Maybe she was right to be ashamed. . . .

I saw Miranda only occasionally now, and when she peered into the dining room I looked the other way. Whenever she was recovering from one of her recent attacks she turned giddy, almost silly with the joy of temporary relief. I wanted her to be happy but I could not stand to see her then. Voracious after not having eaten for so many days, she would shovel potatoes onto her fork with her hands and splatter gravy in her beautiful hair.

One December morning as we were walking to Harvard Square, Miranda dropped a contact lens in the snow. Unable to find it, she simply collapsed and started weeping uncontrollably. She insisted that we continue to look as the snow fell thicker. Whatever happy stories other women tell about their college days, I have none that could compensate for the memory of watching my friend begin to unravel in the middle of Radcliffe Yard. She asked me to hold her hand but I said no. I feared that her illness was contagious and that if I got too near her, perhaps I too might go mad.

The note on my desk said, "Call Miranda, it's urgent." I called a number that I did not recognize as hers and was connected to the third floor of the University Health Services, the psychiatric ward. The nurse told me Miranda would be spending the night and that she had asked for me to bring her a few things. I put a pair of pajamas and a toothbrush in a bag and started the dreadful walk to Harvard Square.

She seemed happy to see me, her disloyal friend, and relieved, too, for she and the psychiatrist she had been seeing had decided she should go home. I was relieved, too. I felt better believing that there were differences between us, that she was really sick and I was not. Her dropping out proved it.

Still, I wanted to avert my eyes or turn away. Everything she did frightened me. "And then the funniest thing happened," she said. After she and the doctor had decided she should drop out, she finally felt well enough to wash her hair. When she stepped out of the shower, she looked in the mirror and saw ugly red blotches on her arms and face. This was proof: she was finally going mad. She thought she would faint until the nurse came in and reassured her. Miranda was so relieved—she was not crazy, only allergic to some silly chemical in the shampoo—that she started to giggle hysterically. She approached me for a hug. I handed her the bag in which I had packed her belongings and kissed her on the cheek. It was my fervent prayer that I would never have to see her again.

IN February I was walking out the back entrance of the dining hall when I noticed a room with an empty bed. "Is anyone living here?" I asked. "I'm not sure," a woman answered from her perch on the opposite bed. She was a tall red-cheeked woman with a long dark ponytail. I had seen her only casually, in the dining hall. She looked a little too wholesome, but Miranda's departure had left me wary of sensitive interesting types. I wanted a girl who was stable to the point of being dull, who drank milk, who went to bed at eight. "I did have a roommate," she answered in her calm even tone, "but I think she's left to join the U.S. Olympic Ski Team." "Is she coming back?" I asked, hoping the answer would be "No." "I don't know," she answered, but she was sweet and friendly and already I felt reassured. She looked slightly astonished but not displeased when, two hours later, I piled all my clothes into the elevator, rode down to the second floor and steamrolled into her room.

The world changed the day I moved in with Eleanor. It took on a cheerful sunny countenance that I could only attribute to her. "You see? You're much stronger than Miranda," my mother said when I told her how much better I felt. "You made a practical move." But I was convinced it was only on the basis of Eleanor's strength that I rallied that term.

She was happy to have me as a roommate as well. It had been a difficult first semester for her. She had gotten a C-minus on a calculus exam, which made her feel inferior to her classmates. "Tell me, really," I asked her, after the second month of my stay. "Why did you let me move in that night? I must have seemed crazy, trying to barge in like that." "You didn't sound so crazy," she replied, "and besides, I was lonely." (I loved this about Eleanor, that she did not say she was "crazy" or "depressed" or "screwed up," but described her feelings in more genuine terms.)

It was a relief then for both of us to have someone to walk into the dining room with and to check in with at the end of the day. We were not soulmates—I would not have the conversations with her that I might have had with Miranda or with Daisy, whom I hardly saw now that I had moved off her floor—but the tie between us was closer. It was the plain, dumb animal tie, the tie of constancy, of loyalty, of support, the tie of knowing that in the dark night, another body is there.

I was so happy to be with her that first week that I was content just to sit on my bed and watch as she went about her chores. My favorite activity was the early-morning hair wash, a ritual she performed with such consistency that I could guess the time by noting what stage of the procedure she was at. Blow-dry: eight-fifteen; forty-five minutes for breakfast and to make it to class. Every morning she would return from the shower in her long quilted robe, a towel wrapped turban style about her head. She moved with a slow plodding gait for which she sacrificed a certain grace. My brother used to joke that she was like a giraffe, that is, tall and impassive, but Eleanor was more complicated than we thought. For all our wisecracking, we were no more acute. The difference between us and Eleanor was that Eleanor observed but did not judge.

Her father was a theologian who taught at a well-known university in the Midwest and she was accustomed to the privileges his position entailed. He had been granted an honorary degree by Harvard and Eleanor was occasionally invited to dine with President Bok. I used to love to coax out of her the details of these dinners, but she was reluctant to talk about them, as if she felt awkward trading on her father's fame. I had no idea of her connection to him or of the extent of his reputation until one night, three months after I had moved in, my brother asked her over dinner, "Are you *the* Frank Remson's daughter?" Eleanor blushed.

Blushing or not, she seemed to radiate health. She wasn't muscle-bound, but she was a big tall woman with ruddy good looks. Every memory I have of Eleanor is in a ski parka, just coming in from the cold. She loved the seasons. Winter seemed to invigorate her but then so did spring and summer. She drew a certain comfort from nature that was as baffling to me as certain facts about me were to her. "Felt?" she asked, incredulous, when I told her about the curtains I had made. "Of course you use cotton. It lets in so much more light."

I wanted to be with Eleanor constantly, so that her calm good sense could infect me. But in fact, just the reverse took place. When I first moved in, she lived like a farm girl. She rose early and went to bed early. She confessed to me once, sheepishly, that she could hardly study past nine o'clock at night, a terrible admission at Radcliffe, where the action only began at Hilles Library after ten. She ate well, her system could not tolerate coffee, and she was the only girl in the dormitory I knew who didn't drink Tab. But the C-minus on the calculus exam and her exposure to me kicked off in her a campaign of self-improvement that, as with most of the women in our dormitory, seemed to involve a fair amount of self-abuse: starving, studying too hard. If she didn't learn to drink Tab, she did start to eat in a way one could trace directly to our cheery sun-filled room that Eleanor had enlivened with pretty curtains and prints: to me.

Since high school I had had an eating problem. It started innocently as a contest between me and my friend Angela La Plage as to who could achieve the lowest weight and the highest SAT scores (the two numbers by which we gauged our success). It ended in my becoming anorectic and Angela's running off to Mexico with a filmmaker twice her age. By the time I left for Radcliffe, I was five-feet-five and barely ninety-five pounds. My parents knew that something was wrong, but dismissed my malady as merely an exaggerated version of the traditional female preoccupation with dieting and weight.

At Radcliffe the problem grew worse. I had been thin when I arrived at Radcliffe, but lost even more weight as January crept by. By the time Miranda left, I was extremely thin, hardly ninety pounds, not quite so low as to qualify me for the hospital but low enough to accelerate the loosening of my hair (this made it easier to pull) and to keep me from getting my period. I lived on sixteen cups of coffee a day and just enough chocolate chip cookies to get a "high" from the sugar and still lose weight. In 1981 it was reported that as many as twenty percent of college women suffered from some sort of eating pathology, either anorexia or bulimia, the syndrome in which one binges on food and then throws up. But we did not know then that these were diseases or that they had names. I merely looked around the Holmes Hall dining room and felt annoyed that not even my irrational behavior with food was unique.

The surroundings—those large sunny dining rooms in which we took our meals—were civil enough. They had the country kitchen look of a girls boarding school, with their Queen Anne mahogany tables, a bowl for the sugar and a pitcher for the cream placed daintily on a doily in the center. We ate and drank on china, not on plastic, and in summer with the windows opened just a crack, the pretty cotton curtains fluttered in the breeze. Our meals were served to us by sweet gray-haired ladies who probably had the biggest hearts in all of Radcliffe. They actually noticed when you looked sad, and if you had a problem with your stomach or a bout of indigestion they took you into the kitchen, with its giant pots and pans, and counseled you, "Try a cup of tea and a piece of burnt toast."

And they noticed the curious ways in which we ate, how some of us took only eggs or grapefruit but would suddenly run amok, consuming whole gallons of ice cream or a half-dozen pieces of pie. Many women starved, for days, for weeks, and then suddenly would dump huge quantities of caffeine and sugar into their systems. In girls who were nervous and high-strung to begin with, the effects weren't good. Of the three women in our class who eventually killed themselves, two had eating disorders. I was not a vomiter, but some of my neighbors were. The starving, the bingeing, the running to the bathroom late at night (one heard the constant flush of the toilet down the hall) was a wretched ordeal. Bingeing was a physical addiction but it had a mental, perhaps even a spiritual root. Had we grown up in the ghetto, we might have turned to drugs. Had we been men and drinkers, we might have turned to booze. But we were women and the easiest way to abuse ourselves was with food.

The compulsion was most obvious in one of us because she started out so tall and thin. Blinkie Bernstein had big brown eyes and was from Beverly Hills. Every day she ate an enormous plateful of lettuce, spiced up with various noncaloric condiments: A-1 Sauce, mustard (not ketchup, too many calories there), lemon juice, salt, pepper and Accent just to bring out the flavor of the other stuff. But when Blinkie broke up with her boyfriend, she very suddenly started to swell. Her eyes widened and her smile became even more bright as if to draw attention away from her weight. It was painful to see her then, waddling into the dining room with a cookie in her hand or a box of toffee or endless packs of Trident gum. Blinkie got so heavy that she finally had to drop out of school.

I continued my regimen, subsisting on sixteen cups of coffee and a couple of cookies a day. But as the semester wore on and it was clear that school wasn't getting any better, I decided to try to gain weight, on the ridiculous assumption that if I had at least my weight gain to worry about, then perhaps I would feel less frightened by other, less tangible fears. At first people encouraged me, "C'mon Fran, have a little more." But as ten pounds became twenty pounds and twenty became thirty, the comments changed. "You look terrific, Fran, but hold it right there." And then, "Are you sure you haven't had enough?" Whether hormonally or chemically, I had messed up my system to such an extent that I could no longer do anything but starve or binge, and in a matter of months moved from haggard to slim to normal (I didn't stop there for even a day) to the far side of plump. My weight and my SAT scores, kept far apart in high school, were now approaching each other.

Unfortunately Eleanor was not immune to any of this. Instead of clinging to her own better, more sensible ways, she adopted my worst habits. She started lessening her intake of food and torturing herself with slivers of cake. In the past, she'd have swallowed a blueberry muffin in a couple of healthy mouthfuls and thought nothing of it. Now she picked at it crumb by shameful crumb, accompanying each with a chorus of "I shouldn't" 's, and then felt so guilty that she, too, started to binge.

By the end of the semester, our room showed a net weight gain of thirty pounds. I was responsible for (+) forty and Eleanor for (−) ten. But if I looked a little better, Eleanor looked worse. She had an unfortunate tendency to lose weight just where she least needed to (that is, her upper torso). Her backside became disproportionately wide and her figure took on the appearance of a cello.

Toward the end of the second semester, Eleanor and I made friends with the woman across the hall. Tess was short and dark-haired, with a slightly beaked nose and liquid brown eyes. She and Eleanor were enrolled in the same biology course, and their common language of zygotes, ribosomes and chromosomes—terms that wafted over from the dining room table where they sat studying after dinner—drew them close. Except for Eleanor and me, Tess didn't have many friends. She was a scholarship student from Providence, Rhode Island, and had decided very early in the first semester that all the girls at Radcliffe were "snobs." By the time I knew her, she was already slamming doors. You could tell when Tess moved down the hall, the flip-flop of her terrycloth slippers like the thumping of army boots.

She had a boyfriend whom she met the third week of school, which violated everything that I held to be fair. I thought if you were sensitive, introspective and had deep insights into yourself and the world, you should be rewarded by meeting a handsome, affable, intelligent man. But the only man chasing me was David, and if trashing the upper classes was what Tess was interested in, she should have gone out with him. But Tess was more fortunate and also had better taste. She had been talking to one of the men down the hall (she got along better with the "guys") when Jeffrey walked in. He was tall and dark and with his neat black beard, cool and self-assured. Tess was sure she would never see him again. She said he was "out of her league"—brighter, wealthier and more attractive. But the next week she saw him at a lecture, he asked her out to dinner, and after that neither of them ever dated anyone else.

They were so different it was hard to imagine them falling in love. Tess was narrow, provincial, almost a human machine. Jeffrey was calm and easy-going. He did things because he enjoyed them, not like Tess who had to get things done. He had his own interests, Italian culture and especially Renaissance art, and happily fled Harvard for Rome every June. He wrote Tess wonderful letters from wherever he was, and all Tess said was, "I wish he'd come home." Once I saw her in a robe he had brought her from Venice. It was silk with a tight-fitting belt. She was sitting on the lawn sunning herself, and when she leaned over I saw she had soft white skin and beautiful breasts, surprisingly ample for a girl of her size. You didn't expect that kind of softness in Tess.

They were different in other ways as well. Jeffrey was naturally inquisitive and enthusiastic about the world. He liked to eat well, was an inventive cook, and loved to try new things. Tess liked tuna fish. We used to joke with her about her lack of adventurousness when it came to food. "Whadd'ya have for dinner tonight? Tuna fish?" "What else?" It was only at that level that any of us could joke with Tess. Otherwise all her good humor was reserved for "the guys." She had one good woman friend from high school, Ruth, and they used to visit each other all the time. Ruth went to Boston University, and rather than go to visit Ruth across the river she liked to import Ruth to Radcliffe, surrounding herself with as many reminders of her non-Radcliffe world as she could. Otherwise she made Jeffrey her life.

She was almost always in his room, having left careful instructions with her roommate as to what to do if her mother called. "Jeffrey," we'd hear her baying into the phone on the few nights when she returned to our dorm. "Oh Jeffrey," a sound that had a certain pleading, sexually submissive tone, as if this girl had discovered something we had not.

Eleanor had a boyfriend, too, that spring and he introduced the first note of tension in our room. His name was Willie and it was my fault they had met. Willie had been my great true love in high school, but by the time senior year approached we had already drifted apart. We had both been accepted at Harvard and somehow it seemed like a natural time to break up. If anyone precipitated the rift I did, being curious about all the new men I would meet. But marvelous men did not descend upon you right away, and after two hours of stumbling around at a freshman picnic the first week I was relieved to see Willie making his way to me through the crowd. "So how's it going?" he asked, smiling. "Okay, and you?" I smiled back. We saw each other casually up through the spring, but it took me a while to realize it was Eleanor he was coming to visit and not me. He was no longer my boyfriend but I still viewed him as my property. He and Eleanor would go off hiking for the weekend and I don't know if I felt worse for having lost Willie to Eleanor or Eleanor to Willie. I remember coming into the room and seeing Eleanor sitting on her bed, smiling shyly as she always did when I was being difficult and rude. "Does my being with Willie bother you?" she asked in her very simple and straightforward way. "No, of course not," I replied, but it did and I started to resent her and grow impatient with her languid ways.

Eleanor knew her being with Willie bothered me and short of ending their relationship she tried to make it up to me. I went on aîtrip with my family that spring and when I returned there was a vase of daffodils on my desk with a note. "I missed you," it said.

THERE two decisions to make at the end of freshman year, what to major in and where to live, and the second decision generated far more concern. Both male and female freshmen had a choice: we could either live in one of the Radcliffe dormitories (all of them were co-ed, except for my former residence on the third floor of Holmes Hall) or move into one of the Harvard houses. There were nine houses, and we chose one over another on the basis of their stereotypes: Eliot House for preppies, Winthrop House for jocks, Mather House for people who didn't get admitted to any of the other eight. Women could move to the Harvard houses only in "groups," so naturally Tess, Eleanor and I coalesced. Tess and I had never been too friendly, but as the housing issue loomed into view she started dropping by our room after dinner to "chat."

Our first and only choice was Adams House. It was the most difficult house to get into, partly because of its reputation for being the "artsy-fartsy" house (it attracted people who were active at the Loeb Drama Center, the *Crimson* or in leftist politics, which was interesting, since it was also the most luxurious house) and partly because it was the closest to Harvard Yard. My brother lived in Adams House, where he was a revered elder statesman, famous for his discovery that on the day the dining hall served chow mein, you could turn your plate upside down and none of the gelatinous mass would fall off. Partly on the basis of nepotism (and a perfunctory interview in which three nervous men awkwardly inquired after our "interests"), we got in.

Applying for a major was a much more serious decision, but it could also be changed more easily. There, too, one had to be admitted on the basis of an interview. This was not true of all Harvard majors, but it was true of the three that were considered "elite": Social Studies, History and Literature, and the History of Science. My first interview was with a young assistant professor who could not quite elicit from me why I of all people wanted to major in Social Studies, which was a difficult field and demanded a high level of interest from its students. He seemed to feel I was majoring in it because my brother had. On my way out, the chairman of the department, who knew my brother, asked how my interview had gone. "Not very well," I answered. The next day I was called back for a second interview with a different professor, and when the list of new students was posted the following week my name was on it. Unfortunately, I was placed in the Social Studies tutorial taught by the young professor, and worried all spring that I would have a dreadful sophomore year.

I hardly thought about my old life anymore. Miranda was gone, and although whenever I spoke to my mother I asked for news of her, I blocked out most of what she said. My mother continued with her cheerleading campaign. "Don't worry. You're stronger than Miranda. You survived." As for David, he had mysteriously dropped out of sight. His campaign had let up, and by the middle of the spring semester finally came to an end. The only time I saw him was at the *Crimson,* where he was about to embark on the spring "comp." He looked very cocky, sitting on top of a desk, licking an ice cream cone. We talked a little bit about the traumas of my abortive comp (I had dropped out after three weeks), and then I left and David stayed. The *Crimson* apparently now exerted more of a pull over him than I did, a change I noted with a certain regret.

I only wanted to be distracted, so when the warm weather came and Eleanor and Tess, who had declared themselves chemistry majors, retreated to their books (one could not procrastinate as much in the "hard" sciences as in other fields), I began playing tennis. I whacked the ball with a power I hadn't known I had. I played hard and with little grace, which was my style, but it passed the time. My partner, Missie, a sophomore, was considerably more lively than anyone else I had met in the Holmes Hall dining room. Breakfast always found her staring into her coffee, regretting what she had done the night before. Usually she had done it at the off-campus apartment of a Harvard dropout, a professor's no-good son who lived on a trust fund and drove a Maserati. Missie, a renegade from Miss Porter's School, could always be persuaded to play, and between showers and buying balls and drinking gin and tonics before and after the games, we made it through the rest of the term.

I hardly saw Daisy anymore. She was always with Maureen, and when I moved from Holmes Hall I dissociated myself from my previous life. But the signs of our friendship were still there, a smile during an incidental meeting in Harvard Yard, a look that acknowledged the "bubbie" bond was still strong. I did not notice how occasional our meetings had become until I saw her in the dining room one morning during spring final exams. I was shocked by how terrible Daisy looked. She was pale and thin, and the circles under her blue eyes suggested she hadn't slept for months. "Daisy, what's the matter?" I asked. "Fran," she replied, fixing her eyes upon me as if maybe I could help. "I'm just so nervous about my exams."

It had been a difficult year for her, too. From the time she arrived at Harvard, Daisy was terrified she would fail. She stayed up all night studying for her first exam and was relieved when she got back a B. She studied even harder for her next hourly, and received an A, but instead of reassuring her the grade only made her feel worse. Now the better she did the more she studied, but it was never enough. Even Daisy now saw there was something obsessive about her fear. She clung to her books with the same tenacity with which I clung to my tennis racket, but while I was getting fat and tan, Daisy was getting pale and had dropped fifteen pounds, not because she was one of us who played crazy games with our weight but because she was too nervous to eat. The worst of it was that she knew her fears were irrational but her awareness only frightened her more. Now, in addition to worrying about her exams, she worried about her mental health. Sophomore year she told me it made her sick to look back on the notes she took at the end of freshman year. They read like transcripts of lectures and the tiny handwriting filled the entire page, even the margins.

BY June we were all relieved to be getting out. Tess planned to spend the summer at camp, an exception to the rule that only allowed us to spend time "constructively." I could just see her, in her Topsiders (because that was what anyone who grew up outside Boston wore, the preppy influence being inescapable), a whistle about her neck and a volleyball in her hand. "Go team! C'mon guys. Play ball." She loved those summers because they got her away from the snobbishness of Radcliffe, and because at camp she probably let herself relax. Eleanor went to her parents' summer home, a pretty rustic cabin on a lake. "It's so cheerful with its red gingham curtains," she said. I felt a pang of envy because she had taken Willie there and not me. And where was Daisy going? Home. School, especially that last semester, had been such a nightmare that she could hardly wait to get home and take stock of herself.

A lot of women went home to get recharged. I felt I could not do that, and took a research job in Cambridge instead. Something about my experience at Radcliffe made me feel as if I had no home, and seeing the old one would only have made it worse. I had done well academically, but what mattered more to me was how I looked. I was embarrassed that everything terrible I had experienced freshman year seemed to have manifested itself in my expanding frame, and did not want the people I loved to see it. When I stepped off the plane for a brief visit home that summer, my mother didn't know whether to laugh or cry, but finally she hugged me because at least I had survived.

The reports she had heard about Miranda weren't very good and she passed them along to me. Miranda was living with an aunt, barely supporting herself. My mother asked me if I wanted to call her but I didn't. A week later I was relieved to be getting back on the plane because I feared—and I might have been right about this—that if I left Cambridge, even for a summer, I might never come back.

CHAPTER 2

Sophomores

Sex is not one of the things you take SAT's in.
I think the possibility for ignorance in this area is quite good.
—DR. WARREN E. C. WACKER, DIRECTOR,
UNIVERSITY HEALTH SERVICES

I arrived back at college a few days before Eleanor and a day after Tess, who, true to form, already had all her clothing put away. There was nothing much to do until classes began, so we embarked on a tentative exploration of our new quarters next to Harvard Yard.

We soon realized how shabby our surroundings up at Radcliffe had been. Compared to the Harvard houses, the Radcliffe dorms now seemed like nurses' quarters, or worse, state institutions for the insane. Here there were no gloomy yellow corridors with emergency exit signs but labyrinthine entryways and rich mahogany walls. The architecture said it all: Women up at Radcliffe shared rooms, the implicit assumption being that two women could dress in front of each other, cry in front of each other and think (as much as necessary) while another of their species was yakking into the phone. Harvard had more civilized groupings of suites, each with a living room, several bedrooms (depending on how many people were sharing the rooms) and a bathroom, with—now that there were women in the dormitories—occasionally a urinal sprouting plants. (The main floor had elaborate ladies' rooms, a vestige of the days when women were "guests.")

The houses, named after great Harvard men—Adams, Eliot, Lowell—resembled Oxford and Cambridge colleges in spirit and style. But the arrival of women at Harvard and men at Radcliffe had a moderating effect on both campuses. Women up at Radcliffe no longer suffered through Jolly-Ups, those dreadful Saturday night ordeals where one was offered cider and doughnuts in compensation for not having a date, and men down at Harvard abandoned the custom of striking their glasses with cutlery when an attractive woman walked into the dining room.

House life was fun. Every Friday we had cucumber sandwiches and tea, poured with great fanfare from a silver urn presided over by the housemaster's wife. I came for the banana bread, served by ladies with white aprons and purple-rinsed hair in nets. Others came for the company. Adams House harbored a crew of very sociable assistant professors suffering under the hardship of imminent unemployment (tenure was next to impossible to secure in those days), who appeared at every social function at which there was anything to drink. Friday afternoon "tea" was succeeded by Friday afternoon sherry, followed by Friday night oblivion.

A handsomely appointed Common Room was where house events took place. Our house was distinguished by its annual black tie reading of *Winnie the Pooh* at Christmastime. Perched on high stools in the dining room and fortified by egg nog, a mix of distinguished faculty members and students read their assigned parts. Forever after in Adams House, I was known as Roo.

Because it had a "mystique," Adams House attracted people who were attracted to "mystique," which lent it a certain smarmy atmosphere. It was also the oldest and most luxurious house, built to accommodate wealthy students who, in a previous era, had brought their servants with them to school. And some of the luxury survived. The son of the mayor of a midwestern city lived in our house, and on his twenty-first birthday a group of his friends were treated to oysters, champagne and a planeload of debutantes imported for the occasion. But what really made Adams House the "Gold Coast," as it was sometimes called, was its swimming pool, a decadent Grecian tub of marble and tile with its own Gorgon's head. In the days before coeducation, the men in Adams House swam without suits, so when women arrived we did, too. (For some reason, it seemed more liberated to prance naked in front of a group of men than to wear a bikini, considered a symbol of oppression.) It was remarkable what a depressing effect all this had on sex. I once heard a fellow in the Adams House dining room say, "My God, there's Gracie Davenport. She looks fabulous in clothes."

Tess and I decided to play a game of tennis before unpacking our bags. (We played with the same style: all power and no form, although at least Tess's shots went in bounds.) We put on our little white tennis skirts and skipped out the main entrance of Adams House, where a man in dark glasses was waiting for us. "You girls live here?" he asked. "Uh huh." "Mind if I take a few pictures of you?" Tess and I looked at each other. "Why not?"

The following Sunday my mother phoned. "Did I wake you? I'm sorry." She wasn't, she called every Sunday. My mother believed it was an indulgence for young people to sleep past eight. "Have you read the *Daily News*?" There, beneath the headline trumpeting Harvard's "Nudie Co-ed Pool" was a picture of Tess and me looking fetching in our tennis skirts. The caption, not untrue but stretching things a bit, read: "With the pool not yet open for the season, these co-eds head off for a drier sport." The truth was, Tess had never set foot in the pool. I was more adventurous, but soon regressed to the all women's swims. I think what did it was Sunday night co-ed water polo, with breasts and other free-wheeling parts flapping about. ("I'm surprised grown-ups let us behave like that," a friend commented in later years.)

THE three of us, Tess, Eleanor and I, were assigned a suite in H-entry. It was a double, so Tess volunteered to sleep in the living room first. It was like Tess to want to get the worst over with right away.

Once we had settled into our various rooms and unpacked our belongings, the three of us dispersed into our wider and more separate worlds. Mine was dominated that fall entirely by Paige.

I met her the third week of sophomore year in the Dunster House dining room. (Dunster House: artsy-fartsy, avante-garde, the left bank.) I recognized her face from the "pig" book, although it took me a moment to match the photograph with the face. She was a fine-looking girl, with long brown hair and soft gray eyes, but in person she had a tendency to go limp, as if she were awkward or scared. Then those fine, long-lashed orbs and that perfectly precious nose would recede into the backdrop, and all that would remain was a face bleached of color—even her freckles wouldn't show—and a look of fear. But in her picture she was radiant. She had a mischievous look, suggesting a daring she otherwise did not reveal. It was as if the camera freed her.

"Oh you're the one," she said as I approached her table. She had heard my name, from David as it turned out. She wanted to know every detail of my relationship with him, which I readily supplied. She was more reticent about her own connection to him. They had had a brief flirtation but everything that drew me to Paige—that she was delicate, beautiful and privileged—had pushed David away.

We talked, that morning in Dunster House, on the pretext of having our majors in common. Paige, too, had drifted into the social sciences for dubious reasons. She was in history, she said, because she did not want to be one of those girls who majored in anything as ordinary as English. In later years, it was obvious her interests were more in the humanities—she liked music and art—but her father was a well-known trial lawyer and she was always trying to recapture the excitement of his work in her own. Besides, the early seventies were more "political" times. Literature and art could be accused of "irrelevance" in a way that history and government could not. So Paige and I, who in later years could hardly recall a word of the Marx we had read, had that as a connection, our feigned interest in these spuriously populist fields.

We became close friends overnight, which was a pretty fair indication of the passion our relationship aroused—love, hate, loyalty, treachery, nothing in between—and of why it couldn't last. I was her friend, and also her rival, which is pretty much what most women were. Our problem was not that we were jealous of one another, although we were, but that the bonds between us were so strong and the boundary lines so weak. At times I felt it was almost impossible to distinguish Paige's soul from mine.

What made us such instant friends? The way she spoke, perhaps. She seemed to know everything. I did not guess then what a debilitating lack of confidence she felt, so great that once she had to have a friend type a paper for her because she could not bear to read over what she'd written. But in conversation she was a goddess, issuing edicts, handing down opinions on all kinds of subjects, politics, literature, art. Whether she was not an especially original thinker or a girl who wrestled with ideas, I did not know, but her manner of speaking suggested that she was. She had a certain breezy manner that implied an intimacy with the world. Her father's celebrity ensured that she had seen a lot. She spent her thirteenth year living with her family in London and her sixteenth in Hong Kong. Because of her father's practice and connections, her family had plenty of famous friends. If we were discussing theater, Paige would mention that Lillian Hellman had visited the house; if we were talking about literature, she would mention a correspondence her father had had with W. H. Auden. Compared to her I felt like a mean little grind from Brooklyn, whose family was not only unintellectual but worse, "nouveau smart."

It was her background that fascinated me. Paige talked about the fanfare the day they took her to meet her father after one of his most famous trials. She described the throng of cameramen and reporters on the courthouse steps, the swordplay among the microphones. Everyone was shouting questions and vying to get close to her father. He and his client were serene and smiling, descending the steps as the crowd of newsmen and cameras roiled in their wake. The steps were huge and white and dazzling in the sun. She was only eight then so it must have made an impression on her.

She was proud of her father's accomplishments and yet they weighed on her. A perfectionist, he did not make things easy for Paige. Once in junior high school she showed him a paper she wrote. "That's very nice," he said. "But I'm not sure I would have taken that approach." She never showed him a piece of her writing again. And then there were the vicissitudes of his work. He loved his family but was rarely at home, constantly out of town on this case or that. Weeks before a trial, Paige would start to feel the tension in the house.

We had wonderful times. Paige could be such an engaging, endearing clown. We both liked to sing and I remember us, meeting in an underground passageway in Adams House, singing songs from *Kiss Me Kate.* For my birthday that year, she bought me two albums, *West Side Story* and *Auntie Mame.* She played Mame and I played Agnes Gooch. Performing brought out the best in Paige and it was not surprising that when Dunster House cast her as the comic lead in its Christmas play, people urged her to consider an acting career. Yet she never did. Musical comedy seemed far too frivolous in terms of the life her family led.

As the weeks passed, though, strains developed in our friendship. Paige was seeing a psychiatrist and I had the feeling my name came up more than once. We were both victims of the same terrible pressures to achieve, only my way of handling it now was to get my work done in a blind frenzy and hers was not to work at all. I knew her weak spot: she was afraid to try, to say, "This is my best." She could not finish assignments. She rarely handed papers in on time, and when she did, the writing was curiously staid. Paige dressed her writing like herself, in browns and grays, yet she was too bright to let all her talent go to waste. A transcription of any of her conversations with me would have made a brilliant piece. Did I exaggerate her talents? Perhaps, but not the discrepancy between her skills and her output. There were censors in her head that thwarted her.

She was troubled and, like everyone else, looked to other people and their family backgrounds for clues to her own problems. Away from our families for the first time, we could begin to see them in a critical light. But we were not cool or objective about this. We saw them as larger-than-life characters, villains or victims in Greek tragedy. Paige, who was extremely perceptive, could see the strengths and weaknesses in anyone. You merely had to mention someone's name and we would pull out our treacherous analyst's knife and start cutting. This was fine when we did it to all our friends, but then we started analyzing each other.

In some sense, Paige saw me and my brother and family as being like her father—bright, rasping, aggressive, and achievement-oriented. In this light, she viewed even David as a threat. Our very energy frightened Paige, who, on the brink of any challenge, would suddenly go slack. At the same time, she knew no other way of measuring success, for no one was more taken with her family's accomplishments than Paige. In trying to cut her ties with her own family, she constantly told me what was wrong with mine, what my mother and father and brother had done to me. I resented it, yet it was tempting to feel that everything might be my family's fault. I'd go back and forth in my head, from Paige to them, waging a terrible war. I wanted her to talk to me like this, then hated it when she did.

On a lark, a misguided one it turned out, my brother asked her out. She went and they had a good time because Chuck liked to have fun and Paige could appreciate that about him, but he came back saying, "She's not pretty. She has big teeth." And she came back saying, "Oh, Chuck, quite a guy," in that way of hers, implying that he was yet another character whom, if he weren't my brother, she would love to dissect. It didn't take long for her to overcome her inhibition and tell me what she thought: another ambitious, upwardly mobile Schumer.

Not long after Thanksgiving, I brought her home to meet my family. I took her on a walking tour of Brooklyn, but after five hours she held up her hand and said, "Enough." I let her rest but suddenly felt a fresh, malevolent burst of steam. "C'mon Paige, let's run," I said, knowing she was tired. She recovered from our walk, in the basement-den of my family's house, fortifying herself with pieces of cheese. She liked chocolate, but favored protein. She was the only woman I knew whose favorite food was meat. Somehow it touched me the way this pale, thin girl could tear at a piece of steak. And then I saw what my brother meant: she did have big teeth.

When we got back to Harvard, she gave me a full report. When she said something unfair about my family, I resented it. The trouble with Paige was that her comments were usually right on the mark.

In November we got a job working on the Currier House dish machine. It was Paige's idea. She thought if we had something tangible to do, our mental condition might improve. Besides, working with one's hands was politically "in." So on Saturday afternoons we'd don our food-stained white coats and trek to

Currier House. There we scraped cigarette ashes and mashed potatoes off lunch plates, felt the server's superiority over the served ("what pigs students are") and helped ourselves to as much free ice cream as we could eat. But the real attraction of the job was the rest of the dish-washing staff. They were tired older women who talked about their families and smoked L&M's. Did they have as many problems as we had? Were they as nervous? It didn't seem so. We wanted to sit and stay with them forever.

One evening after work at the dish machine, I came home homesick and depressed. I had managed to control my weight for most of the semester, but as the pressure built up I had started to binge. Paige couldn't stand the way I went to extremes. "Here, put a packet of sugar in your tea. One package of sugar won't hurt." Though I knew she was right and it made perfect sense to do what she said, it was the way she said it that bothered me, with such anger, as if we were fighting for control of my soul.

That night I ran up to my room crying and packed my clothes, determined to take the next plane home. Paige watched while I packed. She tried to talk me out of it and I continued to cry. "You've got to do it now," she said. "If you don't cut your ties to your family now, you never will." I looked at her as if she had just suggested I kill myself or worse, and with her reddened face and those terrible eyes imprinted on my mind I fled.

Paige and I were growing cool toward each other, and the sniping grew worse. But if my tendency was to have it out, hers was to cut the tie. She was the one who set the tone of our friendship then. When I'd see her in the dining room I'd go running up to her, "Paige!" eager for the next heavy dose of analysis. But no sooner did I approach her than she would make a gesture that was a cross between a wave as if to say "Hi," and a hand being raised as if to say "Stop." I felt I had been dismissed.

One day in January she told me she was taking a bus to the Cape. "I have to get away and think," she said. When she returned our friendship was not the same. It was as if she had determined to steer clear of troublesome objects, and one of those was me.

We made it through that first semester but our friendship did not survive. After exams she decided to take a semester off. Her psychiatrist and she had agreed that she should get away from all the pressure she felt.

I tried to put other things in the space vacated by Paige. I decided to give pre-med a try, since pre-meds were the only people at Harvard with a purpose, however narrow. I devoted much of second semester to molecular theory and atomic bonds, but by the time Professor Nash got to stoichiometry I gave up. I might have spent more time with Tess and Eleanor, but they were among the pre-meds with purpose. And Daisy had Maureen. So I ended up competing in the unlikely sport of crew.

Actually, many woman went out for crew at the beginning of sophomore year. They were tickled at the notion of trying out for such a traditional gentleman's sport, and in response to an invitation printed in the *Crimson,* dozens of Nordic types with thunderous thighs showed up at the Harvard boathouse. Also, Tess, Eleanor and me.

Our first test was on the ergometer, a stationary rowing machine. The meter measured how much pressure one could apply to the oar. The coaches, a matched pair of Boston Brahmins with fair skin that reddened in the late September chill, were dismayed at my effort, unimpressed at Eleanor's and dumbfounded when Tess's skinny chicken legs pushed the needle on the scale past the 45 mph mark (50 was the limit). Barely five-feet-three and 105 pounds, dark little Tess outrowed boatloads of women twice her size. Eleanor and I were retained for the B-boat (as everyone was), but Tess made first team. Every evening at five the three of us headed down to the boathouse, where we subjected ourselves to various tortures. In ascending order, from least to most unpleasant, they were: first, running stadiums (that is, up and down the bleachers); second, the actual act of rowing itself, which, during the Indian summer days of September and October, was enjoyable enough but by November, in the near-freezing chill, was absolute hell; third (and the reason we finally quit), the possibility that we might miss dinner. By the time the boats were hauled in and the oars put away, it was almost six-forty-five. As the dining rooms closed at seven, this was barely enough time to get back to Adams House if one rushed, but who felt like rushing after working so hard? Not Eleanor and I. The B-team would have to get along without us. Tess, however, persevered. She got along better with men than women, and she got along particularly well with men who were jocks. After an evening out on the Charles, her cheeks were suffused with color and her liquid eyes shone. The only time she looked prettier was when she was mad. Crew gave her something to be proud of at Harvard.

During the three months I was tied up with Paige, Eleanor had embarked on a rather unpredictable affair. Reuben was a star of the lunch table at the Signet Society, the pretentious undergraduate literary club. An instructor whose judgment I respected said there were only two students he had ever disliked—his mother's cousin and Reuben. I didn't know anything more about Reuben than that he fell wildly in love with Eleanor the first week of sophomore year, and that must have meant he had goodness somewhere in his heart.

One did not fall in love with Reuben without marrying into the rest of his crowd. Its ringleaders were Reuben and a graduate student named James, two bright funny cynics. Their table was a fixture in the Quincy House dining room, the noisiest table except if my brother happened to be around. Reuben's crowd were miserable people, so naturally they laughed a lot. Others could join them and they were always gracious to "guests," but never once did they fan out among the wider mass of diners.

Life in the fast track wasn't easy. Eleanor had many virtues, but she was not the kind of person you would envision at Reuben's Algonquin Round Table. She was neither clever nor miserable, though she felt pressure to be both. She saw Reuben and his friends as faster, smarter, better than she. And while they might never have said anything, they oozed judgment. They looked upon Eleanor as the good intelligent woman that she was, but their attitude was condescending, as if her goodness made her bland, or even worse, dull. "Simple" and "boring" was what someone said about Eleanor and it got back to her.

Yet Reuben made up for it by adoring her. He liked to tease and it was charming to watch him and Eleanor at meals. Every so often he would turn to her and make a joke or pinch her cheek, and then her face would light up, delighted to have the attention he sometimes withheld. There was no doubt he was in love with her, and she responded to his affection in a most natural and uncomplicated way: she loved him back. It was probably startling to this group of misanthropes to see a woman behave this way.

Like Tess, Eleanor spent most of her nights in her boyfriend's room, but occasionally she and Reuben and Tess and Jeffrey would converge upon our room. Tess and Jeffrey were always quiet (Tess was very discreet); but the strangest sounds sometimes came from Eleanor's room. It was the only time Tess and I ever shared a smile. What a tigress our mild-mannered roommate turned out to be! (We later found out it was a leaky radiator.)

I was not entirely indifferent to Eleanor's affair. Not long after we had moved down to Harvard, I had had a brief encounter with Reuben's mentor, James. He was tall and gangly, with long crooked arms that protruded from his sides like the handles of a sugar bowl. He was miserable and funny about his misery. His father was a psychiatrist, which may have explained his aversion to therapy. He believed that basketball was a better cure and went out to shoot hoop whenever he was depressed. His problem, he told me almost the first day we met, was women. He seemed to fall in love with women who were neurotic, beautiful and unavailable. One night, against my better judgment, I knocked on his door. He answered, in his underwear and acne cream. We spent a few nights rolling around on his floor but after several sessions, he indicated it was not to be.

Not long after our flirtation, I noticed James with Paige. She was the perfect candidate for his obsessions, beautiful and unavailable, not because she was seeing anyone (Paige had virtually no boyfriends during most of her college career) but because she was troubled and seemed particularly resistant to men. She would call them to her with her eyes, but when they got within touching distance she backed off. Most men resented it, but not James. I thought I could predict the outcome: James would become "obsessed" with Paige, who would reject him, and in bitterness they would part. But I underestimated the extent of their tie. They remained loyal friends for the rest of that year.

In some ways, I felt it was a divine evening of the score: Paige was infatuated with David who was infatuated with me who was infatuated with James who was infatuated with Paige. Except I was not infatuated with James. I just liked him and would have made him happy, which would have made him miserable. Which is why it was better that he lusted after Paige.

WHILE I tangoed in and out of scrapes with Paige, and surveyed the seats in my classes for cute and interesting-looking men, Daisy applied herself almost exclusively to her work. At first, the old freshman year compulsiveness reasserted itself. But Daisy was a year older and determined not to give in to it. Even before she walked into her first hourly exam, she reached a kind of mental truce with herself. Nothing was important enough to make her as miserable as she had been freshman year. In that more calm and controlled frame of mind, she extracted what so few of us were able to during our third and fourth semesters at Radcliffe—knowledge.

Sophomore year she blossomed. All the anxiety she had felt as a freshman now reasserted itself as intellectual excitement. Before coming to Radcliffe, she had read only three novels. Now she read stacks of them. She majored in Government and distinguished herself even among that very egocentric breed. Harvard Government majors had Henry Kissinger as their model, for he had once been a professor in that department, and thought it was natural to come out of Harvard and rule the world. "Department of Government," the secretary said, as if she were saying "Department of State." Daisy discussed Locke and Rousseau with unabashed enthusiasm, but she was clever, and if people were apt to judge her naive at first, they quickly changed their minds. Halfway through fall semester, she came running up to me in the Yard, waving her arms and shouting, "Franny, Franny, you'll never believe this." "What?" I asked. "They posted my American Government exam on the wall."

This wasn't the girl I remembered from freshman year, for whom every exam was a crisis of faith and grades. She was so much more exuberant and confident now. What had made the difference? Daisy had taken herself in hand. She had spent most of the summer working in a bookstore near her house, and the peaceful rhythm of work, rest and sleep restored her naturally cheerful temperament. She had also seen a psychiatrist who convinced her her anxieties were normal and didn't have to stand in her way.

In Minnesota, Daisy had never been aware of her possibilities; her intelligence had seemed an encumbrance among all her cheerleader friends. But at Radcliffe she sensed a different path was open to her, and in her charming and buoyant style she began to follow it, though with only a vague sense of where it would lead.

We were heading in opposite directions. I sat in the library, and wearily tried to pull meaning out of Weber and Marx, while

Daisy spent the entire night reading Emerson and the transcendentalists, and the next morning told me, "Franny, it was like having a transcendental experience of my own." In fact her enthusiasm could be a little nauseating, and it introduced the first tiny spark of competition between us.

As sophomore year drifted peaceably to a close, I did not think about grades and schoolwork but concentrated on more vital things. I was desperate for some kind of interesting activity beyond tennis. In May, just as the warmer weather set in and the Cambridge Common was starting to sprout a little green, I fell in love, briefly, and that seemed to open a range of possibilities beyond courses on the one hand and hobbies on the other.

The man was named Marshall Campbell. When I spotted him over in the corner of my radical economics course, I felt sexual stirrings I hadn't noticed since freshman year, when David effectively quashed any interest I might have had in men. I knew exactly what did it. It was spring. I was one year older and much calmer than I had been freshman year. And the man I was after had the unmistakable appearance of someone upper class. (Although my sympathies were basically with the proletariat, David had temporarily quashed that, too, at least for romantic purposes.)

As it turned out, my initial impression was wrong. Marshall was neither upper class nor a preppie, as his tortoiseshell glasses and neatly laced Topsiders suggested, but a public school boy from Fremont, California. Marshall and I shared that quality fairly common at Harvard of trying to represent ourselves as something other than what we were: Marshall, a filthy rich preppie with a socialist heart; I, an eccentric sassy type.

Anyway, he must have noticed me, too, for when he spotted me coming out of a side door on Plimpton Street he stopped me and asked me a question about the course. We discovered in that moment that we held exactly the same views. We cared passionately about the subject matter of workers' control but were a little suspicious about the instructor, whom I knew to be a frequent user of the Adams House pool and whose father was a bigwig in the Treasury Department. Both Marshall and I agreed you couldn't trust a born-again radical with upper-class roots. The fact that Marshall and I were not exactly peasants didn't stop us from passing judgment. This was Marshall of the Preppie Proletariat I was dealing with, and if he wasn't as logically consistent as David, he was certainly a lot more fun. We must have gone on talking for much longer than I thought, for when I returned to my room the entire side of my face that Marshall hadn't been shielding from the sun was bright red.

Marshall and I spent our first few evenings hitting tennis balls around, but eventually there was dinner and walking and talking in the living room of Marshall's final club. Final clubs were Harvard's answers to fraternities, similar to Princeton's eating clubs but more exclusive, since only a tiny percentage of the undergraduate body were asked to join. By the time we arrived at college, many were fast on their way to extinction. (One of the clubs, at one time loath to accept Jews, closed for lack of membership and has since become the site of Harvard Hillel.) Most clubs had their token blacks, but no women were allowed except on certain social occasions, and even on those nights certain areas were out of bounds. As a member of one or two of these semi-excluded groups, I naturally felt incensed about the existence of such institutions and was dying to take a peek.

What a disappointment. The food was better than the University Dining Hall Service fare (turkey tetrachloride and anything in cream sauce on toast), but the jokes were crude and the men dull. Most of them dated women from Ashford Junior College (my brother had told me it was called "The Whore House on the Hill"), and their attitude toward Cliffies was a mixture of reverence and disgust ("Boy, are they brilliant," and "God, are they dogs"). Meals at the club were served by elderly "stewards," who were actively patronized by some of the members. "Oh, Roberts. Such a great guy. And you should see what a wizard he is at poker." Marshall enjoyed my brashness, and was looking forward to my humiliating him at dinner, but I disappointed him. I was intimidated in front of all those slick F. Scott Fitzgerald types and tried my hardest to act demure.

Not long after we started dating, Marshall told me there were three types of women he dated: beautiful blond debutantes ("That's not your category," he said); straight, hardworking, studious types (that wasn't my category either); and avant-garde, bohemian, difficult types. Me? "You," he said. Given the choice, it was obviously the best category to be in, but my placement there reflected my social climbing as surely as Marshall's Topsiders and J. Press sweaters reflected his. I let on that my past was a bit racy, in some intriguing but unspecified way. If I didn't exactly lie to Marshall, I intimated that I was more experienced than I was. (I might have told him the truth, but I'd rather have died than relinquish my membership in Category Three.) At the time, I was reading an Edith Wharton novel in which the heroine preferred yellow roses to red ones. I made a great fuss about this, and told Marshall I, too, preferred yellow roses, which were "more European."

We dated all that May, playing lots of tennis and eating lots of ice cream cones. Marshall had an ulcer, and in addition to his morning ritual of Special K and milk, there was his nightcap: three scoops of a Baskin-Robbins flavor called "baseball nut." I didn't like baseball nut but ordered café au lait (the latter being more European). It was a measure of my happiness that I could eat a double scoop and not worry about my weight. I was falling in love, I was playing tennis, and the world seemed full of promise that spring. On the last night of the semester, Marshall held me in the rain. We went back to my room as always and did what we always did, which was everything but. We had known each other for only a month and Marshall wasn't the type to rush. It made our separation during the summer that much more sweet, and made both of us frantic to return in the fall.

That summer we went our separate ways. Eleanor hiked across Canada with Reuben, who had graduated that year. Tess worked as a counselor at a camp as she did every summer. Except for the fact that Jeffrey wasn't there, she preferred the two months she spent at Camp L'Chaim to any she spent at school (middle-class brats being preferable to upper-class ones). A man I dated briefly at Harvard worked at L'Chaim with Tess. He said she was one of the best counselors at the camp, "a real sport, cheerful, always a smile." (Tess?) Daisy decided to stay in Cambridge that year and work as a research assistant for a feminist professor at Simmons College who was as dull as her book, *Unheralded Women of the Plains.* Daisy didn't mind. She was as enthusiastic as Paige was critical, and always found something positive in what she did. There were times I wanted to shake her and say, "Daisy, don't you realize she's a jerk?" But what would be the point? Daisy would only say I was being too critical. Speaking of which, I had hardly heard from Paige since she had left school. As far as I knew, she was living with her parents in Philadelphia and still trying to recover from sophomore year. Rumor had it she'd be back in the fall.

It was my old high school boyfriend Willie, not quite recovered from his loss of Eleanor, who told me about my summer job. His brother-in-law worked for a small but respectable daily newspaper in Winston-Salem, North Carolina, that was looking for cheap help. I had never written for a newspaper before, except for my brief attempt at the *Crimson,* which I regarded as part of the nightmare of freshman year. But I had heard Paige talk about writing for a paper the following fall, and if Paige was interested in journalism then it was something I wanted to try. I dashed off an application and was offered the job.

No sooner did I step off the plane in Winston-Salem than I felt all the worries I had accumulated at Harvard drop from me. Whatever sense of mastery I felt I had lost at Harvard returned to me here. Perhaps it was just feeling interested again, aroused, excited and eager to learn. The first day I moved in, my downstairs neighbor, Delberta Epps, looked me over with razor sharp eyes and asked, "You a Yankee?" "Yes," I replied. "Well listen, honey, don't be bringing any niggers around here." My first redneck. Delberta may have been a racist, but at least she was inconsistent. Not long after I moved in a black family moved in across the street. I spent most of the summer carousing with my white newspaper friends and Delberta did much the same thing with our new neighbors.

The first day of work, with my lunch in my knapsack (packing lunch always put me in a diligent frame of mind) I rode my bicycle to the newspaper building with first-day-of-school jitters in my heart. I knew nothing about writing news stories. Perhaps during my first go-round at the *Crimson* I had overheard someone mention the inverted pyramid (the method of writing not chronologically but with the most important information first), but I was slow in getting the message. In Winston-Salem, the directions were more terse. "Write," my editor said. "About what?" "Anything."

Except cigarettes, apparently. Nobody ever told me to avoid the subject, but the R. J. Reynolds Tobacco Company was the largest employer in town, and in 1972 the newspaper was cautious about running stories on smoking and health. Not long after we arrived the newspaper took us on a tour of the Reynolds plant. Much of the discussion focused on the "other" products Reynolds made: Chun King Frozen Chow Mein, for example. It was rumored that the company was manufacturing reefers in the basement for the day when tobacco was made illegal, but the tour guide dismissed this as wishful thinking. At the end of the tour I was handed a free pack of Salems. I took my first puff and, in the dizzying high that followed, knew what I wanted to do:

smoke, and anything that went with it. News reporting seemed the obvious choice.

No sooner did I seat myself behind the typewriter than it seemed as if I had been born to do this. I wrote stories that were terrible and everyone said were good. I was given the most trivial assignments (a woman who had crocheted the Lord's Prayer into her quilt) and felt as if they were the most interesting stories in the world. Perhaps it was the people. They never tired of cracking jokes about Yankees. "You a Yankee?" a woman would ask before opening the door. "Yeah." "You from the paper?" (People were always suspicious of reporters.) But once they established that you were a carpetbagger and a Communist, they would slap you on the back and say, "C'mon in and have a beer!" Nobody seemed to tire of talking. I sat and listened to Southern liberals who were different from their counterparts up north: funny, drunk, irreverent and sad. Politics for them was more than a matter of wearing painters' overalls. It meant being cut out of Daddy's will.

I never got to know many of my neighbors well, except for Biff, a Vietnam veteran from Kentucky who lived across the hall from me. We met the night that Delberta and her husband, Ray, tried to cook their dog, Princess, a mangy mutt that Delberta, when sober, adored. One night I cut my finger on a can opener. To stop the bleeding, I wrapped a piece of bandage around it as tightly as I could, which only made the bleeding worse. All night it throbbed. The next day I was treated at the hospital but the pain was still intense. That night, Biff fed me bourbon and played me the record of an ex-prostitute he used to know who sang like an angel. I looked for more of her music when I returned to Cambridge that fall, but none of the stores in Harvard Square had ever heard of her.

I liked the interns whom I worked with, too. They came from places like Roaring Gap and Gastonia, North Carolina ("murder capital of the world"). Our friendships were much less entangled than the ones I had with my friends up at school. We played tennis and went camping. Every week we set off in somebody's car with pimento cheese sandwiches and Budweiser in a cooler in the trunk, and drove to the Blue Ridge Mountains. The only person I met that summer who wasn't happy was the editor's son, and he was planning to go to Harvard in the fall.

Still, I kept in touch with my Harvard friends. Every night I would sit on the top of my rickety back-porch stairs and read and write letters to my friends. My fan mail from Marshall, who was studying in Mali, made up for whatever male companionship I lacked. Daisy was happy in Cambridge, in the middle of the *Crimson* summer photography "comp." Her research job was uninspiring but her parents had bought her a camera and she was learning how to use it. As for Paige, she was in Philadelphia still trying to protect herself from the questions that had haunted her at school—work, grades, achievement. But underemployment wasn't the solution. She had deliberately taken an easy job as a paralegal in a law firm but hated being ordered around by a bunch of obnoxious associates and even once being chased around an associate's desk. I suppose my letter upset her, charged as it was with the enthusiasm I felt at finally having found something I wanted to do. The notion of Paige as my audience always loosened something in me and my letter to her contained more than my usual excitement. And I can't pretend I was completely blind to the reaction this would provoke in Paige. I waited eagerly for her reply, which, when it came, was disappointingly brief. She told me I had misspelled her name (I had written "Page" instead of "Paige") and she closed with the chilling suggestion "Let's keep our correspondence brisk next time." When I did get a second letter from her, it was addressed with my name spelled "Frann."

I was sorry to leave Winston-Salem, but for the first time I felt genuinely excited about going back to school. I boarded the plane in a smart khaki suit I had bought at J. C. Penney for $25 and sat and thought about what a perfect summer it had been—the friends I had made, the confidence I now had in my new summer self. On the glandular front, Marshall would be waiting, and if I hadn't yet lost my virginity it was only a matter of time. But more important, I had a goal. With increased determination, I decided to comp for the *Crimson* again.

CHAPTER 3

Juniors

Cambridge's Only Breakfast Table Daily
—FROM A CRIMSON ADVERTISEMENT

Dozens of students converged on the *Crimson* on the opening night of the fall semester "comp." The draw was free pretzels and all the beer you could drink, which was the least the staff could provide since it was the candidates who would do most of the work. Journalism was becoming increasingly popular in 1972. Seymour Hersh had broken the story about the massacre at My Lai, and Anthony Lewis was writing inspiring editorials against the war in Vietnam. Others who showed up for the comp that night might have had these issues on their minds, but I was only concerned with getting on staff.

I spotted him first. I should have known he would reappear to bother me again, but the David I saw, leaning against the Coke machine and stroking his stubbly chin, had an air of authority his freshman self had not possessed.

"Trying out for the *Crimson*?" he asked. A perfectly natural thing to say.

"Yes," I said. "What are you doing here?"

"I'm in charge of this year's comp."

It took me a moment to absorb this fact, which otherwise

violated everything I knew about David. I could not believe that a board of sane and rational *Crimson* editors would place a maniac like David in charge of the comp. But there he was, looking just as arrogant and foolish as ever, leaning against the Coke machine, puffing away at his Kool. For a moment I considered abandoning the comp altogether, but I was much too primed for this to walk away, and besides, perhaps David had changed. I moved in closer with the rest of the crowd of candidates to hear his opening pitch.

No editor ever looked more masterful, standing on top of the night editor's desk in his rolled-up shirt sleeves and faded corduroys. And yet always the populist, David spoke as if he were just another member of the rank and file. A very harsh critic might have called him a bit patronizing, drawing on examples from his own not distant youth, but then there was only one very harsh critic in the crowd. Everyone else seemed thoroughly amused. This, I thought, is how dictators arise.

At the end of his speech he headed my way. "Nervous about the comp?" he asked.

I was, he could tell.

"You'll feel better once you get a tutor." (A tutor was an editor assigned to each candidate, although it was sometimes difficult to tell whether the system worked to the advantage of aspiring candidates or predatory editors.) "Perhaps you'd like me to be your tutor."

Fat chance, you rascal. But on second thought, it might not be such a bad idea. I needed someone to get me through the comp. Besides, whatever magic he had worked on the crowd had had its effect on me. I did not immediately accept his offer but said I'd give it some thought.

Marshall was patient enough during the early days of the comp. He applauded my efforts and enjoyed hearing about my work. But toward the middle, he started to detect David's name dropping frequently into my speech and naturally started to resent both the comp and its leader, whose politics he found a little extreme. At the same time, I was growing impatient with his club, his friends and their attitude of noblesse oblige. But it was Paige who rang the death knell for Marshall and his final club. "Isn't it disgusting?" she said during one of our late-night cut-'em-ups. "All those healthy young boys, and they allow themselves to be served by those tired old men."

But Marshall knew it was important for me to get on the *Crimson* and pushed his antipathies aside, which is more than I can say for David. Marshall, who despised college newspaper revolutionaries, was tolerant in a way that David, who despised final-club liberals, was not.

One night, during the second week of my comp, Marshall came to visit me on his way to a dinner at his club. It was a mistake wearing a tuxedo into the *Crimson,* where the only clean shirt was worn by the printer, Pat (and he was a proletarian, so we indulged him in that). David, who had heard I had a boyfriend, immediately looked up when he saw Marshall heading my way, and with characteristic subtlety, stuck a finger down his throat and pretended to gag. The show, staged for my benefit, had the desired effect. David was a fool but I was a bigger fool for letting him influence me, although Marshall did look a little ridiculous standing in front of a picture of Uncle Ho.

The final showdown came the day of the Dartmouth game. Football games were big deals in the lives of the clubs, especially at Marshall's club, where a big bash was to follow the game. Marshall was counting on me to come, but at the last minute I changed my mind. I had been bingeing all day, which may have been my backhanded way of giving Marshall the old heave-ho. Not showing his anger (he never did, he had ulcers), he went to the game without me. That night I met him at his club for dinner and drinks and after too much of both, accompanied him to his room. My head was in such a daze that I didn't realize what was happening until it was too late. Marshall failed to pull out in time. I was so foggy I hadn't even known he had pulled in.

The next morning I went to the University Health Services to get a prescription for the morning-after pill. The doctor gave it to me with a frown and warned me not to let it happen again. The pill (diethylstilbestrol, better known as DES), which consisted of a steroid used to fatten cows, made you violently ill and had to be accompanied by another drug to counter the nausea. I went home feeling sick and ashamed. People had lost their virginity before, but not usually without even knowing it. And I had never told Marshall I was a virgin for fear of relinquishing my membership in Category Three. My friend Lucy Love, though, decided it was in both my best interest and Marshall's that he know the truth.

That afternoon he came to my room. "You needn't be embarrassed," he said. And then he produced from behind him a bouquet of roses. Yellow roses. Had I had any sense, I would have asked Marshall to marry me. But I was humiliated and besides, there was someone else on my mind.

David did not pursue me now; I pursued him, humbled by the previous two years. Sophomore year had been better than freshman year but not enough. I still felt as if I hadn't quite recovered my balance. My response was to adopt the pose of a nihilist—nothing mattered, anything goes—and in that spurious state of indifference, I took David into my arms.

He, however, had not spent the last two years sulking. I had not been aware of it before, but now I saw how serious he was about his goals, and this lent him stature in my eyes. His political convictions were indistinguishable from his personality (not a pose as they were with so many others), and the same mad passion that fueled his obsession with me fueled them. But still you could dismiss David as a crazy revolutionary if there had not been the suggestion of a deeper common sense and an even deeper intelligence. He had charisma, and like most charismatic leaders, often said things just to provoke the crowd, purposely concealing the more sensible perspective he held privately. Still, he was masterful in the way he got what he wanted, and it was not simply through sheer persistence. His goals were noble but his tactics were earthy. Perhaps that was why Mayor Richard Daley was his idol. Daley was a villain because of his role at the Democratic Convention of '68, but David admired him because of a certain raw working-class strength he exuded and, like Mayor Daley, David liked to win. He got himself elected to the staff of the *Crimson* and began making it into his political machine.

Compared to David, I felt overshadowed and underconfident, yet that was part of his attraction. It was not so much his position on the newspaper that attracted me; it was his confidence, the remarkable way in which he harnessed his ability in the service of his goals. I did not do that, nor did most of the women I knew, so much more ambivalent and self-defeating, so twisted and tortured about their desires.

A week after I broke up with Marshall, I took David on as my *Crimson* tutor and things moved pretty quickly from there. "What's your favorite movie?" he asked. *"Battle of Algiers,"* I replied, thinking this would impress him. (Paige had told me it was hers.) "You're such a liar," he responded, and he was right. There was a touchy moment in my room, when he looked into my eyes ("Such pretty blue eyes," he said. "They're green," I said), but we got past it.

The next morning I was back in the University Health Services in search of another morning-after pill. "Would you like a prescription for birth control?" the doctor asked. This time I said, "Yes."

I had a much more difficult time comping for the *Crimson* than I had expected (David had given me such rave reviews even before I started the comp that some people wondered what all the fuss was about), but in contrast to my comp, Daisy's raced along. When she first started, David said her pictures were flat and dull (five city councilmen staring into the camera while holding a plaque). But his criticism only made her more determined to get on staff. By the third week of my comp, Daisy's pictures were consistently winning "v-v-strongs" in the red-inks.

She was an indefatigable worker. On election night Daisy was sent to shoot one of the Cambridge contests. Everyone was gloomy as it appeared that Richard Nixon would be President again and that, locally, conservative candidates would ride in on his coattails. But in Daisy's contest, the liberal underdog defeated a well-known antibusing leader. It was hard to tell whether Daisy was excited because the good guy won or just from the thrill of covering an election. I could never get out of the building early enough, and when I did stay it was only because I had to wait for David, who practically slept there. But when Daisy returned she asked, "Is there anything else I can do?" She spent the rest of election night doing tedious work in the darkroom. The next morning people stumbled out of the *Crimson,* weary at the prospect of Four More Years, but Daisy practically flew out the door. "It's terrible," she confided. "I had such a wonderful time." It was that night she decided she wanted to be a news photographer.

She was also undaunted by difficult or uncooperative subjects. Someone at the *Crimson* had gotten wind that a well-known Harvard professor was up for an important political job. The trick was to get the professor to confirm the rumor, which it was almost impossible to do. The managing editor who gave Daisy the assignment had already warned her that the professor had chased the reporter away. Other candidates might have given up but Daisy hopped on her bicycle, rode the ten blocks up Brattle Street to his house and saw him talking with a man who turned out to be a White House aide, clinching the rumor. The next morning the *Crimson* scooped the *New York Times.*

People on the *Crimson* admired goodness but they admired talent more. Daisy impressed them with both. Not long after we began our comp, another woman started hers. Her name was

Sarah Worthington and she was as close to nobility as the *Crimson* had. Men made fools of themselves over Sarah, but she had few women friends. I was famous throughout the *Crimson* for my imitation of her: First I'd toss my flowing hair back, then stalk across the room—long, lean, lissome aristocratic strides—then turn my head and, in a voice dripping of money and ennui, say, "How are you, my dear?" It was easy to poke fun at Sarah because she was so rich and pretty and obviously unflawed, but it was her iciness that kept her beyond the reach of our charity. Only Daisy did not assume that Sarah, being perfect, did not need a friend. One day, over lunch in the Eliot House dining room, Daisy cut me short just as I was working up to a really fine imitation of Sarah. "You have it all wrong, Fran. She's really upset." She told me that the previous night Sarah had asked her to come to her room where she was agonizing over a *Crimson* piece, unable to get past the first line.

Sarah's other unforgivable sin was that she was a really fine writer. The first day of her comp she sat down behind the typewriter and wrote a perfect lead. But according to Daisy, she suffered from the same soul sickness the rest of us did: she was terrified of writing and even more terrified of coming into the *Crimson* each day. When Daisy heard that, she made it her mission to guide Sarah through the rest of her comp.

It was a role I could easily imagine Daisy playing, as she often assumed it with me. Whenever I felt disheartened about my comp, which was all the time, I turned to Daisy for moral support. My stories routinely appeared in the red-inks with check marks at best, while everyone else's, it seemed, were winning v-v-strongs (often from Mr. Crime-Ed himself). I complained to David, whose glib generalities only made me feel worse, laced as they were with references to his own glorious comp ("Relax. Calm down. I used to feel that way, too. Let me give you a few suggestions, not that I'm an expert or anything . . ."). But Daisy had a more effective approach. "Your stories are wonderful," she lied, heaping on the praise. Whether she believed in me or just acted as if she did, her boosterism did the trick. I walked away from a conversation with Daisy feeling that my worries were all in my head, which wasn't exactly true either.

There was only one thing missing in Daisy's life. "Fran, why don't I meet someone?" she asked. She felt doubly bad because her roommate, Maureen (Miss Teenage America), went out all the time. Many men regarded Daisy as a friend, but that was all. There was an unsullied quality about her that perhaps they were afraid to destroy. It was as if someone had hung a sign about her neck: "Fragile. Do Not Touch."

Sophomore year she finally started dating a fair-haired, blue-eyed hockey player. I thought they were a perfect pair, both bright and introspective, but with a little bit of the jock. Daisy would have gladly forsaken her schoolwork if only Michael had given her the sign, but he didn't for reasons she and I could never figure out. Junior year she had a crush on a business school student, and his lack of response was even more surprising. All summer she and Andrew played tennis at the B-school courts and joked. Daisy fully expected the joking to turn into something more that fall and, as her loyal bubbie, so did I. September turned into October and winter set in, but nothing happened. In December, he introduced her to his fiancée, a pale, pinch-faced debutante from Chevy Chase. We weren't objective, but then even people more objective than Daisy or I could not explain it. David, characteristically, chalked it up to social class, which in this case was probably right.

By the end of the first semester, Daisy and I were officially members of the *Crimson* staff and David was campaigning for the *Crimson* presidency. All that fall I watched as he practically took over the place, becoming as much of an institution as the *Crimson* itself. People were intimidated by him (he called them "running dogs of capitalism" and worse), but they liked him, too. He was democratic in a way that other people were not. There were inevitably editors who enjoyed telling candidates that they had to be "cut." David did not. His idea was that everyone should be allowed to join, and you often saw him, sitting in a corner, helping the most timid candidates with their work. Two minutes later he would be sitting atop the night editor's desk, calling someone an imperialist lackey. Even before his campaign for the presidency, he had most of the students on the *Crimson* smoking Kools and talking jive.

In December, David was elected president after the Turkey Shoot, the elevated gossip session in which candidates for the *Crimson* executive board make their pitch. David's opponent Eric probably thought as I did, that the board would never elect someone so extreme, but it was always a mistake to underestimate David. While Eric dozed, David hustled votes.

I didn't know Eric, but I did know his girlfriend, Alison. We were in parallel positions, like the girlfriends of the leaders of the Jets and the Sharks in *West Side Story.* We rooted for our men but secretly felt we had more in common with each other. We used to compare notes about how insecure we were and how frustrated, watching our boyfriends grasp for greater glory while we were always wondering if we were "good enough." It wasn't fair to blame our frustrations on them, but then our self-doubt made us angry and sometimes mean.

Not long after the Turkey Shoot, someone threw a party. It was my birthday and David, basking in the aftermath of his victory, was in a particularly ebullient mood. He bought me the Carly Simon album with my favorite song, "You're So Vain," which I thought was particularly appropriate for him. (He liked the cover, which showed Carly looking very fetching in a shirt without a bra.) Both of us were on top of the world that night: me, shimmying about the room in snug black pants (I was just at that crucial stage where the good effects of my weight gain outweighed the bad); and David, drinking and crooning in my ear, "How Sweet It Is [to Be Loved by You]." (People at Harvard preferred Motown to any funky white boy music.) "King and Queen of the *Crimson*," Daisy sighed snapping our picture. She tended to overromanticize, but David and I did look terribly happy that night. And we were, at least for a while.

We lived not as lovers but as comrades in a Communist cell, our nights and days dominated by the work of the *Crimson.* Generally, we would not rouse till noon from the single narrow cot in my suite in Adams House that became our conjugal nest. Love-making was difficult but then the strain only added to the experience, the two of us twisting and turning so that one of us would not land on the floor and wake the other women, risking Tess's wrath. We had fun then, in the middle of the night, howling and laughing at the silliest things. David, beyond his politics, was a generous observer of human souls and could point to a bit of foppery in someone else and view it with kindness and grace. He made me laugh and I loved him then, the only time.

In the morning I would leave early but David would invariably be late for his classes. He did not appear to be the studious type, but in a much deeper sense of the word he was. He read all the time, and there was always a paperback sticking out from the back pocket of his torn and raveled jeans. He handed in his papers months after they were due but he always finished them. He was not like other students who procrastinated for months out of fear. He procrastinated because he liked "beating the system." He teased me about being a "conscientious girl," the same kind of girl, he said, who always had good handwriting in school. He wrote his papers at odd times, like three in the morning, between articles for the *Crimson* or fights with me. At exam time, he found a friend whose father was a doctor and supplied him with tabs of "speed" (as if David needed anything to speed him up). Those were the only times he woke before noon. He would kiss me goodbye, trundle off for breakfast, which he otherwise never ate, and walk into the chilly Cambridge morning, puffing away at a Kool. Inevitably, he would bring back an A.

We fought interminably. We picked on each other over everything. I was always putting David down, jealous of his strength, and he retaliated by calling me "bourgeois." He was intolerant of my upwardly mobile aspirations, and raged when I expressed admiration for anything "upper class." All I had to do whenever I wished to needle David was tell him about Marshall. "I can't believe it. You actually dated a guy who belonged to a final club!" he would rage. There was a lot of screaming and kicking and arguments invoking political ideals, but it was on the personal level that we scored our points. We could hurt each other very much, for each of us knew where the other was weak.

By day the room was a pigsty filled with our cigarette butts and dirty clothes. (Sloth was another habit David inspired. Once my cousin came up to visit me and reported back to my mother that instead of washing my shirts, I sprayed deodorant under the arms.) And by night—it was usually after two when the two of us returned from the *Crimson*—the room was filled with our shouts. Eleanor was too kind to say anything, but Tess regarded us with undisguised contempt. I could not forget the look on her face when she picked up one of David's cigarette butts off the floor. "Tell me. Is it also against your political principles to use ashtrays?" she asked.

Paige had been back at school since September, but she and I hardly spoke. She had joined the *Advocate,* the Harvard literary magazine, but her appearances there were rare. She darted in and out at odd hours, and stuck close to a small group of quiet women who smoked too much. Paige wrote essays on theater, but always about obscure plays. You had to think she chose her subjects deliberately to avoid any that were in the public eye.

Men occupied her time, too, the dozens of curious creatures who were enamored of her and put up with her peculiar ways. Of all the women I knew, she dated the largest number of men once and the smallest number twice. She was alternately intense and aloof and this drove everyone mad. The same *Crimson* editor who denigrated my legs was infatuated first with Sarah Worthington and then with Paige. He had an infallible instinct for unreachable women. But eventually, even he backed off. Paige was only interested in platonic affairs, and men found it impossible to sustain her repeated rebuffs.

My best friend, aside from David, was Daisy, although it bothered me to see her do so well. I, too, used to care about my grades; in high school, they were the center of my system, my grades and my weight, the dubious currency by which I measured my self-worth. But I cared about them no more. Even Daisy's nervousness upset me because watching her get sick over an exam one day and come bounding through the Yard exuberantly the next reminded me of a habit I had given up and, like a reformed junkie, I envied her her drug.

Paige always asked about Daisy. It bothered her, too, to observe Daisy making the most of her talent while she, Paige, could not. And so she did with Daisy what she did with everyone—she found her weakness. "She's so repressed," she would say. "There's something wrong there." Or, "Oh, Daisy," she'd say, as if she loved her but wasn't it sad. "She's just so, well, you want to reach out and protect her, don't you?" And I did—from Paige.

But not always. Now there were two people I envied on the *Crimson,* my boyfriend and my best friend, and I felt sandwiched between them. It was uncanny the way David had come, in one year, from being viewed as a ridiculous sloganeer to being the political boss. He gave patronizing advice and I found myself living with a man whose power and strength I envied, who managed to get things done, and who, from time to time, would try to teach me how to write. I felt the rage of a subjugated colony (David was always railing against imperialists), and he seemed to play on it. "Oh, Daisy," he might say, and I couldn't help but wonder if he knew what he was doing. "She's really amazing. Such a good writer, and so nice!" And if on that day Daisy might come bounding into the *Crimson,* saying, "Gee Fran, look at what

I wrote," I might find myself seeking the cruel comforts of a late-night chat with Paige.

TOWARD the end of our junior year, Matina Horner, the new president of Radcliffe, was featured in a cover story in *The New York Times Magazine* about her theories concerning women and their fear of success. The essence of her findings was summed up in an experiment in which students were asked to elaborate on the following situation: "After first-term finals, John finds himself at the top of his medical-school class." A typical male response: "John is a conscientious young man who worked hard. He is pleased with himself. John continues working hard and eventually graduates at the top of his class." But when the name "Anne" was substituted for "John," the responses from women changed dramatically. "Aggressive, unmarried, wearing Oxford shoes and hair pulled back in a bun, Anne wears glasses and is terribly bright." And even more disturbing: "Anne starts proclaiming her surprise and joy. Her fellow classmates are so disgusted with her behavior that they jump on her in a body and beat her. She is maimed for life." The last respondent may have been kidding, but the point was clear: women associated worldly success with personal disaster.

Maybe this was the answer to why Radcliffe women hadn't done so well professionally in the past. It was difficult to tell. So many theories were starting to come out about women that we were like medical students who every week enact the symptoms of another disease. One week we were afflicted by the fear of success; the next, we felt a craving for the zipless fuck. "Fear of success" became such a buzzword that eventually it became a joke. "Why didn't you hand your paper in on time?" "It must be my fear of success." Or, "Why don't you aim the ball in the court?" "Sorry. I'm afraid I might win." Was it true? We didn't know, but whether it was true or not didn't matter so much as all the attention it aroused. Just thinking about it affected the way we behaved. Now if you were apt to hesitate on the brink of a challenge or falter before a goal, in the back of your mind a finger wagged: "Are you sure it's not just your fear of success?"

By the end of junior year, Daisy was happier than she'd ever been. Her pictures were on display in a gallery in Somerville and her grades were among the highest in the class. Only a handful of juniors are elected to Phi Beta Kappa, but Daisy was among them that year. When she ran up and told me the news, it was with her usual combination of joy and distress. She was delighted with the news but always felt as if perhaps there was something wrong with pushing herself so hard. Her parents' general euphoria about any of her accomplishments always made her slightly uneasy, and she questioned her own motives for working so hard.

Paige was receding farther and farther into the background. At the end of junior year she had slunk right out of the *Advocate* as quietly as she had slunk in. Instead of devoting her energies to the magazine, where ultimately she might have been rewarded with a position on the executive staff, she dissipated them and so now not trying was her excuse. She took a job as an assistant to a newspaper columnist. It would get her away from Harvard and into Boston in an atmosphere that might not terrify her so much. In fact, she made this into an escape the way she did everything else. The woman wasn't half as clever as Paige, who must have been frustrated, writing expert copy for someone else to use. Yet if Paige's name had been attached to the work, she would have reverted to a safe academic style. We reacted as always, with predictably bitchy comments. "Oh she's terribly messed up," I offered. "You wouldn't believe her personal life," Paige said.

My problems took the customary form of a seasonal although dramatic fluctuation in my weight. One afternoon I was running through Harvard Square when I saw a copy of *New York* magazine on the newsstand at Nini's Corner. The cover had a picture of an emaciated woman and the title, "Anorexia, the Starving Disease."

I bought a copy, raced home, and read a description of anorexia and the character defects associated with it, of which immaturity and a confusion about femininity were the least disturbing. I felt so miserable that I threw the magazine away, but not until I had lapped up every word.

But at the beginning of junior year, when I saw how extreme the problem had become (although I was in the bingeing, not the starving phase), I had gone to the University Health Services in search of help. When Paige had first encouraged me to talk to someone I balked, viewing this as yet another of her demonic schemes: Paige was crazy and wanted to see everyone that way. Now I went of my own accord. Even though Miranda had left school, I asked to see the psychiatrist she had seen, attributing special powers to him because Miranda had trusted him. (I still admired her for having had the courage to leave.) During our interview I told the psychiatrist that I feared I was going to gain an uncontrollable amount of weight that year and asked if he could help me. He said he thought he could and that I should come back to see him the following Monday.

When I returned, the psychiatrist arranged for me to see a graduate student working under him named Franklin. I did not like anything about Franklin, from his Mao cap on down, but I faithfully kept my appointments each week in his office on the third floor, which I had formerly associated with Miranda's collapse. He told me not to worry, that his father had been obese and he well understood the problems associated with weight control. His first suggestion was that we try a little behavior "mod." Every time I went on an eating binge, I was to wear the clothes that made me look the fattest. After my first especially bad binge, I put on the tightest skirt and sweater I could find. David thought I looked great (bigger breasts), but my friend and fellow binger Lucy Love, an ex–prom queen's daughter from Oklahoma City who also binged, confirmed, over coffee malteds at Tommy's Lunch, that I looked terrible. The more I drank, the tighter the skirt pulled. I felt so terrible that I finally ran home and flung it off. I was so disgusted with myself and how terrible I looked that I went out and ate again, this time in a flannel shirt and baggy jeans.

When it was clear that Franklin wasn't helping my eating problem, he suggested we talk about my feelings toward him. "Now be frank," he said. "What do you honestly think of me?" "Twerp" was the first word that came to mind. He told me I was resistant to therapy. We waited out the session and that was all I had to do with the University Health Services that year.

But during my courtship with David, the binges got worse. When I first moved in with him, I weighed 125 pounds. But by the time we parted at the end of that spring, I was 155. David, who was indifferent to food and subsisted on one meal a day (a cheese-steak sub and Coke at Tommy's), couldn't understand what the fuss was about. He liked my more rounded self, but even he was aware that this was more than a matter of breasts. He told me once that a mutual friend of ours, a woman with whom I shared a summer house after freshman year, told him that for long stretches I wouldn't eat and then in one sitting I would polish off an amazing quantity of food. I was embarrassed that David knew this and angry at the woman for betraying me to him.

If David did not care about my weight gain, other people did, or at least I thought they did, which made it worse. One day at the end of junior year, I was coming out of Adams House when I ran into a man I had dated the summer after freshman year. Of all the men I'd gone out with up to that point, I'd liked Jack the best. I remember one weekend we spent at Tanglewood. Before we had left his apartment in Cambridge that morning, I noticed a picture of a dark-haired woman on his bureau. I knew he had been dating someone named Patty, but I didn't know how pretty she was. All weekend the Boston Pops played and I binged. Jack didn't notice, but I remember hiding at the back of the shed and being afraid that Jack would find me eating chocolate chip cookies while the orchestra played the "1812 Overture" and an Irving Berlin medley.

I saw Jack for the rest of that summer and during the first half of sophomore year, but by the end of that semester he suggested we call a halt. He said it might have worked between us but I never seemed to give it a chance. It always seemed as if I were trying to hide something. When I saw him in front of Adams House junior year, I made polite conversation and hastened off. Jack was obviously too polite to comment on how much weight I'd gained, which left me to imagine the terrible things he must have thought. With other people, I didn't even have to imagine. Paige, for example.

My problems exacerbated my relationship with David, but he had troubles of his own that June. He was politically out of step. The sixties were finally winding down, and although his classmates parroted his revolutionary jargon he suspected that for them it was only a phase. They would eventually get jobs working at law firms or in business and David would be left alone to save the Third World. Partially for that reason, he lashed out against anything he associated with being bourgeois. "But I'm bourgeois," I said. "No you're not. Your father's a small businessman. Read Malamud (he meant *The Assistant;* David was always telling me what to read). "But I went to summer camp." "So, other students went to France. Besides, it's okay. It's only a phase. It will wither away like the state."

But there was one bourgeois activity that, for some reason, David could not abide, and that was tennis. One morning I roused myself from bed and started to look for my tennis shoes. We were spending most of our nights in David's room then (Tess, and by this point even Eleanor, had gotten fed up) and I had made plans to play with David's roommate. I was not insensible of the reaction this might provoke; it was part of my motivation. I was tired of David's telling me what was right and what was wrong. I was sick of his attitudes and condescending advice. Choosing my weapon, I unearthed my tennis racket from its cobwebby hiding place under the bed. I hadn't played since my preppie days with Marshall, in which I, too, had hoped to escape from the bourgeoisie, but in a more sensible upward direction. Mark, David's roommate, was more or less innocent of my scheme. Mark was an amiable fellow, slightly short and slightly overweight. Well-fed you would say. He had gone to prep school in Connecticut, but despite his ambition and upwardly mobile ways he and David got along. They accepted each other for what they were: a "crazy revolutionary" (Mark's view of David) and "an opportunistic pig" (David's view of Mark), and with genuine affection. I had always suspected Mark of having a villainous streak. He wasn't the sort of guy who would set a house on fire, but then he might like to watch it burn.

David, who was as good as dead in the morning, opened one eye like a sleeping giant. "Where are you going?" he called from his bed. "Out," I replied, rummaging through the drawer to find a pair of shorts that fit. Only when I was within touching distance of the door was I brave enough to drop the bomb, "to play tennis." I may have imagined it, but I thought I heard a voice say, "I'm coming, too."

Ten minutes later we were on the court: Mark in his regulation whites; me, plump and pale, looking ridiculous in a wraparound skirt that flapped open in the breeze (I never found the shorts); and David, red-eyed and unshaven, half a Kool dangling from his lips. "I'll show you how to play tennis," he said, waving a borrowed racket as he followed us toward Soldiers Field. We made it through a couple of rallies, but with David the game took a violent turn. "Stupid game," he muttered, whacking the ball. His shots turned lethal when directed toward me. Barely a point was earned before all the rallying and screaming turned to utter pandemonium. I don't know how it came to this, but after thirty minutes of dodging his guided missiles I felt the sharp punch of a tennis ball in my chest. Mark, seeing that the situation had gotten out of hand, tried to hold David back. With David flailing his tennis racket in the wind, and me ducking for cover, trying to keep my skirt closed, we ran back to the dormitory. Whatever relationship we had managed to sustain was over for good, I thought.

My hope was that a summer away from David and everyone else would restore me to a healthier state. In May, I had won a newspaper scholarship to attend a three-week course in copy editing at Ohio State and then to work as a copy editor on a newspaper in Orlando, Florida. David, who, as editor of the *Crimson,* had to stick around and oversee the summer edition of the paper, seemed indifferent to my going. "It'll be good for you," he said, chucking me under the chin. "You'll see." (David knows best.) "Aren't you going to miss me?" I asked. "Sure," he said, and bent down and gave me an extra wet kiss.

Always before leaving for our various summer destinations, my brother and I returned to Brooklyn, partly to check in with my parents and partly to get our laundry done. I knew my mother hated it when I lost and gained weight, and this time I had really done it. I had spent the previous year living in David's shadow and now that I had stepped out from behind it, I looked pasty and white, my skin the pale green color of the underbelly of a frog —the combined effect of all those cigarettes, the birth control pill and a diet of malteds and cheese-steak subs. "All right. How bad do I look?" I asked my older brother on the car ride down. "Am I as fat as S——?" (S——was a large woman in Adams House.) "Yes." "Am I as fat as K——?" (K——was even larger.) "Not quite, but K——has it in the right places." "How about C——?" (C——had a serious problem.) "Yeah, I'd say you're about as bad as C——." We pulled up in front of the house and my mother ran from the door to greet us. When she saw me her smile froze. "What is it, Fran, do you purposely look miserable just to upset me?" My brother's was the only note of levity in our house that weekend. He coined a new name for me: Tanko.

What a relief it was to finally get away. I loved the three-week editing course at Ohio State and the other interns. They viewed the course as a prelude to getting drunk every night on the main street through campus, appropriately named High Street. Our professor was well meaning but crude. He referred to Latin American countries as banana republics and insisted on calling the one Puerto Rican student in our class José, even though his name was Ray. It was only from Betsy Bloomington, the professor's able young assistant, that we learned anything at all. She was an intriguing combination of brains and beauty. She also seemed a little icy and we were dying to get the goods on her personal life.

We had only been separated for one blissful month when David called. "Listen, I'm hitching out to Chicago for the week. Why don't I swing by Columbus and we can spend the weekend touring my 'hood.' " I was quite sure I didn't want to see him or his "hood." "Well, I—." "Don't decide now. I'll be there tomorrow night." Once David made up his mind to do anything, there was no stopping him. Two mornings later the girl in the bunk bed below mine awoke to see four feet dangling overhead. Later that day, with me as the unwilling hostage, David helped me up into the cab of the truck of a steelworker who had stopped to pick us up. We were en route to Chicago, heading west through Gary, Indiana, where the sky was an eerie shade of pink. Mike said it was due to the steel furnaces that kept going all night.

David's house was modest, a typical Chicago bungalow, five rooms, one floor. His family were the only whites on the block. Once during the course of the weekend, I asked Mrs. Benson why she and her husband didn't move when their neighborhood had changed. She seemed struck by the question. "We were members of the neighborhood church and the congregation told us it wasn't right to leave."

She was big, like David, and worried a lot. She taught school and made mildly deprecating comments about her son, like "You'd think he'd change his shirt" or "I'll bet he's always speaking out of turn." She was also conscientious. She told me she had recently seen a collection of children's books at the Goodwill near their house and couldn't resist buying it to save the school system money. The entire house was filled with books, most of them at least thirty years old, the remnants of David's father's abandoned doctoral work. The house was plain, but it was not at all bleak and the books gave it dignity.

If there was warmth and cheerfulness in that house, it came from David's father, whose gray eyes twinkled as he puffed on his pipe. He was a shorter, pale version of David and walked with a cane. David told me he had been injured in an accident, which was why he had abandoned his doctoral thesis. Now he, too, taught school. I remember a story David told me about him at college. He was in an army unit in which there was one black soldier. Every year the unit held a reunion at a different member's house. The year it was the black member's turn, his wife prepared an elaborate spread with an enormous amount of food. Only David's father showed up.

Before we left, David showed me all the landmark sights of Chicago, that is, the major influences on his youth: the pink stucco country club where he used to caddy and the steel mill where he had had a summer job. And of course we visited his high school, where, he had told me a thousand times, he had been president of his class. The night before I left, his parents took me out for dinner at Stouffer's. David's grandfather, Daniel, came with us. He was Jewish, although the rest of the family was not. David used to joke he'd make the perfect son-in-law for my mother. "A nice Jewish boy." "But you're only one-quarter Jewish," I would say. "It was good enough for Hitler."

Evidently my fellow interns, worried about the manner in which David had hustled me off, had told the journalism professor that I had been "kidnapped" and might never come back. When I did show up Monday morning, Betsy asked if she could speak to me after class. "Don't you know it's against the rules to leave?" she asked. I told her I did not. She said she was "very disappointed" in me because I had seemed promising from my application and she had chosen me to work with her in West Palm Beach after the course. David called Betsy the "reality instructor," after the villain in Saul Bellow's *Herzog.* He took an instant dislike to her and the sentiment was returned.

David went back to Cambridge and I followed Betsy to Orlando. The first two weeks there I did nothing but try to regain her favor. I worked hard and Betsy was impressed with my reformation. She was the only woman of any stature in the newsroom and was obviously hated by the men (sexism aside, Betsy could be stern; that she was blond, beautiful and twenty-five didn't help). But I liked Betsy and wanted to please her. I was so happy being away from David and Harvard that I felt I never wanted to go back. I worked, swam and slept on the beach. My body assumed a more normal shape. By mid-August I had shed thirty pounds. (Paige said I was like a blowfish, pumping up in winter and deflating to normal size by the time I returned to school in the fall.) On the nights that I did not join the rest of the staff for a beer at the El Flamingo, I went home to my tiny garage apartment, which I shared with my landlord's Rolls-Royce, and sat in a rocker and read. The only sound disrupting the peaceful tropical bliss was the phone. Usually it was David.

Perhaps it was too sudden, picking up the phone and telling him, in words that surprised even me, "It's over. I think we should end it before the fall." A pause and then suddenly, a slight metaphysical click, a shift in gears so palpable it carried over the telephone wires. "David? Are you there?" I tried to call him back but the line was off the hook. I thought of freshman year and the relentless campaign he had waged to win me. And then with a sickening feeling, I knew that David would do something bizarre. I calculated the flight time from Boston to Orlando.

The first person I told was Betsy, who was incensed. She saw how much better I looked now than when we'd met, blamed David for my previous troubles and took credit for my current success. It is also possible that Betsy goaded me on, but if so, I'd goaded her to goad me. I didn't know if I could hold out against David but I knew Betsy could, so I planted the seed. " 'Reality instructor?' I'll fix him."

In retrospect, maybe I should have prevented David from being his own worst enemy, but I knew that to see him was to give in to him. So I surrendered myself to Betsy, who plied me with sherry and chocolate mousse, while David put the finishing touches on his own doom. He left Cambridge that night, borrowed money from a friend, and upon arriving in Orlando the next day, rented a car and tried to find me. He strong-armed his way into the newsroom, where some well-intentioned soul told him I had gone to Miami for the weekend. On the way to Miami, he got into a car accident and totaled his car. "Now don't worry," Betsy said, when she told me the news. "If he were that badly hurt, he couldn't have called to tell you he was." I wondered if I should call him but Betsy said no. By the end of the week David went back to Cambridge, wounded. But when David was wounded, he didn't bleed. He wrote.

CHAPTER 4

Seniors

Children of very strong, rich men usually end up playing the piano or being a little mixed up. My children want to outdo me.
—VICTOR POTAMKIN, FOUNDER AND PRESIDENT, POTAMKIN CADILLAC

Every fall the *Crimson* put out a special registration issue warning of the perils of freshman year. As senior editors, it was our turn to fill the issue. One woman wrote a piece that was so intrusive that her freshman roommate vowed never to speak to her again. (She revealed the girl's intimate depilation habits.) I wrote a piece about freshman year too, but I was kinder to Kate. Clearly I had been at fault in that relationship, and what I had heard about Kate in later years made me see how severely I had underestimated her. After rooming with me (and I doubt I was to blame, although you never know) she joined Students for a Democratic Society (then in its death throes), abandoned physics and, in a complete 180-degree turnabout, became an active member of Harvard Hillel.

But the loveliest piece in the registration issue was a wistful elegy written by a man with a broken heart. The author was David and the villain, the thinly disguised "Rhoda from Queens."

The story, on the front page, told how its hero, fresh and raw from Chicago, had the misfortune to stumble upon Rhoda, no less pure and perfect a vision than Dante's Beatrice, but with a much bigger mouth. It chronicled the ups and downs of their relationship and ended on a plaintive note: freshmen, be advised. Stay away from the likes of Rhoda from Queens. And in case anybody couldn't figure out who Rhoda was, my piece and David's ran side by side under a headline that said, FRESHMAN YEAR: HIS VERSION . . . AND HERS.

David swore he had not laid out the page, and I believed him. He probably handed his story to the dummy (the person in charge of laying out the page) and instead of telling him outright to "run this piece next to hers" he probably suggested it more subtly: "Screw the bitch."

It was an interesting piece, which I read at the kitchen table of my parents' home. My younger brother read it when I was through. "What did you think?" I asked, trying to contain my rage. Bob, who has always been more level-headed than I, looked at me with prematurely wise eyes and replied, "Fran, I have to admit. It's beautiful."

And it was. True, I was slightly upset about the subject David chose, but I was more upset that his piece was better and would draw attention to his side of the page. As to the subject matter, I read it hunting for clues to David's state of mind, which was not always apparent from his actions. How could anyone who risked his life in Florida to find me hate me so much, and how could anyone who was capable of holding a tennis racket above my head with intent to kill love me as much as he claimed he did? It was a mystery, and one to which the answer, I feared, was that it was not me David had ever loved but some image he had created whose more perfect embodiment was flawless Rhoda.

The piece also confirmed what I had felt all along about the relationship. Like the article, it reached moments of dramatic intensity only at the beginning and at the end, that is, the relationship came to life for David only when he was winning or losing me. Having me was the dull, lifeless in-between.

Still, I did not mind his public catharsis. Our affair had been public since Day One and any fictional portrayal of it couldn't have been worse than it had been in real life. Also, Rhoda was far more clever (and far more elusive) than any character I had ever been able to create, despite my attempts at fibbing. All I cared about now was to have a sober and restful senior year and I knew that would be possible only if David and I stayed apart.

I didn't even check in at my room that first day but went straight to the University Health Services in search of Miranda's ex-shrink. I was terrified that I was going to gain vast amounts of weight, just as I had done junior year, and graduate looking like a beached whale (David's term of endearment for my sleeping self). But it was hard for Dr. Rogers to take me seriously. I had dieted so strenuously in the tropical bliss of David-free Florida that I was back down to a size six.

"You look fabulous," Dr. Rogers said. "I see your visits with Franklin must have helped a lot." I spent the next half hour trying to persuade him that it was not Franklin but sun, fun and being away from Harvard that were responsible for the change and that it wouldn't last. But here I was on shaky ground. If I tried to prove to Dr. Rogers how incompetent Franklin was he would obviously think the problem was mine, or worse, that Franklin had hit upon the very core of my neurosis, provoking in his patient a natural defensive reaction. On the other hand, I could calmly and rationally lay out my case against Franklin and win Dr. Rogers's support. The only problem with the second alternative was that the first one was correct. I couldn't do it, thereby proving to Dr. Rogers what he suspected about Franklin's effect on me all along.

"Let's put it this way," Dr. Rogers said. "He apparently touched a nerve."

More bellowing on my part. More up-and-down bobbing of Dr. Rogers's maddeningly cone-shaped head. "I see. You think you're smarter than he is? And his father's obesity has nothing to do with your trouble with weight? That's very interesting." Pause, to write that down.

After another equally unproductive thirty minutes, Dr. Rogers looked at his watch. Since I wasn't paying and Harvard was, Dr. Rogers had all the time in the world.

"Perhaps you'd like to see a woman this time."

By now the feminist movement was permeating the culture. Fear of success. Sex objects. It was all part of the jargon. In 1970, Carol Sternhell, the second woman managing editor of the *Crimson,* had written: "Men may sympathize . . . but basically, they're still staring at your tits." But the combative stage was over, and people were starting to become sensitized to the issues. Articles about the psychology of women and precursors to the landmark *Our Bodies, Ourselves* began to appear. The therapist Dr. Rogers introduced me to immediately zeroed in on what she saw was the obvious cause of my eating binges and my ambivalent attitude toward success. Her basic thesis: "You see, you and your older brother may have achieved the same things—high marks in high school, acceptance to college—but because he was a boy, your parents praised him more."

Now this made sense. The truth was, I would have accepted as gospel anything Johanna said. I liked her, for silly reasons: she had long brown hair that kept falling in her face and the deep burnished coloring of an Indian. But what I liked best about Johanna were her enormous feet, which looked even bigger in the little-girl T-strapped shoes she wore. There is something irresistible about a woman who is lovely in every way but one. "It makes me vulnerable," she said when I told her about this.

Perhaps it was simply a matter of having a kind face to talk to each week, but senior year I felt more relaxed about college. I listened to her theories, and just as I had learned to rethink history after reading Marx and Weber, so I learned to rethink my own past, à la Johanna. First I singled out my older brother as the villain but Johanna didn't want to hear about him. She said sibling rivalry was a way to deflect emotion from the real culprit, who was most decidedly my mother.

"It was important to her that you be thin?" Johanna asked.

"Yes," I said.

"Because you were the girl."

"I suppose so, yes."

She never really offered theories, but then her questions didn't exactly leave up in the air what she thought about my case.

"Your mother may have been a basically happy woman but she shared her problems and self-doubts with you, because she identified more with you. That meant everything you did mattered more to her, the way you looked, the way you acted, but mostly, your weight. Was she overweight as a girl?"

"Yes," I said.

"I see."

Whenever they said, "I see," I knew terrific progress was being made, at least in their minds. It gave you the irresistible urge to smash their theory to bits. But I had to admit that Johanna was getting warm.

"Actually, my mother is very thin. A lifetime member of Weight Watchers. The only woman in the history of Weight Watchers of Flatbush to keep her weight off for twenty-odd years. She even has a diamond pin."

"I see," she said. And then it was time to go.

I said nothing about my sessions with Johanna to David or Daisy or Paige. The time I spent in there was mine alone and I rather enjoyed the notion of having one aspect of my life untouched by Harvard or any of my Harvard friends. It was just Johanna and me, upstairs in her cubicle on the fourth floor of the University Health Services, one flight above where Miranda had spent the worst of her days. In a way I envied Miranda. By breaking down completely, she had afforded herself the opportunity for a complete body job, whereas I was only caving in enough to let them touch up the paint.

"The most psychotherapy can ever hope to accomplish for the neurotic individual is not to rid him of his problems but to let him learn to cope with them," I had often heard my Uncle Harry say. (He was a psychologist who did not practice because he believed psychotherapy was only slightly more helpful than witchcraft.) It wasn't much to look forward to but it was all I had.

And so I continued to see Johanna. She said if we talked about what was bothering me, perhaps the binges would stop. Every week I came to her and talked about the issues bothering me, and every week I binged.

Qualitatively, senior year was very different from the previous three, solitary and somewhat more purposeful, with the specter of graduation looming ahead. Part of the reason was that many of us had to write a thesis, a mini-dissertation that took up most of the year. In certain departments this was a prerequisite for graduating; in others, merely a means to obtain additional honors. Characteristically, almost all the women I knew decided to undertake this burden. The thesis was like an anchor, tying us to our rooms, cutting drastically the time we spent at the *Crimson* or playing Pong at Tommy's Lunch. The papers would be preserved for posterity in Widener Library, but I doubt many of us wrote them for the fleeting pleasure of seeing our names in the card catalogue (though this was not bad for cheap thrills. I later found my card stuck among the other *Sch*—legends: Albert Schweitzer, Delmore Schwartz, my brother). More compelling was a last chance to take from Harvard tangible evidence of what we'd learned. A diploma was one thing, but two hundred pages of weighty prose bound in black leather—that was proof of knowledge. On that theory, my two hundred pages should have been blank, but I was hoping that the same knack that had gotten me into Harvard—a talent for speaking about subjects I knew nothing about—would get me out. I also wanted to salvage one thing from my Harvard education of which I could somehow be proud, and with the help of Johanna and my thesis advisor (a female graduate student who helped, me more than any professor I ever had), I set to work on my opus. It helped that all of us had the same goal, so even if one wanted to do a little mischief there was no one to do it with. In the section of Adams House where most of the seniors lived, one heard only a gentle clacking noise and a low electronic hum, the sound of a hundred Smith-Coronas going full blast.

THE threesome that had moved so cheerfully into Adams House sophomore year had filed for a divorce, long overdue. Tess wanted a single. Basically, she had wanted a single ever since David entered my life, and now that she was a senior it was possible. She packed herself efficiently into a suite in A-entry and was hardly heard from again. All I knew of her life was what I saw of it in the dining room. Jeffrey was in Italy, having graduated the previous year, and in response to her newly widowed status, Tess was forced to make friends. This she did with a group of pre-medical jocks, who were as single-minded as Tess. But they seemed to have fun. The pressure of getting into medical school did funny things to people and it was the pre-medical students who now were among the biggest food-fight enthusiasts.

I had also heard rumors about Tess and crew. Not long after Harvard started a team, Wellesley, Smith, Princeton and Yale all spawned women's crew teams of their own. The Radcliffe team emerged not only as the pioneers but the best. The boat had done so well that senior year it was invited to compete in a special event to be held during the Moscow Olympics. Tess was dying to go; she had never been anywhere other than Cape Cod. But for some reason, the details of which I didn't know, the bespectacled Brahmin coaches did not see fit to put Tess in the A-boat. When I asked her about this she merely shrugged, but her expression suggested something rotten was up. Crew was the one arena in which Tess had risen above her dark little conception of herself and felt the equal of any woman in our class. But the coaches had cheated her, or so she thought, which confirmed everything Tess felt about Harvard: it was not a place for a girl of humble birth. With Jeffrey gone, all she wanted to do was finish her thesis and get out.

Eleanor, too, found more comfortable quarters, but not by herself. Unlike Tess or me, Eleanor actually knew how to conform to the civilities of living with people. Some of her friends, however, suggested that Eleanor's tolerance had its dubious side. A case in point was her cousin, a perfectly horrible girl who, like Eleanor, was dark and tall but unlike her was surly and mean. If plenty of other people at Harvard believed that white Anglo-Saxon Protestants were superior, no one was foolish enough to say so except William Shockley—and Rowena Coe. Rowena was from a small town in western Pennsylvania, and although I don't think she had anything more refined than Chamber of Commerce in her blood, she acted as if she were of *Mayflower* stock. A duller woman I never met. Her father was president of the local bank and her mother secretary of the garden club, which probably explained why her conversation was limited to Swedish ivy and government bonds. Why Eleanor put up with her I couldn't understand, except that Eleanor did have an amazing capacity to endure boredom.

When I saw who Rowena's boyfriend was senior year, I figured it figured. Originally I had known Ed only vaguely as a friend of my brother's. He and I had taken the same seminar junior year.

Ed was reputedly the author of one of those terrible comments you believe is true and so never forget: "She [me] has all of her older brother's bad qualities and none of his good ones."

Ed, too, believed white Anglo-Saxon Protestants were superior, except that he wasn't one. He came from the same Jewish middle-class background I did, but during his sophomore year at Cass Technical High School in Detroit had won a scholarship to Groton, and ever afterwards was never the same. Now he spoke with a slightly affected British accent, hid the truth of his background and toyed excessively with his pipe, an instrument that required more maintenance than a Lamborghini. During reading period his collection of pipe-smoking apparatus really grew. I could finish my meal by the time Ed got the tobacco in the bowl. But he loved the distraction and Rowena loved the whole idea. "Ooooh, I just love the smell of English tobacco, don't you?"

All Eleanor and Rowena had in common, as far as I was concerned, was their WASPdom and the fact that they were "widows," their boyfriends having graduated the previous year. Ed was at Princeton and Eleanor's boyfriend, Reuben, was in law school at the University of Georgetown in Washington, D.C. Other than seeing him on long weekends, Eleanor stayed in her room and tried to finish her thesis. Then I could see why she made such progress with her studies senior year. Reuben was gone and one would almost certainly rather work than listen to Rowena's verbal mulch. As I said to Eleanor, "She has all of your bad qualities and none of your good ones."

I heard vague rumors about Eleanor in those days, no less surprising than the ones I had heard about Tess. According to gossip, she had been admitted to Harvard Medical School that fall. I was surprised. Harvard was a pressure cooker and I was sure Eleanor had had enough. She must have reacted more violently than I had thought to that C-minus on her freshman year calculus exam and felt she had to prove herself still more.

Tess spoke to Eleanor now even less frequently than I did. By the end of junior year, relations between the two of them were starting to wear thin. For one thing, Eleanor's boyfriend, Reuben, did not like Tess. "Bitch," he would say under his breath whenever Tess stomped into the living room and made her desires for silence known. (By then she didn't even have to ask; her presence was warning enough.) There had always been a little competition between Tess and Eleanor anyway, from which I was mercifully exempt. (God knows they didn't envy me; they viewed David as a lunatic and the *Crimson* as an appropriate home for our kind.) But their interests were more intimately tied, and they couldn't help comparing notes. Eleanor in particular used Tess as a gauge. "You finished the problem set already? Gosh, you're fast," she would say to Tess. And it was true. Tess was fast and compared to Eleanor, seemed especially so. Tess could traverse the length of the Adams House dining room in the time it took Eleanor to meditate upon the menu of the day (always posted on the door to the dining room along with other bad news). It was also true they were probably simply irritable—from the effects of living with anyone for two years.

But it was the decision about medical schools that really started the rift. Both were applying, a grueling ordeal and one that inspired backbiting among even the closest of friends. Tess and Eleanor did not give in to that; neither of them was small-minded or envious, but that didn't mean they didn't have their private gripes. Tess didn't even want to go to Harvard, but it bothered her that Eleanor got in. It was James who suggested, not with malice but as if it were a fact of life, that perhaps her father's being in academia had given Eleanor an edge. I did not make much of this theory, but Tess, with her nose for sniffing out privilege, may have resented it.

If it was true, it probably disturbed no one more than Eleanor. She was humble in a school of people with swelled heads and was sensitive to nepotism, of which she did not approve. Eleanor was the last person who would "pull rank." But if she had caught wind of the rumors, other issues bothered her more. She felt a certain pressure to "compete," which she associated with Reuben, Harvard and the whole Northeast. She was ambitious but driven in a more internal sense, always trying to do the "harder" thing because in some ill-defined way, it was "purer." Like Daisy, she, too, wondered if all this striving was so good.

I must have picked a high number in the lottery (the means by which seniors were allotted rooms) because I ended up rooming with a junior I hardly knew. She, in turn, had a friend who had no place to go and so the three of us haphazardly settled into our suite. From the little I learned about them, my roommates were not studious girls. One was from New Orleans and one from Washington, D.C., and both wore black tights and very short dungaree skirts. There was a new career advisor in Adams House (a position with advantages, not the least of which was the opportunity to counsel the growing ranks of women interested in medicine and law), and he was very fond of them. Whenever I mentioned their names, he made a sound like a slurp.

We got along famously because we were hardly friends. Nan's boyfriend was a jazz musician and he and Nan spent most of their time in a piano bar in Inman Square. And Betsy, although she was more often around, was harmless enough. Because I was a senior she liked to ask me for advice and it was nice to have someone think of you as wise. As the "extra" she slept on a faded Indian bedspread on our couch but that didn't mean her presence was limited to that part of the room. Our room was a disaster, and for me to say that meant the problem was pretty much a matter of public health. Betsy took photographs for the *Crimson,* so there were canisters of undeveloped film in addition to the underwear, hair clips, Hägen-Dazs containers and tufts of brillowy blond hair (she too picked her hair). Most people used their empty film containers to store marijuana but Betsy's actually contained film. There was a brief period in which everyone in Harvard Square walked around with a dozen or so photographic lenses dangling from his neck. Betsy, a real trendie, followed suit. But her real passion was men. She had crushes on vapid beach-boy types who preferred vapid beach-girl types to her. For once, I actually cut short the time I spent in conversation in order to settle down to work.

I spent most of my time working on my thesis in my room. My floor was so piled with books that one had to take a running leap in order to get from the doorway to the bed. My roommates were much more considerate of me than I had been of Tess. Every night I worked on my thesis and listened to Barbra Streisand sing "The Way We Were." I chose as my topic C. Wright Mills. Harvard sociologists viewed him as "mediocre," but he was the only sociologist whose prose I could understand. Talcott Parsons was held in higher esteem, but his prose was so dense it demanded an hour per page. Mills hated Parsons, which is why I liked Mills.

I liked to sing and sometimes I would get carried away. I didn't realize the floors were so thin until one day I walked into the dining room and the straightlaced gentlemen who lived below me greeted me with a rather nasal rendition of "The Way We Were," scored for male voices and kazoo.

THE women's movement, the antiwar movement—these were nothing compared to the revolution in health. One day we were eating mean-looking turkey tetrazzini; the next day, yogurt and rolled oats. The change, like all the changes made by the University Dining Hall Services, was introduced with all the fanfare of the christening of a ship. One day, as we were dutifully swallowing the Adams House version of Welsh Rarebit (Day-Glo orange cheese on rubbery toast), a team of dish ladies wheeled in a long serving table holding eight silver tubs. Clockwise from left: three flavors of yogurt—pink, purple and gray (the gray was "plain") —raisins, rolled oats, wheat germ and honey in the same little plastic packets the mustard came in. The only change that stirred up as much excitement was the news of an intruder in the Adams House pool. (Rumor had it that he had sat at the edge of the pool and fondled a stocking.) The amazing thing was how little the new menu additions had to do with health. Men ate platefuls of potatoes and the dull gray matter that passed for beef, and only when that didn't fill them up resorted to bowlfuls of yogurt into which they added everything else. Women ate their usual toxic combination of yogurt and Tab.

Even as I dug into my thesis, there was *Crimson* work to be done. We were seniors and could play hotshot, a role for which three years of toadying to other senior editors had thoroughly prepared us. I was a better reporter than I was a writer, but mostly I had nerve. Thinking nothing of it, I would ring up Professor John Kenneth Galbraith at his chalet in Switzerland and ask, "What's new?" Something was always happening in that department. Either a senior economist was being awarded a Nobel Prize or a junior faculty member was being denied tenure because (we thought) of his Marxist views. I took it upon myself to champion the cause of the banished Marxists and tell the Economics Department how to run its life. I wrote terrible things about professors I had never met.

David was remarkably subdued and, for the most part, left me alone. When we met he merely nodded, then hurried on his way. Penitence was written all over his face. I trusted him and so slowly, as the weeks wore on, began allowing myself gestures that I had ruled too provocative before: a nod, a smile, even a communication as lengthy as "Good story today."

On the Saturday after Thanksgiving, I arrived on campus a little ahead of the rest of the school. Harvard Square was eerily deserted as it always is on holidays. No matter how comfortable we felt here during the year, on Thanksgiving and Christmas it became suddenly forlorn. This part of Cambridge was home to nobody, except for the winos who prowled about the Square. I went to the *Crimson,* where I found a note from the police. A woman had been murdered and raped in Longfellow Park in the affluent Brattle Street neighborhood. She was a thirty-year-old fellow at the Radcliffe Institute, and just at the point in her career where her research was beginning to form the foundation for a lifetime's work. She was also married to a professor in the History Department, which may have been why news of her death hit the university especially hard. Usually, the news format did not come easily to me, but this story touched me. David looked over my shoulder at my lead. "Great," he said. Usually his compliments were transparent attempts to cheer me up or shut me up, but this one sounded real. On the strength of it, I finished the piece and wrote a sidebar. The next morning David called me over to the "red-inks." In big red letters someone had written, "V-V-strong."

We didn't immediately become lovers again, but we did over time. David's acknowledging my story had little to do with our reconciliation, which was more a matter of my being worn down. I was back at school, and despite the fifty-five minutes a week I spent in Johanna's care, my tan, my figure and the confidence I had felt in West Palm Beach were fading. Maybe a psychologist smarter than Johanna could have figured it out: When I was thin I didn't want anything to do with David, and when I was fat, well, what the hell.

And so one night I saw him hurrying into the *Crimson,* his face ruddy from the cool November air, his bony wrists protruding from his much-too-short coat sleeves. David was pretty sexy but much of the time he looked forlorn. He didn't own a decent jacket and walked hunched over, an old man bracing for the cold. It wasn't poverty so much as negligence. He never paid attention to what he ate or wore, didn't own a hat, and the minute he hit the street, lit a cigarette, which would have made gloves an encumbrance anyway. He might have looked totally pathetic to me were it not for the black-inspired lilt in his walk, a vestige of his high school basketball days. "Need help?" he asked. I was editing the "dump truck" (the monthly supplement), a job I did poorly and despised. In the next two hours, he rustled up copy, helped me edit and whisked me off to our favorite love nest, a red plastic booth in Tommy's Lunch.

The whole gang was there: Sean McNally, one of those perennial Harvard Square hangers-on (he had graduated years ago, but kept deferring his actual departure) and the rest of the low life. Even Daisy, not one for hanging around a joint as crummy as Tommy's, was there with her new boyfriend, Curt, a science genius from MIT. He was a classic underachiever, but because he was not a woman, people didn't say he had a fear of success; they said he was lazy (although in Curt's case, I think fear of success was more applicable). He had won a Westinghouse science award in high school but now applied his intelligence to electronic games. Daisy, so happy to have finally found someone, invested all her heart and soul in prodding Curtis to do his work (and all her quarters in feeding his addiction to Pong, which is why they were so often at Tommy's. Tommy had just gotten rid of one of the old pinball machines and replaced it with the eerily blank-faced Pong). But Curtis was immune to her efforts: the more she tried to help him, the more he resented her attempts. In the end, Daisy didn't rescue Curtis as much as he succeeded in distracting her. Her grades slipped, and although she would have preferred to be writing her thesis, she spent her nights watching him match wits with the Pong machine at Tommy's.

With all of our friends within earshot, David began his pitch: "Of course if you never forgive me, I'll understand. I'm so ashamed of myself. How could I have hurt you like that?" He stared into his coffee, every now and then taking a quick peek to see if he was making progress. "And certainly if you never wanted to speak to me again, I could understand that, too. But if you would consider . . ."

He didn't even finish the phrase. What was the point? One thing about bad relationships: there's only one other person who understands what you've been through. So when the moment of reckoning had passed and David had finished his Coke and I my English muffins, Tab (milk shake, oatmeal cookies, Cheez-its . . .), the two of us went quietly back to my room.

Perhaps because we were calmer that year, and both of us had our minds on other things, David and I resumed our affair at a much less passionate pitch. I spent most of my time in my room and David spent most of his time in his, where he was also struggling with a thesis. He chose as his advisor one of the more conservative historians at Harvard, a feisty ex-leftist. Each of them thought the other was the bigger fool. The professor viewed David as a "misguided youth" and David considered the professor a typical City College leftist who, having been disillusioned by Stalin and the postwar years, took out his disappointment on the student left. They fought over everything—the old left, the new left, the proper way to knot a tie. The only person David fought with more was me, and it was beginning to dawn on me that this was his way of showing love. Now I did not bristle so much when he called me a toady or gave me unsolicited advice, which he did less frequently in those days. He was scared of himself, I think, and humbler, if such a thing was possible. He had gotten Rhoda out of his system. There is something, though not much, to be said for this ebbing of passion. In its absence, we became friends.

And so I waited for David's return home from his thesis battles and amusedly took in his changing moods. As much as he and his adversary dickered, their method worked. David wrote a commendably reflective thesis and received a magna plus.

AS always, I was on the lookout for Paige, but it was as if some god mercifully timed our comings and goings so they did not coincide. She was only a semester behind us, but withdrew from the competition by surrounding herself with members of different classes. Her younger friends included some of the barbershop quartet downstairs from me and a group of pale, dull Dunster House boys who adulated Paige. Her older friends were two old friends of mine, Missie, my tennis partner from freshman year, and her sidekick, Georgianne. By now Paige had a better sense of whom to choose for friends.

Missie and Georgianne were bright and nice but they weren't any threat to Paige, and perhaps only because I was and I missed her (eternally) did I believe she suffered for the lack. But I was wrong. Paige would have died if not for this injection of levity into her life. Missie was one of the few women I knew who sloughed off not because she suffered from any kind of psychological malaise but because she preferred to have fun. She and Georgianne lived off-campus in an apartment on Craigie Street. Their living room, with its upright piano, had all the gaiety of a brothel or a border-state saloon, minus the men. Missie and Georgianne were abstaining from boys that term and Paige was her usual aloof self. On a moment's notice, the three of them would hop into Missie's convertible and drive to Somerville for ice cream cones. And then there were their midafternoon breaks for "tea." Breaks from what, I'm not sure. Missie certainly didn't study, and with the slightest encouragement Paige would refrain. Only Georgianne worked. Poor Georgianne. The summer after junior year she went to Sweden, and when she returned she walked around looking like a character out of a Bergman film. She was pale and thin and had that sickly vegetarian hue. But Georgianne was a good and loyal friend to Paige. I liked Missie and Georgianne, too, but they straddled the fence between Paige and me and when they had to decide, chose Paige. Perhaps I made them uncomfortable, always steering the conversation to topics by which I might innocently inquire about Paige. They sensed, probably rightly, that the less they told each of us about the other, the better.

. . .

THERE was one other woman we got to know at the *Crimson* senior year, although it would be inaccurate to speak of her as a friend. Her name was Felicity Barrett and she attracted almost as much attention as David did. She was called, on occasion, "The Duck," an affectionate nickname that I could not make much sense of except that sometimes her voice had a nasal, quacking tone.

I noticed Felicity but then everyone did. Perhaps it was her hair, frosted, glittery and gold. Which of us would do anything as unliberated as dye our hair? But Felicity was oblivious to rules and arrived at Radcliffe with brazenly frosted hair. For a skinny girl who was not classically beautiful, she managed to look like a movie queen. She had small greenish eyes and a wide pouty mouth, features that in themselves were hardly prepossessing, yet the total effect was powerful. Her nose was her most distinctive feature, not small or self-effacing as in the typical model's face, but large and arresting. Perhaps she had broken it once or twice in the many tennis competitions she was in, and even the fine hand of the most expensive plastic surgeon in Shaker Heights hadn't managed to smooth out the bumps.

She was from oil money, but that was about all I knew of her past. Her picture in the freshman register shows a plumpishly fit girl, but by the time we knew her she was dramatically thin. One might have presumed anorexia but it was not a term most people knew then; and besides, Felicity was always so tan that she appeared in good health, even at five-feet-eight and ninety-five pounds. Though perilously thin, she exuded a certain sexual allure. She walked with her bones protruding, pelvis first, Elvis Presley style. She wore jeans that were so tight and threadbare that in more than a few places her tanned flesh showed through. And always the fabric was most filigreed in areas of high risk—the small half-moon of her hard but rounded bottom, the slant running from pelvic bone to crotch. Her shirts were always silk or cotton, opened at the neck and for a few buttons beyond. And with her sleeves rolled up and her earrings dangling from slightly protruding ears, she looked like a reformed starlet, just back from Cannes and ready for work. You expected cameras to roll but, instead, heads turned. Felicity did not enter a room silently. She screwed up her face, rooted around in the enormous satchel she carried on her bony shoulders and, speaking as if those few stray souls in the *Crimson* had gathered expressly for the purpose of listening to her, muttered some incomprehensible garble about not having change for the Coke machine. Her voice was shrill, a cross between a scream and a whine—not a pleasant sound. But it evoked the desired response. Coins would be proffered, she'd press the thin dimes into the slot and, catching her reflection in the vending machine's face, yank out a Tab. A few people would be waiting to see her; she had a following even then, and giving the satchel one last jab with her elbow to knock it out of her way, she would stride into the room to the left of the managing editor's office and sigh hugely, collapsing on to the couch. And from that position, knees on the level of shoulders (all the couches sagged), hands flung out, she might expound on some subject, a film, a book, with intelligence and disdain. Always with disdain. I never heard Felicity talk about anything she "liked."

She was a junior by the time I knew her, but she had taken a year off. The rumor was that she had had a nervous breakdown; none of us knew her well enough to say if this was true. Still, it was indicative of the atmosphere at school that we thought it was "romantic" to (nearly) crack up. Nicole and Dick Diver. Virginia Woolf. It was said that Felicity had been among the best amateur tennis players in the country and that if it weren't for her nervous breakdown she would still be on the Radcliffe team.

But what impressed all of us the most about Felicity was her talent. She was among the most promising writers on the *Crimson,* and whenever she wrote an article it was a major event. Her big subjects that year were Erica Jong's *Fear of Flying* and the tennis match between Bobby Riggs and Billie Jean King. It wasn't from a strictly feminist point of view that she analyzed these events. "Feminist? Felicity isn't a feminist," a friend of hers said. "She wouldn't ally herself with any social entity other than the self." It was the battle of the sexes she loved. Sexual games, hanky-panky, suggestions and innuendo were her forte. She wrote about sex in the same way that some children use dirty words, incessantly and with a certain mischievous thrill. Yet one suspected that behind all that bravura was a certain fear. She was a female Prufrock, constantly taunting herself "Do I dare?"

Her piece on the Riggs-King tennis match was memorable, an excuse to take jabs at the suburban upper middle class. Felicity was most vicious on home turf. Her essay, entitled "Libbers and Lobbers," was pitiless about suburban sirens who, called to arms by women's lib, saw the match as a vindication of their decadent way of life. "She's come a long way baby," Felicity wrote with bitter irony: her epitaph on the liberation of the suburban upper middle class.

When she wasn't a social commentator she was a film critic, writing for the avant-garde on the latest art films. With what authority she hacked Eric Rohmer to bits! But my favorite trouncing was the one she reserved for a Ken Russell film. Only a college junior could be so cruel. The critics inside her were as harsh on her own work and yet they did not silence her. Paralysis was not the result of her exacting standards; good writing was.

It was upstairs, in the "inner sanctum" of the *Crimson,* that she did her best work, her head engulfed by a cloud of smoke. She smoked Gauloise. At the end of a long spell, in which she ate and drank nothing but Tab, she would emerge, a sheaf of yellow papers in her hands, a pencil stuck in her gold knotted hair, her large tortoiseshell glasses perched on her bumpy nose, and howl, "My Gawd. This is awful." And you knew it was going to be good.

She had her academic side, too. She was not a scholar the

way some students are. Felicity was much too flashy for that. But she was bright and read voraciously, now tackling all of Russian literature in translation, now taking on Joyce. She could get so immersed in her books that on occasion, it was rumored, snatches of phrases and dialogue from famous authors appeared in her articles and in the term papers she wrote. Once Felicity was said to have reproduced an entire passage of Henry James on an exam. When questioned by instructors, who couldn't believe a writer as fine as Felicity would stoop to plagiarism, she seemed genuinely surprised to see her words so finely commingled with her hero's. People said she had a photographic memory, and that she read with such intensity she couldn't distinguish James's words from her own. That sounded credible and the matter lapsed. A "quirk of genius," people said. She did well enough on her own to make the point moot. The year before she appeared at the *Crimson,* she had won the English Department's highest prize.

I met Felicity through Marshall, but I really became interested in her because I thought we had something in common. One of Marshall's friends, a tall languorous preppie with dark good looks and deep sad eyes, was indifferent to most women but had a crush on Felicity. His name was Jim Whittaker and he was by far the most interesting man in Marshall's club. Jim looked like F. Scott Fitzgerald and wrote beautiful poems. One night Marshall and I were on our way back from a dinner at the club when I saw a woman dashing out of the Baskin-Robbins ice cream store on the corner of Bow Street. She was painfully thin and walked with the fiendish pace of a woman possessed. She held a container of ice cream in one hand and a bag of M&M's in the other and ate as if she hadn't had a meal in days. "Who's that?" I asked Marshall. "She's the only woman who ever broke Jim Whittaker's heart," he said. For reasons of my own, I knew I needed to speak to her.

Not long after the start of senior year, I approached her.

"Duck," I said, "you know the thing some women do with food, starve and then throw up? Do you ever do that?" I presumed she might want to talk about it. She looked at me as if I were mad. "What?" she said in that shrill voice. "I don't know what in the world you're talking about."

So, like everyone else, I had to be content to watch her from afar, and the farther away one got, the larger the legends about her grew. In March there was the rumor about plagiarism. In April she burned down her room. People said she had fallen asleep with a cigarette in her mouth. She nearly killed herself, aside from destroying her room, but there were rumors, too, that she had tried that before. Felicity made a big joke of it. "Oh, I was just so careless," she said, the sentence dissolving into one of her ghoulish cackling laughs.

The only way you got to know anything real about Felicity was through her stories, for it was in these that her humanity emerged. She wrote about winners and losers and people who could not survive. In the spring of our senior year she wrote a piece about a tennis player from Ohio, who had killed herself. Some of us did not like the piece. David thought it was trivial; a few people questioned whether it was honest journalism. The girl had no name and people suggested she might have been made up. When I saw her byline on the story, I left the *Crimson* office, went back to my room, pushed aside the notes for my thesis and made room to read. When I finished I was dumbstruck. I thought it was the most moving piece I had ever read.

I can still see her, standing in front of the Coke machine at the *Crimson,* yanking out a Tab. She was desperately thin, but she drank only Tab. Or iced coffee in summer, large waxy containers of it, black and sweetened with a hideous amount of Sweet 'N Low. If they ever found out human beings died from artificial sweetener, Felicity would have had problems, but then she did not care much about health. Healthy people were boring, she might have said.

. . .

A marked change took place in all of us as graduation approached. Whatever introspective turmoil we had wrestled with during our undergraduate years, we now had more external things to think about, specifically jobs. We did not think so much about careers then. There was talk of people with Ph.D.'s driving taxis and so we worried a little. Nobody was going to an ashram, but on the other hand nobody was going to business school, either. What little added emphasis there was on careers was most pronounced among the women, not because they knew what they would do after graduation but because they knew very clearly what they wouldn't do—get married. Traditionally, courses in Fine Arts and English at Harvard were filled with women and the rich, two groups who were expected to have independent means of support. Women did not abandon English now, but it was not as popular as it had been. Paige said she would have majored in English if not for the stereotype of "all those women reading *Jane Eyre.*" Pre-law and pre-med sections attracted more women, and all-female sections of science courses were created on the theory that women were too intimidated to ask questions in seminars dominated by men.

Slowly doors started to open. Harvard was among the last of the law schools in the country to admit women, but by the early seventies the number of women started to inch well above the traditional five percent mark. Harvard nominated three women for the Rhodes scholarships our senior year, and although none of my friends was among them, Felicity, Daisy and Maureen were nominated for other prestigious fellowships. For a hundred years, most of these scholarships had been restricted to men, and in forwarding the women's names Harvard was openly challenging the rules. Yet it was hard to identify the truly "progressive" position as to the awards. David was proselytizing against them. A few had been bequeathed by people David considered "robber barons" and "imperialists." He felt that by applying for them, one was condoning the history of exploitation and racism associated with them, and set an example by not applying himself. (This was no great sacrifice as he had no interest in further formal study.)

Daisy was affected by David's argument but other factors were involved. There was a slightly condescending attitude toward "getting ahead," which was ironic, since at Harvard one had to value achievement pretty highly to have gotten admitted and gone there in the first place. Many felt ambivalent about success. On the one hand, they had been driven to achieve and resented it. On the other hand, they were dying for it. In addition, there was a lingering notion at Harvard of a gentleman's education: it was considered gauche to strive or at least to be obvious about it. But the situation was even more complex for a woman. Now, if one hesitated on moral or any other grounds, one could easily be accused of "fear of success." Daisy wrestled with all this but in the end the issue was moot. The trustees of the scholarship for which Daisy had been nominated decided not to accept the female nominations (though they changed their minds soon afterwards).

Eleanor, too, wrestled with ambition. More than any of us, she would have loved to have taken a year off between college and medical school, but she was influenced by her pre-med advisor, a nervous little man whose horror tales of medical school rejections added to the pre-med hysteria in the house. When Eleanor expressed as radical a notion as taking some time off, he told her that medical schools would never approve. "It shows a lack of purpose," he said. There were lots of scare tactics, causing you to think that if you did not chase after this fellowship or that award your chance at a decent livelihood would be ruined. Looking back on it, I wonder why we stood for it.

Tess had fewer doubts about her career. It would never have occurred to her to do anything so frivolous as take a year off. What she did was more radical. She got married at a time when marriage was a dirty word. More than half the women who graduated a decade before us were married within the first two years after school, but nobody I knew was headed in that direction except Tess, who acted with her usual disregard for trends. What did she care what the rest of us thought? She was motivated mostly by love, but also by insecurity. Tess had inherited the Depression mentality that nothing was certain until it was nailed down. Ironically, her parents wished she would postpone her wedding and push ahead with her career. "What's the point of going to medical school if you're going to get married?" her father asked. "I'm going to medical school, too," Tess answered. "Don't be ridiculous. You'll get pregnant and then before you know it, eight years of schooling down the drain." And who was Tess to convince him otherwise? Which of us knew women who had tried it this way before?

Toward the end of spring semester, the *Crimson* hosted a dinner to celebrate the purchase of its own press. The newsroom was flooded with famous alumni that night and David talked with many of them, particularly the major antiwar figures. I stood by him, having little to say. It was difficult at any of these functions not to feel like his wife. After dinner a group of us retreated for beers to the Wursthaus in Harvard Square. There were many famous writers and editors, and a lot of uncharacteristically shy *Crimson* editors. Only Felicity acted with aplomb. She was standing off to the side with the handsome and flashy editor of one of the newspapers at which many of us hoped to work, and his girlfriend, a lawyer wrapped in mink. The three of them were joking and laughing like old friends. Felicity later sent the editor her clippings, and although the paper rarely hired students directly from college they made an exception in her case.

I had gotten two offers to work at newspapers and one to work at a magazine (*Time* needed to hire women in some position other than that of reporter-researcher or copy desk drone). It wasn't my fear of success but my fear of David that caused me to choose the lowest-paying and least reputable of the three. He had given me a biography of Henry Luce, just in case I wanted to change my mind and give *Time* a second thought ("Luce: yellow peril, cold war, Chiang Kai-shek"). I chose, instead, to work at a small upstart newspaper in Wyoming. I preferred the grungy environment of a grade-B newspaper and the West sounded exciting. David applauded my going into journalism even though my alternatives were limited—I didn't have the grades for fellowships and being a doctor or lawyer required additional years of schooling. For utterly "wrong" reasons, I was doing the right-on thing.

David planned to head back to Chicago in June, where he intended to get a job as a bus driver or work in a steel mill. His goal was to make money to fund a trip to Latin America. Salvador Allende Gossens had been shot in the fall and the news of his death intensified David's interest in that part of the world. While the rest of us took "gut" courses to free up our time for writing our theses, David walked around practicing his Spanish verbs *("Imperialistas morirán, Imperialistas mueren, Imperialistas estan muriendo!")*. His instincts were leading him south. He liked to be wherever the political heat was.

The night before my thesis was due, four friends with identical Smith-Corona typewriters typed the last few chapters in my room. With their help, plus the half tab of speed that David had slipped under my door, the thesis was all but finished. Still, I knew it would not be possible for me to hand it in on time unless I had use of the car. I didn't have a driver's license, but given the way people drove in Harvard Square that could hardly count against me. The morning the thesis was due, I careened through the Square to the Social Studies office, double-parked, and slapped down the thesis on the secretary's desk, five minutes before the deadline. The Social Studies office, which was decorated with blowup posters of Freud and Marx, was a day-care center during certain hours and it was very funny to see all those toddlers frolicking under their watchful gazes. Fortunately, I did better on my thesis than on my road test that June.

I have snapshots of our graduation, June 1974. Me and Daisy. Daisy looks so adorable with her dark hair, reddened by the sun, pulled back in a clip. Daisy and I had been planning for weeks for our families to meet, but when they did it was a terrible disappointment. We thought that because we liked each other so much they would, too, but it was not to be. The women didn't take to each other and the men looked weary and bored. The next morning, as if to ignore what had happened the previous night, we toasted each other with our cans of Tab and took pictures of our mothers toasting the camera, too.

Daisy would be in Moscow the following year. The professor whose photograph she had "scooped" for the *Crimson* was now ambassador to the Soviet Union and had offered Daisy a job as his assistant. Daisy did not speak a word of Russian, but she planned to spend the summer at Berlitz and fly to Moscow in the fall. I admired her spirit of adventure; I was restless and eager to start my job, but Daisy saw herself as the heroine of a Bildungsroman and thought it might broaden her to spend the year abroad. She, too, did not think about careers so much as adventures.

And there's a snapshot of David, smiling sheepishly into the camera from the red front door of the *Crimson.* Sheepishly, I suppose, because he knows what a bastard he's been. And he knows that if he smiles in a certain way, I can't resist him. David, who led so many protests against Harvard, managed to get himself elected Class Day Speaker. And so up there, in a navy blue blazer borrowed from his roommate Mark, he gave a rousing speech about equality and human rights. It was unnerving to see how fine he looked in a jacket and tie. I had a heretical thought: what a handsome capitalist he'd make.

Even David-skeptics applauded his speech: my mother (who told neighbors after the first time I brought him home, "Of all the men at Harvard, my daughter had to bring home one as poor as a church mouse"); my brother (he predicted that in five years David, like all "middle-class radicals," would "sell out"); and his mother, who seemed to have a pretty good handle on her son. At the end of his speech, she cried.

The female Class Day Speaker was Sonia Tumanoff, whom I befriended in my radical economics course. Everyone else was much too intimidated to interrupt those cool arrogant Marxists except Sonia, who, in the middle of the lecture one day, stuck up her hand and said, "I don't know what you're talking about." Of all the political activists I knew, I admired Sonia the most. She came from the same upper-middle-class suburb that everyone else did, and went to the same posh all-girls school (in her yearbook, the girls posed like wood nymphs, smiling coyly from behind trees). But even there, she stood out. She was a passionate and earthy woman never afraid to say what she thought. At the end of her sophomore year, fed up with Harvard students and their prattle about working-class life, she got a job with the miners down south. The experience changed her life. She returned the following semester to help Arnold Miller defeat Tony Boyle and was now on her way to Harvard Law School. "The miners told me they needed lawyers more than organizers," she said.

Sonia reminded us not to get complacent, that there were miners' children who went to bed hungry and that although we might seek fulfillment by trying to satisfy ourselves, we would find it more in addressing other concerns.

There was one more speaker at graduation, but his was the least distinguished speech. We heckled Elliot Richardson because he had been secretary of defense during the bombing of Hanoi (although at the time of our graduation, he had resigned from the Nixon Administration during the Saturday Night Massacre, when Nixon fired Watergate prosecutor and Harvard Law professor Archibald Cox). Other students who had been active in the antiwar effort heckled him, too, but already an era was drawing to a close. Later that afternoon, Daisy and another friend of ours went to the Fresh Pond Golf Course and played nine holes of golf because it was the afternoon of our graduation from college and it seemed like an appropriately crazy thing to do.

I have no pictures of Paige. By the time senior year approached, she had dropped out of my life. She was no longer a member of our class, having chosen to graduate with the Class of '75 instead. I kept waiting for her to do what she was capable of, have a boyfriend, score a brilliant coup at school, but she didn't. The second semester of our junior year, which was the first semester of hers, she started to write a thesis. She chose as her subject a nineteenth-century vice-president none of us had ever heard of. She never wrote the thesis, it turned out, and did not graduate with honors, which she otherwise easily would have done.

I saw Eleanor only briefly, to give her a hug, one sandaled foot protruding from underneath her graduation gown. And if Tess saw me, she wouldn't even have come up to say "Hello." I was one of the people she was eager to leave. I did not see Felicity, who wasn't ever a close friend, but I heard, lo and behold, that she had parents, too, and that they looked just as proud and silly as the rest of our parents did, hugging their daughter and taking pictures of her in her cap and gown.

I have pictures of my family, too: my older brother, laughing into the camera; my younger brother hidden inside my big brother's gown; my parents, smiling happily, although on my mother the smile looks forced. She was shaken by what had happened to Miranda, whose mother still confided in her. Miranda had cut off all ties to home and was living at the "Y" in Manhattan and working as a typist for a company that manufactured ladies' underwear. My mother said she was nervous about Miranda and about all of us. "I just hope you girls know what you're doing."

And me. There I am, looking angry and mean. Johanna told me I should dress how I feel, which, I suppose, I did. I am wearing a green halter dress that is much too short and no bra, although at that weight I needed one. There's not a piece of anti-Harvard paraphernalia they handed out that day that I didn't wear: the red armband signifying the demand for equal admissions and the cardboard sandwich sign saying "Harvard Unfair—" (I forget to whom). We demonstrated over two issues that day: for Harvard to improve the ratio of men to women, which then was approximately four to one, and for the dishwasher ladies at Radcliffe to get higher pay. The ratio did improve—from four to one to almost one to one. But I'm not sure the good women in the dining rooms ever got their raise. "Let these girls go out there and see how it is to work," one of them said when I came back for a visit in later years.

Which, of course, is what we did.

PART TWO

Women

1974-1984

For the affection of young ladies is of as rapid growth as Jack's bean-stalk, and reaches up to the sky in a night. It is no blame to them that after marriage this *Sehnsucht nach der Liebe* subsides. It is what sentimentalists, who deal in *very* big words, call a yearning after the Ideal, and simply means that women are commonly not satisfied until they have husbands and children on whom they may centre affections, which are spent elsewhere, as it were, in small change.

—WILLIAM MAKEPEACE THACKERAY,
Vanity Fair

CHAPTER 5

Tess

"The time-honored bread sauce of the happy ending"
—HENRY JAMES, *Theatricals: Second Series*

It was the winter of 1983 when I called Tess. I was living in New York at the time with a man I thought I might marry. His parents lived in Westport, Connecticut, and we often spent weekends there, in their pretty little two-story house, empty now with all of their children gone. There was little to do during those long Sunday afternoons other than catch up on reading or answer my mail. Once I was flipping through the telephone directory, looking to see if there was anyone I might call in the 203 area code, and it occurred to me that Tess lived here, in Westport. Hadn't I heard someone say she and Jeffrey had moved here not long after she had finished medical school?

I had tried to find them before. I had heard they lived in New York, but when I checked with Manhattan directory assistance I never had any luck. It should have dawned on me that, of course, Tess would not live in the city, at least not for long. The suburbs might have fallen out of favor among most people I knew at school; they grew up in them and saw moving back as a retreat, Scarsdale redux. But Tess grew up in a cramped apartment in Providence and suburbia had always been a fixture in her notion of the good life. In this and other ways, Tess had a 1950's outlook. And anyway, I suspect Tess always aspired to be a snob.

I checked under Mayer in Westport and sure enough there she was, or rather there was Jeffrey. Jeffrey F. Mayer. It was like Tess not to use her own last name.

I called her on a Tuesday in December. Though we had never been especially good friends, she was as eager to see me as I was to see her, out of curiosity if nothing else. We arranged that I would take the train out to Westport the following Monday. She was working only part-time at the pediatric clinic near her house, she said, which would give me a chance to spend some time with them and also to watch her a little as she worked. I said I'd like that. My ex-roommate Tess, the doctor.

She was ten minutes late. That wasn't like Tess, who had always adhered so rigidly to a schedule. I felt a little funny waiting at the depot in Westport. An attack of paranoia set in. I thought about what pigs David and I had been, how wild and disoriented I was back then, and felt embarrassed for it. What if Tess had changed her mind and decided not to come?

Five minutes later a shiny green station wagon pulled up. "Say hello to Fran, Dora," the woman in the front seat said. She had short hair and dark eyes, unmistakably the old Tess. The directive was issued to a very pretty girl who I can say without being catty had her father's good looks. "Hi, Dora," I said. "She's really very shy," her mother interjected. I bent over to give Tess a kiss, but I felt like taking her in my arms and crying. So many feelings well up in you when you see an old friend, even an old roommate who never liked you very much. We shared a past, the stormiest part of our lives, and that would always count for a lot. She was like family, and whether we had been close or not was irrelevant.

She looked good, I thought, with shorter hair but otherwise was not much different. The beaked nose, the thin dry lips, all made up a face that was prettier than the sum of its parts. Her eyes were her best feature, so dark they looked black, wet and glowering when she was angry, which was almost all the time at school. Looking into them one could see how Jeffrey found her beautiful. In August they would be married ten years.

"So you still love him?" I asked, the direct approach; also, it was the one thing I was most curious about. "I do," she said. "If anything, it's gotten better since school." It turned out Tess had other problems, and although they were not problems on a grand scale, they made me feel much more understanding of her.

After a few treacherous turns on the ice, we pulled up to the house, modest by Westport standards but large for anywhere else. The exterior was made of stone. The three stories were stacked on each other like an uneven layer cake, which gave the house a cheerfully ramshackle feel. One of its many advantages was that it was a ten-minute walk from the train. "Jeffrey takes the train to work," Tess told me. "He leaves early for his seven a.m. squash game." Jeffrey was pushing for partner at his law firm so it was unlikely I would see him that day.

Before we went inside Tess walked into the garage, grabbed a snow shovel and started clearing the driveway. I watched her quick energetic movements. I had forgotten what a powerhouse she was. Little Tess, the demon of crew. But more than power she had determination and focus. She knew exactly what she wanted —to marry Jeffrey and be a doctor—and in that order she seemed to have accomplished those things.

"People say I have it all and they're right," she said. "I'm happier than I've ever been."

All I knew about Tess's life during the year after graduation was that Jeffrey was in Venice studying Titian and she was coaching volleyball at Camp L'Chaim, trying to earn a little money for medical school. I never knew why Tess wanted to go to medical school in the first place. "I loved science, I was good at memorization and it was practical," she said. But Jeffrey came first. She never questioned that. Where he went to law school she would study medicine, and not the reverse. And yet it never seemed that Tess suffered. In the middle of the summer, Jeffrey cut short his stay in Italy to come home and marry her. He missed her, he said.

Where she was married and what kind of wedding it was, I didn't know; she did not share these facts with me, or Eleanor or any of our friends. Not a single woman from Radcliffe was there. Her maid of honor was her high school friend Ruth. When I later saw wedding pictures they were just what you'd expect. No quotations from Kahlil Gibran, no tossing of granola instead of rice. Just a traditional modest-priced affair in Tess's parents' house. She looked like every other bride in the Providence *Journal* Sunday pages.

It was the fall of 1975 when the three of us, Tess, Eleanor and I, had our mini-reunion of sorts. I had just returned from North Carolina where I had opted for early retirement from my second job (I had lasted two months in Wyoming). Eleanor had just completed her first year at Harvard Medical School and she and Reuben were breaking up. Of the three of us, only Tess had the future in tow. She looked radiant that day. Her hair was cut short and she wore a skirt and blouse, a little dressy compared to Eleanor and me in our corduroys, and a dainty pearl in either ear. Wedding presents, I supposed. We talked about what we had done since we'd graduated and it was Tess who seemed the most content. It wasn't only being married she liked. She was also flourishing in medical school, which she felt was a total contrast to Radcliffe. "The people aren't as snobby," she said. And also it was more structured—like the army. I always thought Tess would have made a terrific WAC.

Eleanor and I were tempted to trade our lives for hers. Maybe all those myths were true: you married the right man and life was settled. Were Eleanor or I any happier—I, wandering around Boston looking for work, Eleanor visiting Reuben in Washington on weekends and coming home Sunday nights depressed? But we dismissed the thought as soon as it arose. It wasn't good to think that way, even if it was true.

Their first years in Cambridge were idyllic. Each day Jeffrey would ride his bicycle from their apartment on Dana Street to Harvard Law School and Tess would take the Green Line to Boston University. She was happy then, memorizing human anatomy and fooling around with the students in her class. At BU the student body was of a more practical bent, like Tess. BU was also the school that her father had dropped out of, so it probably gave Tess a great deal of pleasure to complete the education he was denied.

She and Jeffrey lived in Cambridge for another two years and, when they graduated, decided to move to New York. This involved some compromising. Tess preferred to stay in Boston. New York was frightening and much too big, but the better law firms were in New York and Tess could easily get an internship at a hospital there. The decision was made: they would live in Manhattan but only for as long as necessary.

Both she and Jeffrey worked late hours and saved as much as they could. (They were still paying off Tess's college loans.) When Tess was twenty-eight and in her second year of residency, they decided to have a child. The sight of other residents waddling through the halls in their eighth month inspired her. "I would never have done it if I hadn't seen other women doing it. I'm not a pioneer," she said. But she was efficient. By the time Dora was born, she had accumulated so many favors of owed time that she was able to spend her first three months of motherhood without going on call at night. Tess scheduled her vacation to begin on the date that Dora was due and, not surprisingly, Dora arrived on exactly that day.

Four weeks later she was back at work. In retrospect it was too soon, but at the time she anesthetized herself against the tug of maternity. Other women couldn't. Two months after going back to work, they found themselves inexorably pulled back home, their careers no longer so significant. But Tess was remarkably unspoiled in that way: once she undertook a commitment, she stuck with it. "The woman's a machine," David used to say. I thought she was strong.

Yet there were times when even Tess broke down. She was appointed chief resident the following year, a mark of her extraordinary ability to get things done. She hated the job. "I'm not a politician, and some of those doctors can be arrogant bastards," she said. A large part of the chief resident's work is administrative and she had no patience for that. "I started wondering if this is what I spent all those years at medical school for, scheduling some prima donna's vacation while my daughter is waiting for me at home." She had a housekeeper but the woman was "selfish," Tess said. "If I walked in a minute past six, she yelled. What did she want me to do, drop my stethoscope in the middle of an emergency and run?" Then if one of the doctors started complaining about his schedule, Tess might crack. "Some nights I'd come home and the housekeeper would yell at me for being late and I'd just burst into tears."

But Tess, as always, looked ahead. She had been sending out feelers for a non-hospital job after her residency expired. Three of her teachers at the hospital were partners in a pediatric practice in Westport. That was Tess's dream: to live in the suburbs and work close enough to home to be able to feed her kids lunch. The doctors liked Tess (who could always be "one of the guys"), and by then it was considered an asset to have a woman in one's practice. When a position in the partnership opened up that spring, they offered Tess the job. Jeffrey might have preferred to stay in Manhattan but that was their bargain, to move when they could. They never argued or even talked it out; it just seemed to work that way for them. Tess had followed Jeffrey to New York; when it was important enough to her to do something, they did it. Tess wanted to live in suburbia so Jeffrey agreed to commute an hour and a half each way.

"When you marry as young as we did, you grow up together. You build your life around each other's needs. My friends who married in their thirties have more trouble than we do because they're more set in their ways."

I hadn't known much about her background, but she filled me in that morning. Tess grew up poor; her mother worried and her father worked. He was a bill collector but he hated his job. He had hoped to finish college but kept having to drop out. "One week he didn't have money for books, the next week he was fifty dollars short of tuition, that kind of thing." His dream was for Tess's brother to go to medical school, but with so much pressure on him to achieve, the boy rebelled naturally enough. Instead, it was Tess who quietly started bringing home the A's, and her father began to invest his hopes in her. "The day I got eight hundred on my physics Achievement Test was the happiest day of his life." But Tess was emphatic on one point: "It wasn't that I was any smarter than my brother; I just had better study habits." "Oh come on, Tess," I said. "That's what all women say." I told her about a section man at Harvard who told me all his women students complain if he gives them an A. "They argue with him that they don't deserve it." But Tess disagreed.

The weekend we all arrived at Radcliffe, Tess came alone on the train. For some reason, her father couldn't come. Maybe that set her off on the wrong path, all of us in family groups and Tess alone with her book bag, standing there in her Jordan Marsh skirt and brown loafers, a shade too new. Did she take one look at us and decide she didn't belong? She said we were all snobs, which wasn't true. There were plenty of us who felt as out of place at Radcliffe as Tess did, but she never let her guard down long enough to find that out. Instead, she stayed in her room and slammed doors.

"And then I met Jeffrey," she said. Even Tess said she didn't know what she would have done had he not sensed something about her that he liked. Maybe it was the fear, erotic to a person as seemingly unflappable as Jeffrey. It was in October and Jeffrey and a friend had come wandering up to Radcliffe. He noticed Tess was wearing a Union sweatshirt and they talked about people they both knew at Union. "I was sure he'd never call me again." "And then what happened?" I asked. "I saw him at a lecture. We started talking after class and he asked me out for dinner that night." "And then?" "You know the rest."

She was still bitter about Radcliffe, especially because of what happened on crew. "What really did happen?" I asked. "I don't know. It was hard to explain. I weighed even less than the cox, which surely should have made me an asset to the boat. But someone knew someone who knew someone who had a daughter they wanted in the boat . . . I never forgave Radcliffe for that."

When Maureen called her last June to give money as part of the college's Tenth Year Reunion drive, Tess was barely civil to her. "I told her I was perfectly happy to contribute to my medical school, but I wasn't going to give a penny to Radcliffe."

NINE A.M. Car pool, Tess at the helm. "I always make up the driver list. It's easier that way since I'm the one with the complicated schedule." Of the five women in the pool, only Tess worked full-time. The others, represented by a hand, an elbow, an arm holding out a box of lunch from behind a partially opened door, worked part-time or not at all. "What do they do all day in those big empty houses?" I asked. "Think of illnesses to bother their doctors about."

Officially, Tess worked part-time but the designation was deceptive. If you added up the nights and weekends when she was on call, she worked at least a fifty-hour week. She spent Mondays at the hospital, and half of every Tuesday, Thursday and Friday at her office a few blocks away. But on at least one of those days and part of every other weekend she was on call. On a bad Sunday her day would start at six A.M. By the time she phoned the office at seven, half a dozen parents would have already called with complaints about their kids. A pediatrician on call in the suburbs gets a lot of emergency calls, but not everyone has the same definition of an emergency.

"Pediatricians are notoriously abused. People call you in the middle of the night for all kinds of reasons. I had one woman call me because her child had diarrhea. Now couldn't that wait until the morning?" "How does Jeffrey react?" I asked. "He just rolls over and goes back to sleep."

There were three hospitals in her jurisdiction, and on a bad weekend on call she might have to drive to all three, the closest being twenty-five minutes away. On a recent Sunday there were newborns to examine at a hospital that was forty-five minutes away, a Caesarean delivery to examine at another and a complicated respiratory problem to look at in town.

"People make all sorts of fun of doctors for playing golf in the middle of the week, but really, you live for that one day off."

A notion prevailed for a brief time while we were in our twenties that the stresses of being a super-mom were too great. Tess and I talked about one study conducted by two researchers at Wellesley, Dr. Rosalind Barnett and Dr. Grace Baruch, and the writer Caryl Rivers in their book, *Lifeprints,* that found to the contrary. It said that married women between the ages of thirty-five and fifty-five who work are happier than those who do not. The stresses of work and motherhood seemed to buffer each other. Tess said her life supported the Wellesley thesis. "If I have a bad day at the office, I'm delighted to go home and see Dora and Robert (Tess's six-month-old). But if I've been at home and Dora has been whining all morning, then I'm really grateful I have to go."

In summer, when most of the children went to camp, Tess's practice slowed down. Then she could leave her office at five, pick up Dora and go to the municipal pool, which, in Westport, looks more like a country club, the lawn around it mowed like a putting green, chaises longues everywhere. "Oh I love that," Tess said in the voluptuous voice she used when talking about the luxuries in her life. "Some of the mothers make a career of sitting by the pool, but I'd get bored if I did it all day. An hour or two is plenty."

Eleven-thirty. Car-pool time again. I would hate the constant lurching about. Her days had such a jerky rhythm, but it didn't seem to bother Tess. She grabbed her beeper and we drove to nursery school. A herd of three-year-olds piled into the car. "I don't mind doing this," she said, putting Dora into her carseat and breaking up a minor altercation between the girls. "It makes me feel like a mother."

On the way home, we stopped at one of the children's houses so that Tess could use the phone. Dora had been up all the previous night with an earache and Tess wanted to order an antibiotic from the druggist before noon. "Hello, Burt? This is Dr. Mayer. No, not for a patient. For Dora. Can you send me 250 milligrams per five. That's right. 150 cc's. Right. Great. Thanks." Tess sounded like such a pro; I wondered how the other mother in the room felt. Envious? It wasn't easy nowadays to be a mother and not work. "Isn't it nice to have a mommy who's a doctor?" the woman asked Dora, who was busy disengaging herself from around her mother's leg. Dora looked up and shrugged.

Finally, free time at home. Much of the house was empty, except for the den, which was furnished in typical Tess style, Jordan Marsh-colonial: plaid couch, comfy rocker, a brass eagle here and there. The other rooms were empty but had a wonderful smell. Fresh paint, a new home. "We've lived here for a year and we've only just completed the den," she called from upstairs, where she had gone to change. "Decorating isn't exactly a priority, you can tell."

I stepped out of the kitchen and peeked into an adjoining room. It, too, was bare because its inhabitant did not have much in the way of belongings (there was a Bible on the night table beside the cot and a crucifix on the wall). Edna, a West Indian woman, was their live-in housekeeper. She took care of the children while Tess worked. "It would be impossible to do what I do without a housekeeper," Tess said, not the least bit squeamish or guilty about having a maid like upper-middle-class women who grew up with them. Tess was pragmatic. "The quality of your life is really determined by the quality of your housekeeper," she stated.

We talked about Jeffrey, who worked for a small but well-regarded law firm. He had been at a larger one, Tess said, but felt lost among the drones. The pressure didn't suit him. He wanted to do well but not at the expense of other interests, with which he'd obviously kept up if the art books and prints in his study were any indication. The only drawback to his job was the commute. "Do you split the dishes or argue about who does the grocery shopping?" I asked. "Are you kidding? I don't know the last time Jeffrey's seen the inside of a supermarket. He commutes three hours every day for my sake; why would I bother him with chores?"

Before we left, she showed me the pictures in her den. Jeffrey. Tess. Tess pregnant. Newborn Dora with Jeffrey. Tess said Dora was only a month old when she was called back to work. Jeffrey, then between jobs, had two weeks off. "He didn't know the first thing about child-rearing but he jumped in and helped out. It was great. He'd call me every few hours to report on whether Dora was eating or wetting. We had a ball."

There were pictures, too, of their trips. Tess in front of pyramids, Tess along the Appian Way. Tess, who had never been anywhere more glamorous than Cape Cod. When I asked her what she would change if she could change anything in her life, she gave, for her, the most extraordinary answer. "Maybe I'd like to travel more, go to Egypt or France. Otherwise, I have everything I want."

. . .

AFTER lunch (tuna fish) and a little rest (I lay down, Tess bustled about) we went to Tess's office for her afternoon shift.

"I'm afraid you picked a slow day to come out," she said. It was snowing and the roads were icy. "The weather will probably keep most of my patients away and Tuesday afternoons are slow anyway. That's the day I work with Saul."

Tess had never talked to people much about her problems. But she did allow to me that she was having a problem, since it would come up by afternoon anyway.

Saul was the most popular of the four doctors in Tess's partnership and this obviously bothered Tess. On days when just he and Tess were in the office, all the patients went to Saul. The other partners had been in practice longer than Tess and didn't mind having an afternoon off. But to Tess, new and young and eager to work, the idle time was maddening. Here she spent all morning being efficient just to clear time for work, and when she got to work there was nothing to do.

We drove up to the office, a former Howard Johnson's with its orange roof intact. Patients in some pediatricians' offices are assigned doctors on a first-come, first-served basis, but in this affluent suburb parents prefer to select their own doctor. That made the big black appointment ledger the Book of Judgment in Tess's eyes. As soon as we got inside, she ran her finger down the column under her name. Just as she feared: on one side of the ledger, two dozen patients for Saul. On the other, four for her, and two of them had already canceled because of the snow. "Well, looks like it's not going to be too busy today," Tess said to the receptionist with false good cheer. "Not entirely," the receptionist answered, tilting her head in the direction of Saul.

You didn't see Saul at first, but you heard his strong booming voice carrying down the hall. When he did appear, it was with a trail of anxious, nervous parents behind him, vying desperately for a second of their doctor's time. You can see why some doctors start to think of themselves as God. Even from where we stood, we could hear Saul expound. He wasn't patronizing, and although he overexplained, parents probably appreciated a doctor who gave generously of his time. Tess scowled. "Even the routine cold elicits a sermon from Saul."

We retreated into her office but Saul's voice carried even there. As the new person on the team, Tess had the worst quarters, a room no larger than a utility closet, but she didn't mind. All she wanted was work and that she didn't have. She wasn't the type to hang up posters or surround herself with hanging plants, but I was curious as to why she hadn't hung her diplomas on the wall. All the other doctors had (including Saul, whose walls boasted a thousand credentials). "Oh, I haven't gotten around to it yet," she said. And then, "Suburban women aren't impressed with my degrees." "JAPs," she called them, and she was one of the few women I knew who could cast that stone. Whatever Tess was, she certainly wasn't a JAP.

While we sat glum-faced, waiting for something to do, the older woman nurse came in. Tess said I was interviewing her about her career, which prompted the woman to talk briefly about her own. "I didn't start out wanting to be a nurse. I applied to veterinary school but got back a letter that said: 'We don't feel it would justify the expense the state would have to pay to train a woman.' Just like that. I should have saved it. Of course you girls wouldn't believe that now."

It seemed trivial then to talk about the remaining obstacles for women doctors, but I was curious and Tess was in a mood to complain. "For the first time, I'm acutely aware of being a woman," she said. (Tess, at college, regarded feminists with the same bewildered air as she did antiwar demonstrators and people who liked tofu—a little off.) "In the emergency rooms in the city, parents are grateful for any doctor, male or female, they can get and ghetto kids are more hip. Here, they call me 'the lady doctor' and the children are always surprised. 'Oh, it's a lady,' they say. Sometimes I answer the phone and I say, 'Dr. Mayer, may I help you?' and the person on the other end will say, 'Is this the receptionist?'

" 'No, this is Dr. Mayer. Can I do something for you?'

" 'Are you the nurse?'

" 'No! This is Dr. Mayer. Doc-tor May-er. Now what can I do for you?'

"I've had women walk into this office and say, 'A woman doctor? I'll never be treated by one. Where's Dr. Berman?' That's Michael, one of the partners. According to Mike, half the women in suburbia come to the doctor's office to flirt.

"On the other hand, some of the mothers are delighted to have me. They say I'm a good role model for their kids. And once the adolescent girls develop, they won't see anyone else. 'Oh, thank God it's you, Dr. Mayer,' they say. When it's time for camp physicals in June, they practically queue up at my door."

"What about the adolescent boys?" I asked.

"Oh, I suppose the boys are shy at first, but then I ask them, 'What about your sister? She's been seeing a male doctor for years.' They think about this for a while and then they say, 'Yeah, that's right.' It's their mothers who are the problem."

"How about your mother? Is she proud of what you do?"

"Oh yeah. She thinks it's great. Terrific. A woman doctor. But she wouldn't go to one."

A half hour passed. Still no work. Tess picked up a stack of folders and started to file. Another doctor might have been too impressed with his title to pitch in with the clerical work, but Tess always had a laudably democratic view of work, which was why the nurse and receptionist liked her.

Tess was embarrassed more because of my presence than anything else. "Here I am this big doctor and nothing to do." Finally, a few calls. "Yes, Mrs. Doyle. No itching? Then I'd just give him plenty of rest." "Chicken pox? The blisters look like a dewdrop on a leaf. No? Well then he probably doesn't have them." Much of the work seemed routine. "Bread and butter," Tess said. "I'd say it would take the person of average intelligence not more than a year to learn ninety percent of the things he would need to know to be a good pediatrician." But what makes pediatrics rewarding is not the kinds of cases one sees, which tend to be mundane (measles, chicken pox, the litany of childhood ills), but the doctor-child relationship. "When it's going well, you feel terrific. When it's not, it can ruin your day."

"What's a bad day?" I asked. Tess looked at the nurse and smiled. "Last Tuesday," they both agreed. Saul was bustling around, a swarm of mothers in his train, while Tess sat idle. A few hours later, she saw the mother of one of her regular patients leave Saul's office. "What's she doing in there?" The receptionist wouldn't answer but eventually Tess wheedled it out of her. "When she called for an appointment this morning, she asked specifically *not* to be seen by Dr. Mayer."

Tess thought she knew why. "A few weeks ago the woman called at three A.M. She was all upset because her son's joints were starting to swell. I told her the swelling was common with that kind of medication and would go down in a couple of days. 'Can't you at least take a look at it?' I told her it wasn't necessary. The next morning she called one of the other doctors, who prescribed a steroid. I told Mike, who said he would've done what I did. But the woman wasn't convinced. She thinks I just didn't want to be bothered at night. How can you defend yourself in a case like that?"

But there were good days, too, that made her feel capable and confident. Recently, Tess examined a patient who complained of an ache in his foot. Tess said it was a sprain. The mother, incredulous that nothing more serious was wrong, took the boy to a specialist. A few days later she called Tess. "You know Dr.

Mayer, we're quite upset. We took Richard to a specialist who told us we have a major problem on our hands." Tess suggested she call in a third doctor. When she saw the woman in the office a couple of weeks later, she casually inquired, "By the way, how's Richard's foot?" "Oh that. We took him for a third opinion. You were right. It was only a sprain."

Doctors often disagree on treatment, so it is their manner that usually determines what patients perceive as the quality of their treatment. But Tess wasn't used to being pampered and didn't pamper her patients. Saul did. He coddled them. Tess saw Saul as condescending and his soliloquies as a waste of time. But what she saw in her own manner as efficient, her patients may have viewed as abrupt.

It was ironic: here was Tess in suburbia, where she most wanted to be, and yet it was here that she was most likely to encounter the kind of people she disliked at Radcliffe, women she regarded as pampered and spoiled. "You wouldn't believe it," she said. "The ones who drive the expensive cars—the Mercedes and BMW's—they're the ones who are the worst about paying their bills."

One more patient came before we finally left. "She's a doll," Tess said. The woman, obviously not as affluent as the rest of Tess's clientele, spoke softly and deferentially. Tess was at her best—cheerful, methodical and brisk. "All right, Mrs. Cardullo. Why don't you and Jennie step in here for a while." I watched Tess's quick forceful movements, hands flying from glands to throat to chest. But those eyes. Tess had gotten what she'd always wanted and yet they still looked as if there were some place more to go.

In suburbia, everything, including Tess's office, shuts down at six, the northbound lanes starting to swell with traffic from the city. Just the prospect of seeing her children and Jeffrey put her in a better frame of mind. "So what if you have a bad day? It makes me that much more grateful for my day off tomorrow." She would probably take Dora shopping and buy her new clothes. "The other mothers ask me, 'Why would you want to be with screaming kids on your day off?' But it's different. I really enjoy a day like that. I know if I didn't work I wouldn't appreciate it as much."

When she first moved out here, she intended to work full-time. But now, even if a full-time position opened up at the clinic, she wasn't sure she would take it. "I really enjoy working half-time. I remember one day last year. It was in the middle of the worst year of my residency and we'd just moved out here. I took an afternoon off, just like that, and Dora and I went out for ice cream. There I was, with four hours on my hands, and nothing to do but watch my daughter eat ice cream. It was ecstasy. I felt so happy, I could have sat there all day."

THE office seemed a million miles away that evening. Tess changed back into her jeans and we sat in the den. We could have been roommates back in Cambridge. It was cold outside and we were cozy and warm in front of our Adams House fireplace. The only difference was that now we spoke in a much more cordial, though impersonal, way and Tess sipped sherry instead of soda. "Girl!" I said, reverting to David's ghetto-ese. "You never drank anything stronger than Coke!" Whether it was the liquor or just old age, Tess struck a philosophical note. "You know, the best part about it is that the striving is behind me. First there was getting into Radcliffe. Then medical school. Then internship, residency, an endless stream of exams. There always seemed to be one more step. But now? What's left, really? The last tests I had to take were my pediatric boards, and I passed those last November.

"Well, sure, there are always going to be problems," she said. "But what are the bad days at work compared to the big things in life, the really important things? The constants. You know, last night after dinner, I sat there and looked at my kids. I've got two terrific kids. And Jeffrey's really such a wonderful guy. And I thought to myself, there's not another thing I want. Life could stay exactly this way and I'd be content."

I asked Tess if Jeffrey was helpful about her problems with Saul. She said he was, but only up to a point. "Jeffrey doesn't complain as much. When he comes home, he's usually in a pretty good mood." "Do you think he understands?" "I don't know. He doesn't have my self-doubt."

And then I wished that we could start all over at college. This time I would march into her room all the time, and laugh with her over all those snobby Radcliffe girls. "Oh Tess, you're such a panic. You with your dopey old tuna fish. Get a little class, girl. C'mon. Don't be such a bitch all the time." But I was glad to see her anyway. Certainly, she was happy with the way her life had turned out. Dark, scrawny, tough little Tess. I wished I had just once gone to cheer for her when she was rowing crew.

I was on my way out when Jeffrey came in. Same Jeffrey, maybe even a little more handsome at thirty-three. You really could fall in love with him, even a complete stranger could, sitting in the kitchen. He was congenial in a way Tess never was, and asked me about my work. (Tess hadn't asked me a single thing all day, which didn't surprise me. She had the same narrow approach as my immigrant grandmother: only her needs and those of her immediate family concerned her. The rest you saw on TV.) But Jeffrey was more curious. "How's so-and-so?" and "What have you been doing all these years?"

Before we left he put his arms around Tess. He could tell from her look she hadn't had a good day. "Another Tuesday with big bad Saul?" he asked, kissing her cheek. Tess sighed. A married person's sigh, full of exasperation and love.

I wondered as I left Tess's what might possibly go wrong. Jeffrey, who is awfully handsome, might have an affair. Tess might alienate all her patients with her no-frills manner. But both seemed unlikely. I suspected Tess's manner would soften with time, as she became one of the suburban matrons she scorned. And Jeffrey: Even now, when Tess spoke of him, it was with adoration in her eyes. I don't think Jeffrey, or anyone, would easily give that up.

CHAPTER 6

Eleanor

Even when the East excited me most, even when I was most keenly aware of its superiority to the bored, sprawling, swollen towns beyond the Ohio, with their interminable inquisitions which spared only the children and the very old—even then it had always for me a quality of distortion.
—F. SCOTT FITZGERALD, *The Great Gatsby*

"So how's Tess?" Eleanor asked.

"Good," I said. "I think she's really doing well. You know, still in love with Jeffrey." But Eleanor, who was also a pediatrician, was more interested in the practical aspects of Tess's life.

"How does she manage it all, working and being at home with the children?"

"Well, she works only part-time and they have a live-in housekeeper, which helps."

"Can they afford it?" Eleanor asked.

"I think so. Jeffrey works for a law firm in New York, and I'm sure he makes more than fifty thousand a year."

"Wow," Eleanor said, a long incredulous "wow." And then she laughed because where she lived, numbers like that weren't casually tossed around. "I don't think Sam and I could ever make that much put together."

Just as I knew Tess was destined for suburbia, I knew Eleanor would probably end up living in a small town, some place with trees and grass and plenty of open spaces for long walks in the afternoon. When I found her, finally, she was living in just such a small town in Vermont not far from a well-known college. The town was like all the other towns Eleanor had ever lived in, peaceful and scenic but not entirely out of the mainstream. As the daughter of a renowned professor, Eleanor was too cosmopolitan to wander totally off into the woods.

We hadn't seen each other since her medical school days. There had been that breakfast in 1975 with Tess and then once, briefly, we'd bumped into each other in Cambridge during the great blizzard of 1978. Suddenly, there was Eleanor with a couple of friends, gliding along Massachusetts Avenue on cross-country skis in the clean white snow. We kissed and spoke for a few minutes, but there wasn't really much to say. We were both too absorbed in the present to take much interest in people or places from the past.

But I knew Eleanor was practicing medicine and had gotten married later that year. She said she sent me a wedding invitation but I don't remember receiving it. At the time, marriage and weddings were the farthest things from my mind. None of my friends was even close to "settling down."

Finally, years later, she sent me a packet of letters she had written but never mailed. The postmark was Manchester, Vermont, where she now lived with her husband and their two-year-old daughter. The operators didn't know what to make of her last name—RemsonBorg. "One word," I tried to explain. But it was hopeless. Directory assistance was having enough trouble with joint listings, let alone nonhyphenated last names seamlessly joined like Siamese twins. I called her mother, who gave me the number, and Eleanor and I arranged for my trip.

. . .

EVEN before I got off the bus, I saw her, a pretty ponytailed mommy with her ponytailed girl. "Say hello to Fran, Becky. This is Mommy's old roommate from college." Maybe ten years isn't a long enough time to age because we all looked more or less the same to me. She was wearing a ski parka, as always, and was four months pregnant, although it hardly showed. Winter always brought out the best in Eleanor, who was hardy in ways I was not. Every night she'd rouse from her bed and open the window that I, accustomed to the overheated apartments of New York, had shut. "God, it's stuffy in here," she would say.

We walked a little around downtown Manchester, which was a pretty town. The ski industry and nearby Bennington College set the tone; why else would there be shops that sold gourmet food and imported clothing in an area otherwise inhabited by poor farmers? Young teenagers walked around with book bags and long lugubrious expressions on their faces, as if they were eternally troubled or stoned. Eleanor was probably used to it, having lived around campuses for most of her life.

On the way back to her house, she gave me a brief synopsis. She was pregnant with her second child and working at a pediatric clinic a ten-minute drive from her house. Like Tess, Eleanor did not work a full shift but normally worked three-quarter's time, which in practice amounted to a sixty-hour week. Her husband, Sam, was an artist, but he had taken a part-time job in an architectural firm, partly to bring in extra money and partly because it got depressing hanging around the house waiting for inspiration. Eleanor was methodical; Sam could take apart a stereo and put it back together six times, make a clay figurine for their daughter, Becky, and bake a batch of biscuits (anything to stave off the muse) before finally getting down to work. I liked Sam for all this, but it meant that Eleanor's work was their main source of support.

We pulled up to her house, the first house on the block. The address was "A" Market Street. "There already was a one and a two on the block and we didn't want our first house to be 'One-Half' or 'One and a Half' so we persuaded the Post Office to give us a letter." A broken-down MG was parked out front. "That's Sam's," Eleanor said. "He likes to fix it."

Eleanor parked the car and we went inside. Walking into Eleanor's house was like walking into her room almost ten years ago. I felt I was in the most cheerful spot in the world. It was bright and sunny and everything in it was homemade. I stopped especially to admire the curtains, made of a big splotchy garden print, the backs thermally lined. They reminded me of the curtains she made for our room freshman year. They were cotton and let in plenty of light. She had a genius for brightening life, hard to find at Radcliffe.

She led me past the wood-burning stove, past her desk with its unanswered mail, up the wooden staircase to yet another sunny room. I wanted to put down my things and stay here forever, just as I did freshman year.

It had been a long time since Eleanor and I had sat down and had a heart-to-heart talk. I forgot what a pleasure it was talking to her. She had such sensible, down-to-earth ways, and her instincts were always so good. I sat in that kitchen for a long time, listening to her opinions and watching the sun do spectacular things to her rich dark hair.

The best thing that had happened to her since college, Eleanor said, was being a mother. "It's wonderful having Becky. There's someone there who needs you and loves you regardless of how your day went. She also adds an evenness to our lives. The ups are just as euphoric but the downs aren't so low." But it was working in a clinic with adolescents, which she did briefly after she finished medical school and moved back east, that had taught her the most. "Sometimes I lie awake at night, in awe of how humans grow. I tell you, Fran, I have new respect for all the traumas we went through freshman year."

When Eleanor first moved back to Boston in 1982, she worked

at the infirmary of a private boarding school. She told me then she saw the role of a physician in much broader terms, as someone who nurtured health, even if that meant holding a student's hand because he was depressed or reassuring him because he was so far away from home. She was sympathetic to those students, children of doctors and lawyers, who felt themselves under pressure at this competitive school. "The infirmary was the only place where no one expected them to perform." The students at St. Andrew's loved her but their parents were slower to respond. She was young and the school had never had a female physician before. They preferred her predecessor, who was in his seventies, despite the fact that his training was "probably thirty years out of date." So Eleanor had to suffer the ignominy of having her work reviewed.

But the point was that she appreciated the pressure her students felt. "Even as a parent," she told me, "I've had to watch myself. Sometimes I'll be observing Becky in a group and I'll see myself having expectations for her, wanting her to be what she's not. I try to really clamp down on that." It was to be the theme of the next three days we spent together. Eleanor felt Harvard put a lot of pressure on her from which she later rebelled, although some of that pressure came from within.

She had been used to hard work in high school but not the eleventh-hour drama of staying up all night to get a paper done. "And all those crazy diets—they made me miserable and I'm sorry I tried to be like all of you." (A twinge of guilt because we both knew who Eleanor's first example of the Harvard hysteric was.)

And hanging around with Reuben's crowd didn't help. "I saw them as bright intellectual northeasterners, while I was some dull slow-witted cow." She felt ashamed of her background. "I came from a quiet, low-key midwestern home. If I ever wanted to say anything at the table, there was plenty of opportunity. I didn't learn to shout."

Academically, she felt hectored from the moment she declared herself pre-med. "They gear you earlier and earlier to choose a professional career. It's like getting married right away. It narrows the road. I ruled out other options before trying them." Even her choice of where to go was thrust upon her, she felt. "My advisor encouraged me to go to Harvard and I did." She said it was in the same passive vein that she had decided to go to Radcliffe. "I didn't really think about where I wanted to go. Everyone said, 'Oh, of course. Dr. Remson's daughter. You must go to Radcliffe.' I figured Boston was a nice city, so why not. But I never really sat down and thought, Is this where I'd like to go?"

Eleanor was much happier in medical school. She lived in an old barnlike house in Newton with friends she acquired during her senior year, free of the influence of Reuben and James. (I thought one of the women was nice but dull and one of the men was a bit of a fool. He clomped through the Adams House dining room in red-laced hiking boots, as if Cambridge were Innsbruck.) By now she was less awed by Harvard and preferred living off campus to life in a dorm. "I felt more like an adult—cooking, cleaning, running to the Star Market once a week." After a friendly dinner of lasagne and cheap wine at her house one night, I remember wondering who of the rest of us could live with other people and get along with everyone so well, sharing the cooking and shopping and eating at synchronized times. Certainly not Paige or I, and we paid a price for it: we were lonely. I wished then, as I had many times, for whatever quality it was that made Eleanor get along so well in the world. I know now it was her goodness, and if it made her "dull" that was because our notion of being interesting was being "fucked up."

She and Reuben had broken up by the end of her first year of medical school, she said. It was too hectic, running down to Georgetown, where he was a law student, and arriving back in Boston Sunday night depressed. She was weary and by that time they were fighting. She would have kept the relationship going but Reuben cut it off. In retrospect, she was glad. "He married Susan Wigham [another of our classmates] and was divorced by the end of the year."

What a relief it must have been for Eleanor to be with Sam, who was so different from Reuben and James. He was quiet almost to the point of being inarticulate, but expressed himself in other ways. He was an artist, although at the time Eleanor met him he was occasionally making some money as a construction worker. He helped her through her painful breakup with Reuben, and when she recovered they fell in love. I remember meeting him just before he and Eleanor left for Iowa, where they were going to be married. She had come to say goodbye, and that touched me. I was giving a party and had drunk a fair amount of wine, but I do remember this about Sam: he was handsome, soft-spoken and nothing like Reuben except for his size—both men were somewhat slight whereas Eleanor was large for a girl. I liked him. He seemed shy, except for his eyes—animated and alert.

Even if she hadn't told me, I would have known that they would be married by her father in Iowa, on the beautiful green campus of the college where he taught. Later, I saw pictures: Eleanor in a plain white dress and Sam in a white jacket, white pants and white shirt open at the neck. It was 1978 and the peasant look was still in style. Sam wore sandals and Eleanor a spray of baby's breath in her hair.

Their marriage was the culmination of a difficult period. Sam moved in with her during her third year of medical school, the nightmarish year in which a medical student learns to be a doctor. "I'd watch one patient die of a heart attack and then two minutes later, it was on to the next patient. It took a while to get used to death." And then her own life became impossibly unpredictable. "I'd tell Sam I'd be home by five and walk in at eight, or ask him to pick me up at three and not show up until seven-thirty. Now he takes it for granted, but then my hours were a constant source of stress." But there were touchier issues. Sam was unemployed at the time. He was irked by all her medical school friends running through the house. "Isn't there anyone we know who isn't a doctor?" he would complain. He was not yet successful as an artist and he felt pressure to have a more conventional career. He came from a traditional and competitive family and, Eleanor said, it still bothered them that she was the one with the professional career. "It's funny," Eleanor said. "As an artist, he has an enormous ego. He'll put on a one-man show and hold his work up to criticism from the entire world. But as a man he has less confidence. It took him years, for example, to believe that I didn't want him to be a doctor."

At the end of Eleanor's third year at medical school, she was offered a position at a Harvard-affiliated hospital. Her advisor ("a real rah-rah Ivy League type") was pressuring her to accept the job, but Eleanor didn't think she wanted to stay in Boston for another three years. Much to the dismay of her advisor, she turned down the offer. Instead, she and Sam piled into his old MG and headed out west. Her advisor gave her a list of five "acceptable" hospitals but she ignored the list. They covered ten thousand miles and visited nineteen cities before she made her choice. "I chose Kansas," she said, "not because of reputation or because of what anyone said but because, based on the people I met and the things I saw, I felt it was the best." Her advisor was so distressed that he wrote a letter to the hospital making sure it would be recorded in her files that she had turned Harvard down, and not the reverse.

It was a major breakthrough, she said. For years she felt she was drifting, doing things because other people said she should. Now she was finally thinking for herself. In a certain sense, she was emulating her father, whose rags-to-riches career bred in him an intellectual vigor that she felt she lacked. "My father grew up on a farm. He didn't go to school until he was ten. He knows things that have nothing to do with his work. He goes off on a tangent if something interests him intellectually. My father came from a background that encouraged him to do that. He had to, if he wanted to survive. I never had to do that. Money, school—it was all handed to me. I could afford to be intellectually lazy."

She said that all her credentials, Harvard College, Harvard Medical School, meant less to her for that reason. She had even played the role and worked hard to obtain them, but never with a sense that this was what she wanted to do. For that reason, she saw herself as passive and weak for failing to resist. She had succumbed to the pressure to be a "northeastern intellectual, which, basically, I'm not."

She talked about a problem a lot of people at Harvard had. They could duplicate all their parents' achievements except for one: they could not be self-made. Eleanor did the next best thing: she remade herself. When she turned down the offer, she felt it was one of those small victories that meant more than any achievement.

Kansas felt like an awakening, the perfect antidote to the smarmy Northeast. "It was wonderful to see very smart, very bright people out of the mainstream," she said. "I'd tell them, 'You're brighter than ninety percent of the people at Harvard Medical School' and they wouldn't believe me. But the really bright people were brighter, because they were independently bright, not just following a set academic course. Harvard people are there because they're good at following the route."

Her years in Kansas had their ups and downs, but basically they gave her back the confidence all those dinners with Reuben and James had taken away. "In some ways I was a good chief resident, in other ways not. I felt the poor person who got sick tonight was going to get worse treatment because I was here instead of someone better. I made mistakes. As you grow more mature in medicine, and you are where the staff people are, you see that they make mistakes, too." She said that paradoxically, accepting her mistakes made her more confident. "I was underconfident at Radcliffe. Reuben and James were brilliant in areas I knew little about: government, philosophy, psychology. For fear of not doing well, I stayed away from those fields."

Their criticisms must have festered in her because here, away from their scrutiny, she strengthened herself in just those areas in which they had regarded her as weak. "I learned to talk in front of large groups, which I never thought I could do. As chief resident, I had to do this often. It was great watching myself handle situations I never thought I could."

Sam prospered, too. The closely knit academic community of Lawrence was less intimidating than gallery society in Boston and New York, and in this more protective environment Sam completed more work. His massive colorful canvases attracted attention; his name began to be known. At the end of his first year in Lawrence, the city bought one of his paintings, and it was later hung in the museum.

Prospering as they were, they decided to have a child. Becky was born the following spring. Eleanor sent me a picture: a pretty dark-eyed girl sitting with her mother on a swing. I was so glad to receive it I hung it over my desk. She was the first of my friends from college to have a child.

At first, Eleanor stayed home and Sam went to work, but six months later they switched roles. "It was just the right time. If I hadn't stayed home for so long, I probably would have regretted going back. As it turned out, I was grateful for my job." That last trying month with Becky gave her new sympathy for her mother, she said. "I doubt she liked staying home all day with the three of us, and when she didn't she probably felt guilty."

Their final year in Kansas was their most successful. Eleanor assumed her duties as chief resident and Sam continued to paint. But at the end of the year, she was offered a prestigious research fellowship in Boston (with the help of her advisor; he had not given up on her yet). The offer forced her to make several decisions: Did she want to go back east? Did she want to pull Sam out of his comfortable niche? Did she want to go into academic medicine, a pivotal decision in terms of the rest of her career?

The last decision was perhaps the easiest. Eleanor had always assumed she would go into research, which was more prestigious, more demanding and less remunerative than clinical work. Few women chose it because of the long hours it entailed. (I knew one woman in our class who went into academic medicine; she and her lab mates worked round the clock and chain-smoked Camels.) But Eleanor was more ambitious than I had thought. "The fellowship was a good stepping-stone into academic medicine, and even if I didn't know whether I wanted to practice or do research, this allowed me to keep my options open.

"Besides, Becky made us think more of being close to our families, who were now back east, and it was an excellent offer. I had turned down Harvard once; it was hard to do again."

"What about Sam?" I asked.

"I felt lousy doing that to him. But we were used to making decisions based on my career. Sam was unemployed when I met him. There was the assumption from the start that my career might be the career for the two of us. This wasn't some glossy second income we were talking about.

"And besides, Sam wasn't painting as much as he had been now that Becky was born and sometimes even welcomed an excuse not to do any work. If he had something pressing to do, I would have followed him. But I think it's partially his nature: he likes having some of these decisions made for him."

Boston the second time around was little better than the first. On Eleanor's stipend of $15,000, even babysitters were a luxury. Sam hoped to find a job at a computer firm but wasn't having any luck. Daily he made the rounds of the firms ringing Route 128 but he had no experience, and the high-tech computer cowboys were unimpressed with his Harvard degree. They were even less impressed when he asked them about child-care and paternity leaves. "If I were you," one of the engineers told him, "I wouldn't bring that up. The industry isn't ready for that sort of thing."

And Eleanor was having her own difficulties at work. "I thought it would be easier to work a more normal, nine-to-five shift but I was wrong. All the good hours, the time when I was awake and alert, were spent at work, and by the time I came home at night I was too tired to do very much. The worst thing is to have time with Becky and not want it. You think what a terrible mother you must be."

Academic medicine had other drawbacks. On paper the hours were nine to five, but if you wanted to make a mark of any kind, you had to put life second and work first. "I saw I could never be as good as I *wanted* to be unless I was willing to give up being a mother and having time with Sam." But she resented even having to make the choice. "My father never had to wrestle with these things. He was able to spend hours in his study because he had my mother. And that's the assumption that's made in certain high-powered professional careers. Surgery, for instance. To be a really good surgeon, you need to have one and a half lives, your own life, and half the life of that person who's going to do everything else for you. My father had that person, my mother. I don't, and having seen my mother's life, I'm not sure I'd want it. I wouldn't want to ask Sam or anyone else to play that role for me."

Money was an even more pressing problem. They had depleted all their savings on child care. And being poor, they found it even more difficult to adapt to urban life. Eleanor missed the outdoors but made adjustments. "I walk the thirty minutes to the MTA so I get some exercise with my smog," she once wrote me in a letter.

At the end of the fellowship, she decided to withdraw from academic medicine. In the spring she applied to pediatric practices in small rural communities in New England. It was a little embarrassing to have so many offers rolling in while Sam was still looking for work. But they were almost completely broke and it became increasingly difficult for her to pass up good jobs. She finally decided to take her present post. A few weeks later Sam was offered a job doing computer graphics at a nearby architecture firm. They arranged their hours so that both of them would have some daytime hours with Becky and looked forward to doubling their income to almost $28,000 a year.

"How did you feel about leaving research?" I asked.

"Mixed," she said. "I felt better in terms of my family but divided in terms of my work. I love seeing kids and their families, but every time I meet someone my age doing research, I feel a pang."

THE pediatric clinic where Eleanor worked was a half-hour's car ride from Manchester, but the half hour made all the difference in the world. The people here were rural poor. Their children went to vocational colleges if at all. Eleanor's being a woman seemed to matter less than her carrying a stethoscope. Even the men, big burly construction workers out of work, were intimidated and distressingly polite. Patients here put doctors on a pedestal, from which Eleanor was eager to step down.

Her situation at the clinic was almost the opposite of Tess's. Eleanor had been at the clinic for only a year and already patients were switching over to her. It was her manner, I think. All the reasons that she felt out of place at Harvard, the fact that people thought she was "simple," maybe slow, caused her to be regarded at the Tri-County Vermont Pediatric Clinic not as a doctor but a saint.

A woman came into the clinic with her son, whom the doctors thought had a heart murmur. (A special cardiac clinic was in progress the morning I was there.) The woman was a telephone operator for New England Telephone and had to miss a day's pay and ask someone to stay with her other children in order to get here. Most patients did not own cars and had to ask neighbors or relatives to drive them. It was hard to imagine how these women did it. Often they came with their husbands but, far from being a sign of shared responsibilities, it more often meant that the men were unemployed. The parents were guarded and reluctant to talk. But when Eleanor spoke to them they lost the polite, fearful manner and got to the point of what they were really worried about. "I thought maybe he might wheeze like this forever."

Eleanor examined her patient with another doctor in attendance. Her partner spoke in jargon. "His X rays are unimpressive, Mrs. Wiznewski. I see an atrial septal defect but it isn't troublesome at this point." The woman sputtered out a few questions but she seemed confused. (She thought "unimpressive" meant "bad," but in the way the doctor used it, it meant "nothing to worry about.") Eleanor sensed the confusion but waited until her colleague left to intervene. When he finally did step out, Eleanor explained that an atrial septal defect is really a tiny hole in the heart and that from the X ray it appeared to have been a small one. But more important, she told the woman how to think about the problem, whether or not to worry, and then she reassured her, for Eleanor is a mother, too. "You know my two-year-old had a heart murmur, too. It's nothing to worry about, really.

"And don't worry if he touches his genitals, it's normal at his age."

In another room, a nursing mother argued with her husband. The woman later confided to Eleanor that her husband got angry at her whenever she nursed their child. Eleanor said it was common. "They're jealous. It's like the baby owns you. And also, there's no way for them to participate."

Eleanor worked with three other doctors, two men and a woman. At a meeting that morning, one of the male doctors described the case of an adolescent girl who had had a case of appendicitis that might have had psychosomatic roots. He concluded his lecture with the crack, "Many a girl who doesn't get taken out has an appendix that does." Everyone booed.

"The funny thing is," Eleanor told me, "his wife is a doctor."

In the three months Eleanor had been working here, she managed to become universally admired by the nurses, something almost impossible for a doctor, especially a woman doctor. At a weekly lunch meeting, two of Eleanor's colleagues (the two men) unwrapped their hero sandwiches at one table; the all-female nursing staff dined on their salads and Tabs at another. I wondered where Eleanor would sit. Eleanor sat with the nurses. Several of the nurses (called health practitioners here) complained about the onslaught of clerical work. "I was hired to do health care, but the filing keeps cutting into my time." Dr. Appendix said what amounted to "too bad." Eleanor raised her hand. "Perhaps we can help the nurses by putting the folders back ourselves."

Later that afternoon I spoke to the nurse who had voiced the complaint. She was young and pretty and talked about what a servile profession nursing had become. But she did not begrudge Eleanor her job. Instead, she admired how steady she was even on the most harrowing days. The previous week, she said, Eleanor had received a call informing her that one of her patients had hepatitis B. It was the last day it would be safe for Eleanor to be immunized, crucial because she was in her first trimester of pregnancy. They called the druggist. He was all out of serum B. They called the hospital. They too had run out. A fresh supply had to be rushed in from out of town. "You should have seen her. They gave her this huge needle right in the rear and she went hobbling back to work."

Sam's parents stopped by the clinic later that day. Retired, they were both on their way to one of their famous whirlwind tours. (Sam's father had been a cardiologist.) Eleanor said she envied them. Now that they were retired, they could do things they both enjoyed, like travel. This was not the case with Eleanor's parents.

I met Eleanor's mother once during our undergraduate years. I remembered the way she said my name, Fra-ahn, as if it were pure gold. She had a gracious way with strangers, probably acquired at innumerable faculty luncheons and teas. But when Eleanor's father retired, her mother lost her job as faculty wife. Her father was still getting invitations to speak all over the country. "My mother goes with him but there's really nothing for her to do." Any interest of her own she wished to pursue would require her to spend most of her time apart from her husband, which, at this point, she wasn't willing to do. "Her only real interest is her family but none of us is home."

What poor timing. When Eleanor's mother was younger, all that was expected of a faculty wife was that she raise a family and help her husband. But then the women's movement put people like Eleanor's mother on the defensive for what they had done. The model faculty wife when we were at college was Harvard's president's wife, Sissela Bok—lecturer, philosopher, author and a wife and mother, too. I thought Harvard could have done with a few more women like Mrs. Remson, but a woman like Dr. Bok was a rebuke to her whole way of life.

I was too tired to traipse after Eleanor at work the next day, so I stayed home with Sam. He was painting. He worked in sort of a neo–Jackson Pollock style, hurling cans of paint in a ceremonial dance that left him exhausted. On Wednesdays he participated in a play group with other parents of youngsters on their street. He was the only father in the group but did not mind. "My father never changed a diaper, but I've always liked staying home," he said. "I grew up watching my mother around the house and I felt much more comfortable with the pace of her life."

But it bothered him, as I suppose it had generations of women who stayed home all day waiting for their men, that work took such a piece out of Eleanor's life. It deprived him of her. "It's a rare day when she comes home happy," he said. "She's harried and complains about work. She needs an hour all by herself, just to relax and do nothing." Both she and Sam needed their "vegetative" time, Eleanor told me. Sam had his; it was built into his artist's life. But Eleanor didn't. "She doesn't even have time to put into her career in a personally gratifying way, like reading medical journals or catching up on the latest research."

They used to have their evenings at least. They would read by the fire, sharing the occasional trivial or not-so-trivial thought. But now evenings consisted of little more than eating dinner and cleaning up. During one of the nights I was there, Eleanor, exhausted (I forgot that she was four months pregnant, too), smiled and apologized to the three of us. "I'm sorry, but I just can't keep my eyes open anymore." It was eight o'clock, too early for Sam and Becky to go to bed. He fiddled with plans for a new bookshelf and she leafed through the pages of her book. They have become used to staying together while Eleanor comes in and out of their lives.

"I wish she'd slow down," Sam said. "What's the alternative?" I asked. "She could work in a clinic where there's less hospital-related work." There is a clinic like that in Boston, Sam said, run by a community health plan, in which doctors work banker's hours and don't do emergency work. The only problem is that the work is uninspiring. "It's dull and I don't think it would suit Eleanor. I've seen her when she's in the hospital, working late on some complicated case. She's happy then. I can tell by the look on her face. I doubt she'd be very happy if she had to give that up."

SAM is a member of a string quartet and one night a week they practice at his and Eleanor's house. We spent an hour, Eleanor and I, listening to them play: string quartets by Beethoven and Brahms. All this and a light snow was starting to fall.

The musicians took their bows and we adjourned into the kitchen for cranberry juice and brownies, real homespun, small-town fare. I thought what a lovely life it was, in between the problems we talked about all day long.

On Friday night, my last night here, Eleanor and Sam decided to go out. They almost never ate dinner out but because I was company they decided to take me to the big barnlike restaurant where all the politicians stopped when they campaigned in Vermont. Becky walked down the aisle of diners as if she owned the place. She is a beautiful child and people turned from their tables to talk to her. Sam said he thought Becky was more even-tempered because of being raised by both parents; their flaws tend to cancel each other out. Becky did get confused at times. "Sometimes she wakes up and asks, 'Who's my mommy today?' " Sam said.

We had to get home early that night because Eleanor was planning to attend a conference in Boston the next day. The subject had nothing to do with her current work, but might be useful in case she wanted to go back into research. "When I first left academic medicine, people said the same thing to me they did when I wanted to take a year off before applying to medical school, 'The profession frowns upon it, you'll never come back. . . .' But I'm not so sure that's true. And besides, with so many women entering medicine, attitudes may soften."

On Saturday, Sam, Eleanor, Becky and I piled into Sam's MG. It was a miserable rainy day and the drive to Boston took longer than we had thought. We pulled up to the arcade of the Marriott, where the conference was being held. Eleanor leaned into the car to say goodbye to Sam and kissed Becky, and then I got out to give her a hug. Both our bulky parkas got in the way so it was more like the embrace of two bears.

"I'm sorry it was so hectic," she said. "I hardly had time to ask you anything about your life."

"I'll put it in a letter."

"Okay. And I'll try to be a better correspondent this time."

Five months later I got a birth announcement in the mail. She and Sam now had two pretty dark-eyed girls. It was a few weeks before our Tenth Year Reunion at Radcliffe and I called to ask if she was going. "Only if I have a day off," she said.

. . .

ELEANOR rescued me from the terror of freshman year and I loved her for it. She had showed me the same loving tolerance that she now showed her patients. I would think that would be enough to fulfill her, to give her some sense of her own worth. People who are of service are happy people, I thought. And Eleanor knew she was liked by her nurses and the rest of the staff. But she worried still, and the pressure came from a different source. It was the old James-Reuben-Harvard pressure to achieve, the bug that had caused her to go to Radcliffe in the first place. It was why on a day she had free, she took Becky and Sam with her, into Boston, so she could attend that conference. But there is enough good sense in Eleanor to keep her from tipping the balance. Hadn't she pulled back when she saw how destructive the way I ate was? Didn't she finally say, "No" to Harvard and head out west? And now, too, when she talks to me, what she likes to talk about best are the picnics she and Sam and Becky take, when the weather gets nice, at a lake not too far from their house.

I was right about Eleanor from the start. Unlike Miranda, she wouldn't crack up. She is a woman who knows something about moderation.

CHAPTER 7

Paige

The last four years have been a slow process of weeding out all the employments and activities I invented for myself as excuses for not doing what I really wanted to do: perform. Radcliffe (and I perceived it more as Harvard, living as I did at Adams House for three years and having mostly male friends) prepared me somewhat in conducting myself properly in the excuses, logically, since Radcliffe itself was the same kind of excuse. I was frightened as hell there, intimidated by everyone, students and professors alike. I dared not fail or excel. I was never sure I would have been there if my father hadn't been a celebrity and a generous alumnus. . . . In no way did Radcliffe prepare me for any of this, but that was a decision I made; I didn't invite Radcliffe to do much of anything for me. I was hiding out. I am much less bitter now than I used to be. I don't "blame" Radcliffe for the shitty time I had there. It doesn't help to say "If I'd gone to X college I would have done Y and Z." And anyhow, I'm doing what I want to now, and heading where I want to go, so why hold grudges?!

—JAMIE BERNSTEIN, '74
Radcliffe Fifth Year Report

In 1979 our Fifth Year Reunion book came out. By then, I was working for a newspaper in Boston, Tess and Eleanor were doing their residencies, and, according to the catalogue, Paige was at law school in Pennsylvania. Some women wrote lyrical passages about their experiences, but I was feeling too awful to do anything other than make a list. That was Paige's tactic, too. Simply and methodically, she listed her whereabouts over the previous five years. She worked for a newsweekly in Pennsylvania. Then she did research work for some demographers in Princeton, and between her first and second year of law school worked as an intern in a Philadelphia firm. Under "travel," she wrote, North Africa, Europe and the American West. Once every bit of information would have given rise to a thousand thoughts of Paige, but things had changed over the years. Oh, so Paige is in law school. That's nice. Oh, so she visited Tunisia, what do you know.

I had had news about her on several occasions. The first was in the fall of 1975. I had just left my newspaper job in North Carolina and had come up north to look for another one. One of the papers I applied to was in a tiny working-class suburb outside of Philadelphia. The editor said that if I wanted to find out more about the job, I should contact my predecessor, Paige Coleman, who was also a Cliffie. I don't remember whether I actually called her. I might have had more sense then and restrained myself. A friend later told me she was working as a research assistant for a population studies institute in Princeton, a holding position more than the start of a real career. I was more surprised when I heard she was dating Alex Cramer. It was the first I had heard of Paige having a boyfriend. I had known Alex vaguely in high school. He played basketball for a school in the Bronx and I had seen him occasionally at citywide meets. He had a big heart and always let kids from the neighborhood practice on the courts. He also had an eye for pretty women, so it was not surprising he would go after Paige.

Two years after the Fifth Year Class Report came out, when college seemed even further in the past and I was happily settled in New York, she called. She was going to be in town and would

I meet her for dinner? I wasn't sure I really wanted to see her, but I was feeling more secure than I had been at school and didn't think we would upset each other as much as we once had. We had dinner at a Chinese restaurant close to my apartment on the Upper West Side and for the first time in our lives, spoke about how good things were. For the first time, too, it did not feel as if we were rivals but two women up against the same ghosts—fear, insecurity and doubt. We believed that if one of us licked them, the other would.

Paige had graduated from law school the previous year and was now clerking for a judge in Michigan. She expected to move to Montana at the end of the year to be with Alex, who worked for an Indian legal defense fund. The recognition that there were new, more important people in each of our lives put more distance between us. (I had had a similar experience with my brother. He had gotten married and suddenly our rivalry had vanished.) There was only one difficult moment, or one that threatened to be. Paige asked if she could read something I wrote. I was both reluctant and eager, as always, to expose myself to her. I braced myself, anticipating her unenthusiastic reaction, and handed her a story. Even before she started to read, I had the same old feeling, as if my insides were spread out on a table and Dr. Paige was surveying them with her critical eyes. "It has a nice ending," was all she said.

I didn't think about her much until two years later when she called on me again. She said she did not like practicing law as much as she had hoped and was trying to ease her way back into writing. Would I give her the names of a few editors? It was a simple request and yet it pained her even to broach the subject, for she turned white and pink and then red, which is what happened whenever Paige felt scared. I felt my old nasty urge not to help her, but compensated by giving her the names of every editor I knew.

By now I was living in Manhattan with Philip. He was everything David was not, which was a relief in some ways, but part of me missed the Sturm and Drang. I told Paige I was in turmoil about whether to marry him or not. Paige said that she and Alex were going to be married. She worried at times if Alex might be unfaithful to her, although she doubted he would. "He knows it would hurt me and he loves me too much to do that." Paige was not the kind of woman who took many risks, yet in loving Alex, evidently she had. Well, good for you, Paige, I thought.

In the fall of 1983, I shared the latest bulletin about Paige with Daisy, the only one of my friends from college with whom I was frequently in touch. "Can you believe it?" Daisy asked. "Paige a mother?" Paige was the last person we imagined being anyone's mother or wife. Daisy was not envious but wistful: her career, which had been an upward spiral from the day she had graduated from school, continued to advance almost in spite of herself. But what she wanted now was a husband and a home.

When I told David, also an occasional visitor of mine in New York, he, too, looked stunned. "That was one woman I thought would never settle down."

I flew to Montana in the spring of 1983. My plane was on time but Paige wasn't. I knew I would recognize her and I did, when she came huffing and puffing into the crowded terminal ten minutes late. She was wheeling her daughter, Louisa, in her stroller. Louisa was six months old but small for her age. Paige was larger than she had been at college, motherhood having made a palpable difference in her shape. The old willowy look was gone. Her slim upper arms were heavier and her basketball player physique—long-limbed and flat-chested—had not rounded out so much as thickened, and this was emphasized by the way she dressed. She was nursing now, and wore long overtops with stains that looked like watermarks around her breasts. Still you would stop on the street and say that is a beautiful woman, perhaps even more beautiful now than she had been at school.

A change was evident in her manner, too. Confidently, she tossed diapers here and there and bent down to give Louisa a kiss. This was not a nervous mother, although her demeanor changed as soon as she spotted me. Her face always turned red with the slightest exertion, and now it may have been the excitement, or disturbance, of seeing an old friend. She lent her cheek for a quick kiss and backed off. Physically, Paige was never warm; there was always that look of fear when you approached her. She conveyed her warmth in words instead, and very quickly began telling me about this town. She poked fun at it, which was a relief. What fun would it be to talk to Paige if she were not still just the slightest bit wicked?

I had called her this time. I knew that her husband, Alex, worked for an Indian legal defense fund in Billings and would not be difficult to find. He said Paige was in Philadelphia. She was seven months pregnant and they were going to spend Christmas with their families back east. She returned my call from Philadelphia, from that house I imagined so many times but had never seen, the site of all those scenes of her growing up that had taken on such mythic proportions in my mind. And now Paige was going to be a mother herself. I told her I wanted to see her and she did not say no. She and Alex felt stranded in Montana and they enjoyed having visitors come down. And then when she told me about all the arrangements they had made for my coming, dinner parties and tours around town, I was flattered and saw how much had changed. I was no longer in the category of "enemy" or "rival" but "old college friend." "Be sure to leave an extra day," she said. "Alex just loves showing guests around."

"Are you still seeing Philip?" she asked as we strolled around town. "No. How is your family?" "Better. Now that the children are grown." Chatter, with the loaded questions buried in between. It was as if we had made a tacit agreement not to delve deep and so we glided more easily over topics than we would have done in the past. That may have had more to do with our age; nothing between us seemed so important anymore.

It was the baby who interested me, the most tangible sign of Paige's new life. "She's wonderful," Paige said. "It's a little like love. When she leaves the room, even for a minute, I feel awful." But she cautioned about making too much of Louisa. "It's wonderful having Weezie, but she doesn't make my problems go away."

The main problem was her work, or more accurately, her lack of it. She had recently quit her job as a lawyer for Legal Aid. "I'm frightened because here I am pregnant and I don't have a job to go back to. Most women worry that they don't have long enough maternity leaves. I'm worried that I'll have one for the rest of my life." Alex kept pushing her, she said: " 'Do this, do that, there are plenty of jobs you can get around here.' But I think I'm spoiled. I'm too well-educated and I won't do work that I don't like."

The problem wasn't with keeping busy, she said. "You can always find something." She had edited a health pamphlet for a nearby Crow reservation and done volunteer work for a local museum. But it was the kind of work wives did and she was sensitive to the negative connotations it had. She still toyed with the idea of writing, ideal in her circumstances, but it required a good deal of self-confidence and self-promotion, "not my strong suit," she said. And she looked at me then as you would an old friend, someone who knows your flaws.

After a brief spin through downtown, we met Alex on the courthouse steps. He was much better-looking now. The ponytail was gone but he still had wire-rimmed glasses which, now that they were out of fashion, gave him a scholarly air. He wore khakis, an oxford shirt and Hush-Puppies, the standard attire for a do-good lawyer. Alex was not handsome but goofy-looking in an appealing way. In college, his hair was greasy, his face broken out, and he lumbered about the halls in a T-shirt and jeans. All he needed was a can of beer and you could see him permanently parked in front of a TV. But now he looked fresh. It was as if Paige had put him through her washing machine and sprayed a little starch into his life. They made quite a contrast: fragile Paige and robust Alex. He seemed delighted to see us and could not wait to begin my tour, but first he had to pet and hug his newborn daughter. Paige said that it was he who had delayed their getting married and he who was hesitant about having a child, but now he was the one who enjoyed them the most. "Right after Weezie was born he said, 'I'm so happy you've given me this, you can do anything you want.' "

"Alex loved being single and on the road," Paige told me later. "A part of him is wild and free; another part is cautious, family-oriented and sober. Alex's mother told me she could see him having kids but not a family. But I think the family part is dominant now, especially now that Louisa is around."

It was because of Alex that they had settled in this city, remote from anyplace Paige would want to live. As one of four attorneys for a privately funded foundation dedicated to improving the Indians' lives, Alex believed he had the perfect job. There was no scrambling for partnership, no hierarchy, and no need to wear a coat and tie. "I don't have to put in hours for anyone and if there's pressure, it comes from the intrinsic value of the cases themselves," Alex said. He spoke about one landmark case he recently prosecuted concerning mineral rights. "Back east, it would take years for a talented attorney to be in a position to do that."

Which meant it would be hard for Paige, who admired his work and believed in what he did, to ask him to leave. "We made a deal," Alex said. "When Paige first came to Billings, we said that in three to six years we'd review our situation and if she wasn't happy we'd leave."

"Would you go if she asked you to?" I asked.

"I don't know," he said. "But in the meantime, it hasn't come to that."

They lived in the older, more established section of Billings. It was not where most young couples live, but after they saw the house they asked their parents to lend them the extra money. Paige said the house was at odds with Alex's style. "Alex is still fighting to keep his distance from the bourgeoisie." (Unsuccessfully, it appeared; his poster of Che was in the garage because Paige would not let him keep it in the house.)

Inside, the rooms were dark, cool as the interior of a Greek temple and furnished with fine antiques. Paige's taste had always tended toward the patrician. We wandered into the baby's room where I stopped to admire a quilt. Paige said she had felt guilty buying it because of its extravagance. "It would be different if I were earning money, but I'm not, which seems to make Alex the arbiter of how much we spend. Now I know how housewives used to feel," she said.

She felt if they were living anywhere else, there would be many more opportunities for her to work. In a larger city, she would be able to teach law, do editorial work in book publishing, work for legal services in a more progressive atmosphere, she said. But here the opportunities were limited. "You could work for the U.S. attorney," I suggested.

"He's in Helena, two hundred fifty miles away."

"Private practice?"

"The handful of law firms here still give women a hard time."

Once Alex suggested she write mystery novels. At first Paige was excited by the idea, but when three days later Alex brought it up again, she snapped at him: "Don't pressure me."

Alex encouraged her to work, for both selfish and nonselfish reasons. "On the selfish side, we could use the second income and he wants to be able to say he has a working wife. On the nonselfish side, he knows I'd be happier if I were working. One thing you learn when you're married: How happy your spouse is has a lot to do with how happy you are."

Paige could draw that moral but not much guidance from the intermeshing of her own parents' careers. "I was a latchkey child," she said. Paige's mother started working during the Depression. She taught music in schools that paid their teachers in rations of coal. She met Paige's father at the University of Pennsylvania, where she was studying for her doctorate in music and he was studying law. She dropped out and worked so her husband could stay.

Over the years Paige's mother helped support the family through various jobs. She gave music lessons in their house and eventually taught music at a local private school, but it was never a career, in the sense in which women now use the term. It was a job, to support her husband while he got his career under way. And if she ever wanted to move from "job" to "career," she was handicapped along the way. One year the high school made her acting principal "while they looked for a man with a Ph.D.," Paige said.

As her husband became established, she worked less on her own and more as his helpmate and sounding board. She became his de facto office manager and occasionally accompanied him to court to give him a reading of the jury's reaction. "Frankly, my mother liked what she did. In helping my father, she worked for love, a better motivation than most people have, and she did something that was socially useful and intellectually valuable as well." I knew Paige was comparing this in her mind to the dull and uninspiring jobs she had had since school. But more important, helping her husband with his work instead of doing her own allowed Paige's mother to conquer her fears of working on her own. "In some ways my mother is even less confident than I am. She never thought she was good at what she did."

But it was not easy being the woman behind the great man. Paige described how difficult it had been for her mother, for all of them, to withstand the pressure of her father's career. The work was contentious and for weeks before a trial, her father would withdraw into a world of his own. But her mother succeeded. She was everything to her husband: wife, nursemaid and handmaiden to his career. Despite his accomplishments, her father was often plagued by bouts of self-doubt. "It was hard for him to think what he was doing was valuable." Paige's mother was always there to reassure him of his gifts.

But there was a nice footnote to all this, Paige said. After her father semiretired, her mother went back to complete her doctorate. Searching for a thesis topic, she discovered that a famous nineteenth-century musician's wife had herself been an estimable composer. Mrs. Coleman then wrote what became an award-winning book about her. In another age, her subject might have existed only as a footnote in her husband's life, but in the more feminist climate of the seventies, she was perceived as being worthy of separate treatment. And what better author than Mrs. Coleman, one wife eclipsed by her husband's grandeur giving another a spotlight of her own?

At first Paige's father balked. "He was disturbed that it might interfere with his schedule or take time from him," Paige said. But when Mrs. Coleman finally completed the thesis, and it was published as a book, her husband was only too pleased. "You should see him. He's so proud of her," Paige said. "He insists on calling her Dr. Meg."

Paige later showed me a review of the book that appeared in the *Washington Post.* Her reaction to the publicity was somewhat ambivalent. It added just another bit of pressure on her to resolve her own career dilemma. In the end, her mother had blossomed despite the considerable obstacles of her era and situation. Paige had fewer excuses.

The next morning Alex left early for work. It was a little frightening to have time alone with Paige. I was afraid we would upset each other as we had so many times at school, but in retrospect it was really very calm. None of the old toxicity was there, though neither was the old thrill.

We returned to our favorite subject—ourselves and how we got that way. I knew all the facts, but they made more sense coming from a more mature Paige. I realized then that what I loved about Paige was her craziness, whether real or in my mind (David said in my mind) and how distorted my view of her in college had been. She urged me to break the one tie I couldn't, to my family and my home, and I couldn't rationally view anyone who did that. But if David wasn't threatened by her, he wasn't moved by her either, and I was. I thought she was the most remarkable woman I had ever met. I saw her potential as he never could.

Up until college she considered herself as having come from a happy home, although she said she was probably repressed. She read almost constantly. "My parents would have to come and tap me on the shoulder to get me to come to dinner."

She attended Girls' High School, one of the most competitive public high schools in Philadelphia. "Everybody was so hepped up about SAT's," she said. Her parents took a more intellectual approach, and yet they cared that she went to Radcliffe. The day the admissions notices were put in the mail, her father, on business in Boston at the time, called the Admissions Office to find out if Paige had gotten in.

"Leaving home was quite a shock." Everything she had repressed in high school now came out as Dr. Paige and her assistant, Dr. Fran, got to work. But mostly, she had problems with men. "I feared that if you gave yourself to a man, he would possess you." Part of the problem was the four-to-one ratio at Harvard. "The men pounced on you," she said, which in Paige's case was true. They were boys and didn't know what they were doing, but it was a bad introduction to sex, and for women like Paige, a further reason to avoid the whole subject.

She was as disappointed by Harvard as she was by Harvard men. She had a hundred reasons: it was too competitive, it wasn't a meritocracy, there was less emphasis on learning and too much on grades. "Alex saw college as a means to an end. If a course was boring, so what? He needed the grade to get into law school. But I was more idealistic, or less practical."

"Why didn't you write more for the *Advocate*?" I asked. "I thought you were so good." "That was so foolish of me," she said. "I came from a background where you had to be the absolute best to be any good at all." Paige was right and for this reason never got to the starting line, either with work or with men.

Right after college, she worked for a demographic research firm in Princeton. The statisticians couldn't put two words together and because Paige could, they deferred to her. They provided the kind of flat lusterless backdrop against which Paige could stand out and it was in that kind of environment that she always excelled. They thought of her as some kind of "creative" type. But the job was tiresome and the pay was low. On long weekends she would drive to Cambridge to collapse and recuperate on Missie and Georgianne's couch, which is where she met Alex.

Missie and Georgianne were giving a party as usual, and a serious relationship was far from Paige's mind. I pumped Missie for the story, but she just laughed and told me I would have to ask Paige. "Let's put it this way," Paige said. "Don't ever flirt with a man just because you know it could never work. You might end up marrying him."

"Why didn't you try to avoid Alex, the way you did all the others?" I asked. She laughed. "I did. He was just too persistent." Alex liked to win. Their relationship was almost as volatile as David's and mine had been. Almost; I did not like yielding even this distinction to Paige.

They dated on and off that year. In certain ways they were compatible: they shared the same outlook on life, the same liberal politics, and both were stubborn and strong-willed. But in other ways, they were incongruous. Paige was cautious almost to the point of being timid. She needed the proper food. At eleven P.M.

she would fold her arms across her chest and say, "All right, Alex, I have to get to sleep." Alex, on the other hand, was wild and reveled in it. He aspired to uncouthness. And though she was tolerant of his ways, he was not so tolerant of hers. When she complained she needed sleep, he called her a "wimp." When she asked him to slow down, not to walk so fast, he called her "weak." "Why did you put up with him?" I asked her. "Well, he was exciting," she said, "and also, I was enormously fond of him" (an outburst, for Paige).

At the end of Paige's year in Princeton, she moved back to Philadelphia and started law school. It seemed like the worst possible career for Paige, given her father's life, but Paige rationalized. She admitted she had no particular interest in the law, but then neither did a lot of people who went to law school. Paige said she wanted the security of a professional degree. What she told me in later years was, "It solved my career anxieties, at least, for another three years."

Even more important than going to law school was her decision to return to Philadelphia. Her father was getting older and she wanted to know him in his calmer years. She was no longer the nervous child she had been and it pleased her to communicate with him on a more even-tempered plane. We both agreed that it was a relief to finally stop analyzing our families and get along with them. Analysis, like therapy, seemed to have prolonged our adolescence.

She was happier at law school than she had ever been at Radcliffe. She later said she did not love the law as much as she loved her own competence at it. She made law review the spring of her first year and helped orchestrate the Law School Show. It was around that time I saw her in New York. She seemed full of hope then. She didn't know what she would do when she graduated but felt there were any number of things she might try—teaching, clerking for a judge, working for Legal Aid. And also, she said, she might even write.

Her third year at law school was her most exciting. She worked in a Legal Aid clinic, which she loved, and took interesting courses. Her only problem was that she kept getting sick. She was self-conscious by this time because Alex often made fun of her frailty. He said it was probably psychosomatic and this made her angry. One winter she decided to figure it out once and for all. She was like a dervish, whirling into action, making a list of every illness every person in her family had ever had so that when she finished her research, it was she who told the internist what was wrong with her. She was hypoglycemic, which a lengthy blood test confirmed. How happy she felt then, knowing that at least part of her fatigue had a physical root. "You know the feeling, you have a problem and you lick it."

To Missie and all their other friends, the Alex-Paige saga was as entertaining as the David-Fran affair had been. They dated on and off over the course of five years, and across the terrain of five states. When she went to Philadelphia, he suddenly showed up with a job at Legal Aid. And she made a detour out west on one of her vacations just to be with him. Once in Cambridge he waited eight hours on a certain street just on the chance that they might "accidentally" meet. When they did, they went off together to spend the weekend in Marblehead, but an argument about the proper way to sew a hem blew them apart. Had it not been for the long stretches of time they spent apart, the relationship would never have survived, Paige once said. "We were such volatile people. Had we stayed in any one place together too long, we wouldn't have lasted."

The big issue over the years was commitment. It wasn't just clean sheets Paige insisted on, it was monogamy. Alex was seeing other women and she would not tolerate that. "I was working my tail off in law school and if he wasn't ready, I wasn't interested." But they continued to crash in and out of each other's lives.

And then, when it was certain that they would be more than two thousand miles apart, each of them started to bend. They were on a summer trip in Paris, celebrating her graduation from law school. Paige was a much more civilized woman on vacation. Even in cities in which she never lived, she was a resourceful guide, so in Paris, which she had visited many times with her parents, she was spellbinding. And being on foot seemed to help. They were such nervous, restless people, it helped sometimes just to walk it off.

In the middle of their vacation, Alex got a call from the states. The job he had hoped to have with the legal defense fund in Billings the following year had come through. Paige had just graduated from law school and had already accepted a job with a law firm in Philadelphia. They were standing by the phone booth. Alex had to make his call. He did not ask her what he should do, he told her.

"I took the job," he said.

"You did?" she asked.

"Yes."

"I didn't know how to feel," she told me later. "In a way I knew he was choosing not to be with me, but on the other hand, we hadn't made any sort of commitment to each other yet."

And yet it seemed they had. They started talking more and arguing less. They made plans to see each other instead of leaving their explosive reunions to fate. Paige had a rather pragmatic view of Alex's sudden change of heart: "It's easy to be a bachelor in Boston and New York. But once Alex saw he was going to be stranded in Billings for a while, he started thinking more in terms of wife and family."

In February, Alex called her in Philadelphia and proposed. It was the fifth anniversary of the day they had met. "Alex can be pretty corny," Paige said.

The first order of business for Paige when she moved out to Montana was to pass the bar exam. Alex was helpful. He brought her meals on a tray while she studied. As soon as she passed, she took a job with Legal Aid in a tiny outpost about a two-hour drive from Billings. Paige had a bad knee so they agreed to move there and Alex would commute. Grateful, she clipped an advertisement from a magazine and ordered "Great Books on Tape" for Alex to listen to in the car. When they eventually did move back to Billings, Alex said he missed his tapes.

"If you asked me then how things were going, I'd tell you 'Fine,'" Paige said. But soon she grew restless with her work. Much of it involved litigation. "I can't stand arguing. I'd had enough of it because of my father. My attitude was, Can't we all just settle this thing amicably?" The office had no library, no Xerox machine and a born-again secretary who decided which clients Paige should see based on whatever "sign" from the Lord she got that day. "We didn't even have a copy of the Code of Federal Regulations, and when I complained about it my boss said he'd never heard of it." Her proficiency in the law was stagnating, limited by the kinds of cases she worked on. She litigated over barroom brawls and divorced drunken lovers. One woman she divorced got married the next week and then wanted Paige to divorce her again. "I told her we'd better think this one through." Paige was great at telling stories like this. She had always had a way of bringing other people's kookiness to life. But it was only in talking about her work that she derived any pleasure from it; otherwise, she counted the days until she could quit, which she did, not long after she and Alex were married.

For a year, Paige kept busy organizing a Great Books society in Billings and acting in a community play. But she was not content with these jobs, which she saw as stopgap measures. It was when she was home and pregnant that she acknowledged she didn't want to practice law. What she wanted to do was write, but there was always an excuse for not starting. She had to fix up the baby's room; she had to order a desk. She herself acknowledged that she wanted to get the words down, if only to conquer old ghosts: her celebrated father, her unforgiving perfectionism.

But what good did any of our insights ever do us? Once, when she visited me in New York, I told her about a magazine article I was writing and how upset I was about the work. "It doesn't have to be perfect," she said. "Just do an adequate job." "Workmanlike" was the term she used. I liked the sound of it—cool, practical, realistic, qualities that neither of us had. Paige was good at giving this sort of advice because she was so utterly incapable of following it.

ONE night she and Alex showed me slides of the wedding and the place where they used to live. Alex made some comment about how skinny Paige used to be before she had the baby. But you could tell by the way his arms encircled her that the attraction was still there. "And of course there was that, too," she said in the kitchen, telling me what I really wanted to know.

Which meant that she was really no longer the Paige I knew because that was the most fundamental thing about her, that skittishness about men. It explained the clumsy gait, the awkward manner, her fearfulness with regard to the world. She did not have them anymore; they had been replaced by the cool and more languid look of a mature woman. Once I asked Alex what the happiest time was for Paige. After the wedding, he said. "She was high for three weeks."

JUST then Alex was concerned I might think of him as an ogre for forcing Paige to come to Billings against her will. (We were having breakfast at his favorite diner in town.) "She never expressed any opposition to it," he said. "I said and felt at the time I wasn't willing to do anything else."

When he arrived at college, Alex planned to go into academia. "My idea was to write books and change the world." But he had been disillusioned. "I had overromanticized academia. I envisioned a group of professors all sitting around and discussing ideas, which wasn't the case. It was all politics."

He just barely tolerated law school, which is where he developed his interest in gardening and cooking. "I needed something to humanize the place," he said. It was about this time that he met Paige. Ever since he'd seen her on a subway platform in Kendall Square, he said, he could not forget her. "She looked so beautiful, pale and innocent." (Paige?) "I saw her as my better half."

The way he put it, Alex was "at war" with himself. Throughout most of his courtship of Paige, he was seeing another woman whom he had met the summer before law school when he was working at a halfway house for runaway kids. She was rebellious like him, whereas he viewed Paige as a symbol of stability and all the bourgeois values he was trying to escape. The stormy period with Paige was a contest of egos, he said, which masqueraded as a matter of lifestyle. Once he had suggested they live in a commune with another couple. Paige refused. Not long after he and Paige had started dating, they drove from Washington to Savannah, Georgia, their first vacation. Alex wanted to sleep in the car; Paige wanted to sleep in a motel. They fought and eventually Paige prevailed. "How come?" I asked. "I saw she was right. It is a lot better than sleeping in the car."

Everything was an issue when they first got married. "We both used to work on the garden, but we got into too many fights. So we devised a solution. I'm in charge of the vegetables and Paige is in charge of the flowers and indoor plants. When I get nervous," Alex said, "I can be difficult to live with. During the mineral rights case, for example, my career rested on the outcome; all I wanted at home was peace. I said I was willing to help Paige on her cases, I just didn't want to chat. I've driven from Boston to D.C. with my father without saying a word. That doesn't seem strange to us, but Paige just couldn't understand it.

"But it's worked out fine. We're both people who need a lot of support from other people. She's great that way for me," he said.

"She tells me I'm wonderful at what I'm doing and that I'm handsome, which isn't true. And I try to be helpful to her. I do stuff around the house: the laundry, dishwashing, anything she wants me to do. If she gets tired staying cooped up in the house, I take her places.

His main worry, he said, was her lack of career. "She has so many talents and skills, probably more than I do. Her problem is making a commitment.

"Paige has a way of displacing anxiety," he said. "In December she decided what she really wanted to do was write. But she couldn't write until she had a desk. My uncle had a beautiful antique desk that he offered to send us from Seattle. But then she kept changing her mind about the shipping arrangements." He told me about an article she wrote about a piano player at a local bar. "It was a wonderful piece."

"Did she ever try to get it published?" I asked.

"I don't think so."

I asked Paige if I could see the article. She said she was too busy to look for it but would find it for me later.

A windstorm whipped through Billings during the middle of that night. Exhausted, Paige slept right through it but Alex, roused by Louisa, stirred about the house. There was something irrepressible about him, the way he prowled about the kitchen at three A.M. With Weezie slung in a Snugli around his neck, he began to assemble the ingredients for hot and sour soup: chicken, chicken broth, tofu, chili oil, sesame oil, mushrooms and eggs. (Only one store in all of Montana stocked Chinese ingredients, at Alex's request.) Now and then he consulted with Weezie—"Need a little more chili oil? A little more broth?"—but mostly the baby slept. In the morning Alex presented us with his soup and told us about the storm we had missed.

The next afternoon I watched Paige prepare for a wine and cake party she was throwing that night (in honor of me, their northern guest). She was making two cakes, an elaborate chocolate cake from Julia Child called Reine de Saba and a carrot cake. Her sister had sent her a food processor for her birthday. Paige was not a devoted cook but an efficient one. She has a way of doing certain noncerebral tasks that makes them seem easy. She reminded me of one of those people who work in department stores, demonstrating Magi-Frying Pan and such. "See?" she said, holding a pound of carrots up before my eyes. "In no time it all turns to mush."

She was equally competent with Louisa, an expert at feeding and diapering and juggling dirty and clean diaper bags. It was almost as if it were too easy; I never saw her get flustered. She must have been reading my mind. "I figured with Weezie I was bound to make mistakes so I relaxed and decided to do the best I could."

She said there was a metaphor that was central to her life. When she was in Dunster House, she attempted to try out for a female lead but when she walked up to the piano, she just croaked. Someone suggested that she try out for the comic lead. Paige, thinking it a joke, began to clown around. She got the part and stole the show. She wished she could apply the same principle to her career. "If only I could just pretend it didn't count."

SHE would not let me go without inquiring about both David and Daisy, the most controversial topics from our old "rival" days. Had I told her that Daisy was doing smashingly, having a wonderful life and career, she might have reverted to her old critical self and started enumerating Daisy's flaws. But I told her Daisy was unhappy, still seeking what Paige had, a home and a family. "Maybe it's difficult because Daisy is so bright," Paige said. "It would be difficult for anyone to live with someone as talented and good as Daisy."

After that it seemed safe to talk about David, but it was nothing like the old days. Then when she would ask me about him, her face would drain of color and she would look like someone who had prepared herself to hear terrible news. And God knows in what misguided way I doctored up what I said, knowing its effect on her. Now when she asked, she looked no more pale than usual and I simply told her the truth. I told her I felt he was a ball of fire, still too hot and intense for me to approach. But with the distance of years and miles—David had spent the last four years in Africa—I liked him better.

I told her how the first day he arrived back in this country, he'd called me from the airport (I was living with Philip at the time) and after consuming an unspeakable quantity of beer at McSorley's in Greenwich Village (he ordered them two at a time; he said in Africa, everybody did), asked me to marry him. I should have said yes. That would have sobered him up. It was a thought I had had as well, but only in the moments when I wanted him to rescue me from my situation. Once he accused me—wrongly—of using him as my "safety" school, the one college we were sure would admit us in case the others we had applied to turned us down. He was calmer now that he was home and his father was ill; I found myself wanting him to call more than he did.

Paige thought the marriage proposal was a gas. Finally we could laugh over David.

WE had fun my last day. Alex would not rest until he showed me the site of Custer's Last Stand. Paige spent the morning at home, alone with Weezie and her own thoughts. I would have given anything to talk to her about what she really thought about, but we did not do that kind of delving anymore. And if we had? Only once did she make a reference to how we used to be. "There were times when I was mean," she said, but it was not as if she were speaking to me but to herself. And that was all.

At lunch on a screened-in porch overlooking the brown flat land, she put Louisa in my arms and took a picture of me. Three weeks later it arrived in New York with a note. It was as nice a note as I have ever gotten from Paige, who never gushes with feeling. Her prose as always was curiously formal and brittle, like her handwriting, but it contained several warm thoughts. She said I seemed in splendid form, as if the life I had worked hard to make suited me. As I could see when I was there, she wrote, whatever her doubts and confusions, Louisa was an unalloyed joy. Still, she had to laugh everytime she recalled my imitation of Tess: "Well, I would like to travel more." Wouldn't we all?

As always, it was I who bent over to kiss her goodbye at the airport and she who inched imperceptibly back. She was flushed that day, probably exhausted by then from all our talking and visiting. Alex was probably going to want to run around a little more, but she would insist that they go home. She would like to rest. Her head was "schpinning," she said.

WAS there anything left between us? I think so. I felt a sort of affection for her now, a word that I would not have used in the past, it being too tame for what I used to feel, which ranged daily from rage to love. I also saw things about her that I would never have admitted in the past. Did she see herself skidding all over the surface of everything and never really taking the plunge? She was as wise and worldly as I had always thought, but it seemed less dazzling in the context of her failure. Her cleverness undid itself. And change would never be forced upon Paige, who could rationalize her way out of anything. That did not mean I did not hold out hope for her. I thought she would strengthen in spite of herself, through Louisa and through Alex. Confidence, particularly of Alex's ebullient sort, was contagious. He adored the way she handled the baby; he believed in her work. I would read Paige's articles critically; Alex read them and said, "Great." It was just the kind of backslapping that might eventually help her settle into the kind of work I thought she was worthy of. She might not be a "genius" like her father but she was talented enough, and she had other joys—Alex, Louisa and stability in her life.

We did not have stability then, in the days when I went crazy and Paige was so afraid. It took us a long time to grow, Paige, Miranda and me, and I'm not sure why. I can remember, and so could Paige, the low point sophomore year when she left school. But she was terrified then, not just of writing papers but of life. Now she was terrified only of writing papers and that wasn't such a bad thing.

Once, before I left, we walked over to the local theater where she had recently performed. The stage was empty so Paige and I began to fool around. First I got up there and started to sing before the audience of empty velvet seats, and then Paige did. She did a splendid rendition of "It's Too Darn Hot" from *Kiss Me Kate,* and once again she was that long lanky girl, clumsy and skittish and yet with an awkward grace. Someone turned on the lights and came in to see who was making all that noise and we were back to our sober selves. No times were ever as wonderful as those when we loved and taunted each other in the Dunster House dining room. I understood then the appeal we'd had for one another: we were each other's stars.

CHAPTER 8

Daisy

Can the heart's meditation wake us from life's long sleep, And instruct us how foolish and fond was our labor spent—Us who now know that only at death of ambition does the deep Energy crack crust, spurt forth, and leap . . .

—ROBERT PENN WARREN, "Coda," *Rumor Verified*

I flew out to see Daisy the weekend of New Year's Eve. We had kept in touch fairly regularly since college so, on first spotting each other at the baggage area, neither of us was very surprised. She looked the same and I did, too, except that my hair was a little longer and hers cropped short. Otherwise, she was still the same Daisy, dark and tawny-haired, with that famous smile.

Of all the women I had known at college, I felt closest to my bubbie, although the years had caused us to drift apart. We were both chasing our careers and so our communications were limited to phone calls, postcards and letters from whatever city we were in. But we knew the facts of each other's lives, if not in detail then the broad outlines.

Daisy spent her first year out of Radcliffe working for the U.S. ambassador to the Soviet Union, whom she had met and impressed while on assignment for the *Crimson* After her month-long crash course in Russian at Berlitz, she traveled through

Europe and parts of Asia while the Justice Department had her credentials cleared.

No student was ever more ripe for such a trip than Daisy. She wrote letters from London, Venice, Prague and Vienna in which I could sense her excitement. Even when she wrote about the rough spots—an incident with a Turkish soldier on a beach, the long spells of loneliness—it was in the spirit of a traveler who knew her purpose was to experience, not just to enjoy. She did not make a pilgrimage to Tibet but a visit, yet the impact was equally profound. She said when she arrived in Lhasa it was as if she were leaving the known world and that was where her trip really began. By the time she arrived in Moscow, she was at home not feeling at home.

The Soviet Union changed her. I cannot say exactly how except that it opened her eyes and continued the broadening process that college had only begun. The bureaucrats had not worn her down, she joked, nor had winter; a native of Minneapolis, she was used to the cold. But the loneliness, coupled with the grimness of what she perceived as Soviet life, had. She spoke movingly, as if she were describing not a country but an old and ailing friend. She read as much Tolstoy, Pushkin and Turgenev as she could and many writers of the post-Stalinist generation whose names I had not heard. She drank vodka with Russian intellectuals and felt a kind of fear and excitement about their life that seeped into her own.

Her job at the embassy ended in June, when she met her parents in Milan. Her mother waved a telegram bearing the news: Daisy had been accepted to work in the Rome bureau of an international photography agency. It was not a happy summer. She loved Italy but was troubled by the lives of the women with whom she worked. They were well-known photographers, so it was both titillating and depressing to hear the details of their lives. Most of them drank heavily. One had children but complained they did not love her because she "had not been around for them while they were growing up"; another was in Italy to flee the fallout of an unhappy divorce. Had they been less impressive, it would have been more easy to dismiss them, but these were interesting, accomplished women who led miserable lives. Daisy was troubled by her experience and talked about it frequently. She was grateful when the summer was over and she could finally come home.

Her first job was at a small newspaper in a backwater part of Texas. It was the kind of paper that, on Easter Sunday, ran a rotogravure picture of Jesus Christ on Page One. I had seen it used as an example in my summer journalism course of how a paper ought not to look. Daisy had received an offer from a paper in Minnesota, but she had seen too many exotic places to be content with going home. The experience in Rome had left a bitter taste in her mouth and she was eager to wash it away with a long cool draught of Texas. If Texas was provincial, she embraced that provincialism now. She wanted to start small, to take things in manageable portions and slowly work her way up to better jobs. She also wished to reexamine "America," she said, to view her native land through a traveler's eyes.

We did not talk very much but she kept me posted on the highlights. On the first day of her first job at the paper in East Texas, her editor asked: "You been to Haaaaavard?" He pronounced it with an exaggerated New England accent.

"Yes."

"And then you been to some fancy bureau in Rome?" he said, each word hitting with the force of a punch.

"Yes."

"Well let's see. I think we have just the place for you here."

And he put her in the most backward rural county of the state. If he meant to dampen some of her enthusiasm for work, he failed. She loved that little patch of wasteland and made art out of its shacks and muddy fields. She wrote about dirt farmers, faith healers and snake handlers. And when the occasional thought,

What am I doing down here? arose, she would suppress it with the notion that she would not be there long.

The small-town hominess, the intimacy of the newsroom, the earnestness of the people she met provided a closeness that the Rome bureau had lacked. Every Thursday the younger staff members would get together for a dance club. The idea was to practice the latest steps. "It was hopelessly hokey," she said, but she enjoyed it. She was dating a boy named Ezra. "Remember?" she said when we talked about him. "You told me you liked his name."

After a year in rural Texas, a newspaper in Dallas came after her. It was a much better paper but still provincial in its way. She laughed when she told me its slogan ("The biggest little paper in Texas") and claimed that its longest section was wedding announcements. But she was hesitant to make the change. She wavered, as she always did, convinced she would fail. And although she never turned down a promotion because of her fears, she always had to play out this little scenario. She balked and vacillated and consulted her sages on the staff. "I'm just beginning to hit my stride; I don't want to leave," she confessed to one of the "older" photographers with whom she worked (Jake was thirty). "You feel you're just beginning to hit your stride?" he asked. "Yes," she said. "Then that's the time to leave."

It was an auspicious time for women in journalism. Newspapers were just beginning to change the way they parceled out assignments. In the old days, women were given the "soft" news, stories known in the trade as the "four handkerchief jobs" (if it really made you weep, it was "five"). Men were given the "hard news": feuds at city hall, zoning board meetings, stories concerning the real issues of the day. Photographers were less circumscribed by sexist rules but few with Daisy's abilities were satisfied shooting Chamber of Commerce luncheons or meetings of the zoning board. Daisy felt she had time to grow and viewed the limitations of her job as challenges. Her editors must have been delighted: a photographer enthusiastic about taking pictures of potholes.

I saw Daisy at our Fifth Year Reunion in June 1979. It was a gloomy affair because of the small number of women who attended and the tragic incident that had preceded the event. One classmate, a much closer friend of Daisy's than mine, had committed suicide. Her name was Sue Bienstock and she was part of Maureen's "freshman herd" that Daisy clung to and I abhorred. She, too, had been among the group at Radcliffe who acted bizarrely about food. Every morning she would come into the dining room with her hard-boiled eggs and grapefruit, which she rolled down the table as if they were bowling balls. That was all she ate, at least in public. She looked so pretty when she arrived at Radcliffe freshman year in her crewneck sweaters and woolly plaid skirts, but she quickly switched to men's shirts and painter's overalls to hide the rapid fluctuations in her weight. Sue wanted to be an economist but had switched to psychology because she thought it would help her find more answers about herself. As far as I knew, her questions were not much different from ours: what to do with our lives, how to make a mark, how to find love and meaningful work. I asked Daisy if Sue still had eating problems at the time of her death. Daisy either did not recall or was too upset to say.

At the reunion I also chatted with Maureen, who, as a matter of principle, did not complain, but that day even she admitted to having problems. Things weren't happening as quickly as she had expected. She had spent a year working for a congressman in New York but the job was largely administrative and Maureen felt she wanted a position with more clout. She'd spent the next two years at the Woodrow Wilson School of International Affairs in Princeton (when all else fails, go back to school) but was still floundering. At the time of the reunion, she was toying with the idea of business school. Maureen had always seemed so sure of herself at college; now that she was not, I felt I could actually like her.

There was one woman who attracted attention because she had already gotten divorced (which was unusual, since so few of us had even married yet). But in general, it was a pretty dull group. The only woman I wanted to talk to was Daisy. She looked pretty that day and had happy news to share. She liked her work but more important, and she said this as if she had been saving it all day, "Fran, I'm living with someone."

As far as I knew, Daisy, like Paige, had been a little slow in this regard. As frank as we were about everything else, we tiptoed around sex. I think I intimidated Daisy. David had not been at all shy in his physical displays of affection (placing a hand indelicately on my breast without checking to see who was around, or doing it deliberately because someone *was* around). Maybe Daisy saw me as "advanced." But in a rare moment, she would imply that she was still "a little shy when it came to that." The situation was corrected the year she spent abroad. "A Russian?" I asked. "No," she giggled. "One of ours." We laughed. Daisy told me nothing about him except that his name was Nick, and he smoked too much. Their affair was cool and businesslike, which suited her purposes just fine, she said. She felt a little roguish after that, a woman of the world.

Her body changed, too, in the way that some women's will long after adolescence. She had been lithe and girlish but now, at twenty-four, was growing thicker and broader. She had not gotten any taller but rather wide across the shoulders and chest. It was hard to reconcile my image of sweet sunny Daisy in her new, more powerful frame.

The man Daisy was living with in Dallas was a photographer for the rival newspaper in town. She told me all this on the porch of my apartment in Cambridge in between Fifth Year Reunion events. I was sullen that day. I hadn't dated anyone in a very long time, except for men who were older or otherwise inappropriate.

And then Daisy brightened up, inspired to tell me the story about her and Lee not as if to boast and say, "See what I have," but to encourage me and say, "If it happened to me it can happen to you."

She had been dating Lee for about a year when she found out she had a lump on her breast. She went crazy, she told me. "I couldn't even think that it might be benign, but anticipated the worst." She was operated on and a small benign cyst was removed. But Daisy was still shaken. She spent two days in bed and then rushed back to work, as if to deny the whole thing had ever happened. "It was a mistake. I hurt myself and had to spend the next week in bed." Lee asked what he could do for her but all she did was scream at him. He was patient and loving and waited for the worst to pass. When it was over, she believed she was in love with him. "I let myself need him," she said.

Lee wanted to get married, but Daisy wasn't ready. There was a slight imbalance between them. Lee seemed pale and slight beside Daisy, who, physically and intellectually, was now beginning to hit her stride. Not long after the reunion, I saw them both in New York. Lee wanted to eat in an Automat, so we sat in the newly refurbished one on Forty-second Street. Daisy, normally such a spirited conversationalist, hardly said a word. I realize now she must have given me some sort of signal, for somehow I knew to concentrate my efforts on Lee, drawing him out to talk about his job in television. Daisy told me afterwards it was a problem between them. "He sometimes feels overshadowed by me."

The problem grew worse the following year. The more excited Daisy got about her job, the more Lee withdrew. Of the two papers in town, his was actually the better one but Daisy's gave her more free rein. She was consistently winning better assignments and was often sent to shoot out of town. She tried to downplay her accomplishments so Lee wouldn't feel so bad but it only made him feel worse. The low point was when the newspaper sent Daisy to photograph Jean Harris. She took wonderfully revealing pictures, but when she came home Lee was in a rage. He argued that the paper was pandering to sensationalism by sending Daisy off to New York while there were more important stories to cover at home. Daisy, of course, agreed with him. She not only took his criticism to heart but developed new fears of her own. She worried she would lose her "small-town" humility. "Maybe with all the attention and fuss I'm getting, I'll become too grandiose." "Daisy, that's dumb," I told her. She must have realized his criticism did not grow out of moral concerns, or that even if they did, it was futile to try to appease him, because eventually she stopped trying.

I remember driving with her in California the following year. She was about to start her new job as a photographer for a national magazine. "I've discovered something and I'm not going to fight it anymore," she said.

"What's that?" I asked.

"I'm ambitious. I really do want to be a great photographer. And I'm not going to pretend I don't."

"Did you ever?" I asked.

"Not really. It's just that all those months of warring with Lee made it seem like more of a conflict than it was. He was always trying to make me spend less time at my job and I was always trying to get him more fired up about his," she said. I remember the phrase she used, too. "Fran, he's trying to clip my wings." As if anyone could.

Their relationship had dragged on for another few months, but with too many ups and downs. When Lee's work was going well they lived together in relative harmony but when Daisy's was and his was not, anything she said might be the cause of a feud. Daisy had graduated to assignments that were attracting national attention. When the magazine offered her the job in its West Coast bureau, it was tantamount to asking her to break up with Lee.

"I knew it might screw up my relationship but I wanted to keep going," she said. "I was still climbing and I didn't feel I wanted to stop yet. I felt as if I were on the threshold of a new takeoff, and I felt Lee would hold me back."

It was about then that I flew out to California to see Daisy. She had just arrived in San Francisco but had not yet started her job. When I asked her if she had any regrets about breaking up with Lee, she said absolutely none. She seemed much more forthright and less self-effacing, and I liked the way she finally owned up to having real ambition in her work. For some reason, I felt easier having dropped out of the race, as I had, knowing Daisy was staying in.

We had a fine weekend, bouncing around the pretty city that was to be Daisy's new home. She had yet to unpack but she did take time off that weekend to visit old friends. We looked up everyone we knew from college who was living on the West Coast and in a whirlwind ride in her little yellow car managed to see them all. Our tour ended at the house of one of our favorite ex-*Crimson* editors. He was chubby and funny and had married a woman who was also chubby and funny. Daisy and I giggled over that and everything else we could think of on the ride home. We were still each other's best bubbies after all these years.

A year later, we had a terrible fight. It was April. Daisy had come to New York. She had just had a promotion at the magazine and was feeling exuberant. I was starting to freelance and was actually earning a living in New York for the first time. She asked me something about how to write fiction. "Oh, Daisy, I'm tired of you always playing so dumb," I said. "You know damn well how to write. Why do you pretend you need me for advice?" I had my realm of expertise and I wanted Daisy to stick to hers; my notion of success seemed to preclude the idea of there being enough to go around. I thought back to my worst days at the *Crimson* and felt, Oh no. Daisy's going to do everything I do but better. "Why do you ask me such stupid questions?" I went on. Daisy looked up from the couch where she had been staring at me, incredulous the whole time, and said, "I can't believe it. I can't believe this. You know what I feel like doing? I feel like packing up my clothes and going home." I said I was sorry and convinced her to stay but it was a dreadful week. Every time I tried to explain to her why I had yelled, the words had a tinny self-justifying air. And she would just look at me with that same hurt and puzzled stare, which hardened into certainty as the week wore on. It was if she had seen a side of me she had not recognized before, and now that she had seen it our friendship would never be the same.

We amused ourselves that week the best we could. My parents took us out one day, which was pleasant. Daisy always loved seeing them. And we visited mutual friends in town. But when she left for the airport it wasn't the same. The only thing to do was to keep busy and try not to think about our fight.

A year or two lapsed in which we did not speak, but our friendship was far from over. There was too much holding us together. From that very first week at Radcliffe when we had sat in the corridors of Holmes Hall, hugging our knees because we were too nervous to sleep, up until now, we were still caught up in the same issues—work, friendship, a desire for success and peace of mind (the last two always seeming to contradict each other), and they kept us unnaturally close. We were in the same race, and although during an off moment we might wish one or the other to swerve off course, basically we would always be cheering the other on. I loved Daisy and envied her but I never wanted her to lose. I knew that her winning was my winning, too.

DAISY started working in San Francisco the following spring. All her progress and accomplishments up until then did not make her any more secure. She was sure the magazine editors would take one look at her pictures and ship her back to Texas. "Don't you realize you always feel this way?" I asked. "Sure," she said. But these judges were much more discerning, so that this time she was certain she'd fail. All she thought about was work. She was ill those first few weeks and lived on a diet of yogurt and Tab. Physically, the new office was intimidating. Daisy was used to ill-equipped darkrooms and noisy newsrooms where the clatter of typewriters and the chatter of reporters seemed to soak up the excess anxiety in the air. Here, in the carpeted offices of the bureau, only the computers made noise, and that, an eerie electric hum.

She panicked during the first three weeks, until the editors started to praise her photos, which meant she could relax. She called all her friends to rejoice. "You'll never believe it. They liked what I shot."

During those first few months she concentrated almost exclusively on her work. Even after she handed in an assignment, she went home and tried to see how she could have made it better. "Anguish" was something other photographers might have felt, but Daisy enjoyed what she did. Finally she was working with people she could learn from, and she learned. During her third month at the bureau, her pictures of illegal aliens crossing the Mexican border were nominated for a national magazine award. They did not win, but she felt the shock of suddenly being in that league.

And then, six months after she had been in San Francisco, she sank into a serious depression. She had experienced similar tail-spins before. She would excel at whatever job she was doing, but when the initial fear and anxiety ebbed, would grow weary and depressed. Our phone conversations then had to do with what really mattered in life and we would say things we did not believe —it did not matter how well we did at our work, there were other things in life besides doing well.

Daisy had a habit, whenever she was depressed, of sweeping a searchlight back over the past and seeing it as all black. Then she believed her career had been a waste. She felt disgusted with the fuss her parents made over her accomplishments and refused to mail them copies of her clips. But then a new assignment would come along and Daisy would get excited, and the work would carry her along until the next period of lethargy.

It was during one of the deepest troughs in this cycle that she thought about Lee. She did not regret leaving him but regretted not having someone else. She saw herself as a drone, a machine that ate and slept and recorded other people's lives. In that light, her apartment looked sterile. She was lonely and often bored. And she was turning thirty, and that benchmark gave her pause. What was the purpose of all this work? She wanted to fall in love. In retrospect, she made it sound more clear-cut than it was: "I'd always assumed there'd be a man up ahead, waiting for me, and now I was starting to realize that by my own choice, this was no longer true."

It was just about this time that she met Ben. He will always be just a name to me because I saw him only once, when I visited her in San Francisco after their affair was over. I tried to peek across a lobby and get a look at him. I may have seen the faintest outline of a handsome man, middle-aged but at a point when he could still be called young. But I did not look for too long. I was embarrassed for even wanting to look at someone who had caused Daisy so much pain.

That evening we sat in the dining room of Daisy's new house. She had moved there after the affair was over. The old house, anything she associated with Ben and their relationship, made her ill, she said. It was an excruciating scene: Daisy, suffering the more she talked, and me, not knowing how to help her. She had taken portrait shots of him, which, despite everything she had said about him ("I was deluded; the whole thing was a horrible mistake"), she had kept. They were in a bundle, lightly bound with a piece of string. There were also a few color Instamatic snapshots he had taken of her. He must have loved her, for he captured the Daisy whom I knew perfectly, especially her smile.

She looked at the bundle as if it were poison. She would not even say his name or refer to their relationship. She just left the space blank. "You mean your relationship with Ben?" I would say, finishing her sentence. "Mmmm," she would nod.

He must have caught her during one of her low periods at work because she was waiting for someone to lift her out. Relationships between newspaper people and the subjects they met on assignment were increasingly common. There were more younger women journalists, single for longer because they had delayed settling down, and an ever-available supply of middle-aged politicians, lawyers and businessmen. Photographers worked closely with their subjects (following them for days to get a sense of their lives) and both were caught up in a curious community of interest. Women like Daisy were terribly vulnerable, having pushed their social life aside for so long. Ben was an author whose most recent book had just won a National Book Award. He lived in Marin County, where Daisy was sent to shoot him for a major magazine piece. He was well known for his writing, was active in liberal causes and was something of a media star. He was also handsome, which might have accounted for his being photographed so much.

I don't think Daisy felt she was in love or allowed herself to admit it, at least not at first. It was difficult for her to accept being pursued by someone so famous. When she told me his name, I, too, was taken aback. But Daisy wasn't the type to be bowled over, or to fall senselessly in love. "Those are always the type that do," her secretary said.

She was fond of Ben when they met, and spent several weeks at his house, coming and going as both their schedules allowed. He was probably charmed by her. People often were. Neither of them seemed to realize that there was anything more going on until a few weeks after the shoot when Daisy was sent to Mexico on an extended job. She was pleased with the assignment, which promised to be exciting. But Ben, alarmed by the prospect of losing her, did what he otherwise might not have done. The day after she left, he chartered a plane and flew down to Mexico to see her. He knocked on the door of her makeshift darkroom and told her he had a confession to make. He was in love with her, he said. "What did you do?" I asked. She looked at me but did not respond.

I don't think they were ever happy, not from that very first day when he showed up at her door and not ever afterwards. She spoke not as if she were in love so much as consumed. But she said she felt powerless to stop herself. When I talked to her—and she hardly spoke to any of us then—she sounded like an addict, doing something she knew would cause her great pain but she could not stop. She was in love, she said.

Their relationship lasted for less than a year, but it was passionate and intense, partially because they tried to keep it out of the press and partly because Daisy was so often out of town. They met at the train station because, ironically, no photographers would find them and it was appropriate, even comforting, to be among other people meeting and parting. Eventually, they took an apartment together. They decorated it with things they loved. (Later, she threw away everything they had bought together.) She had loved Lee, she once said, but that was more a love inspired by habit. Lee interfered with her work. With Ben, work did not exist. In the skewed world she inhabited during those few months, she finally got a grasp on her priorities. Work was what you did in order to live; this was what you were living for.

None of us heard from Daisy during those few months. She didn't call me. She didn't call Maureen. It was as if she had dropped out of our lives. The one time I did reach her, I hardly recognized her. I remembered our conversation because I was living with Philip at the time and still trying to decide whether or not to marry him. "Fran," she said, "the feeling you have when you're in love is that you've been waiting your whole life for this, and nothing else matters." In comparison, my feeling for Philip seemed so much more tepid. She was in love and I was as taken in by the drama of it as she was. I heard about the details not as if I were listening to my friend get herself into trouble but as if she were the heroine of a tragic play.

I think she assumed that eventually they would get married. At first, that was their plan. But he kept vacillating. One week he would tell her to set a date, and the next week he would act annoyed whenever the matter arose. Daisy was torn. She wanted to be with him but if he loved her, wouldn't he wish to marry her and settle down?

In the end, it was not Daisy who stopped it. It was Ben. One day she came back to their apartment and found a note. He said he was having trouble writing and needed to be alone with his manuscript. For a month she entertained the hope that he would call her when he returned.

There was a final scene, not with Ben but with his likeness. Daisy's editor had submitted her photographs for a national magazine award. This time, her photographs won.

At first it did not sound like Daisy's voice. It was low and raspy and difficult to hear. But after a while I got used to it. That was what it sounded like when you were that severely depressed.

Days, whole weeks, she blocked out. She dragged herself to work each day, but with only half a mind. She stopped playing tennis; she left the house a mess. She took pictures but without any real interest in them. Once, months later, I called to complain about my own work. I told her I could not stand being nervous all the time. She told me she no longer got so nervous. "How come?" I asked. "I learned to be a hack." "You mean you finally learned to calm down?" I asked. "No, I just learned not to care."

For months she was despondent, and when she emerged from her despondency it was with a tremendous anger about her entire life. It was Ben who had betrayed her, but it was her background, her parents, the ethic by which she was raised that was more deeply at fault. "The whole pattern was of someone who made her work her life. I always got enough chits being the best to sustain the system. I used achievement as a substitute for love. I was a crack performer. Give me a test, I get an A. Give me an assignment to shoot, I cover it. Give me a job to try for, I get it. It wasn't healthy. It wasn't good."

She told me she felt she'd been "had." "All my life they'd been telling me, 'Be a good girl and you'll be rewarded,' and now look at this: I had been successful and I was miserable and alone."

After almost a year, when there was no sign of any progress, her psychiatrist suggested she take some time off. Daisy did not relish the idea but she was desperate. Once, when I asked her about this—it was toward the end of her leave—she said, "I had no choice. I had gotten myself into such a low state that I couldn't function."

Six months later she sounded better. It was unmistakable: the spunk was back and so was the laugh. She said it was partially the rest but mostly just time. She had just moved in with a roommate, a tremendous improvement over living alone, and was on her way to Greece. She and a friend had arranged to take a real vacation, something she had not done in years. They had a wonderful time. They swam and walked and at night drank ouzo and complained about men.

In autumn, when she was feeling better, she started dating again. She had just moved back to San Francisco (a transfer at her request) and was starting to see a doctor for a community health clinic. He was thirty-six and had never been married. He told Daisy he had a problem getting "close," but with her, he felt inspired to change.

I flew out to see Daisy the weekend of New Year's Eve. I was no longer living with Philip and didn't want to spend the holiday alone. Daisy's voice on the phone was not as buoyant as it had been the last few times we spoke, but she encouraged me to come. She was having problems with Jay, she allowed. She did not go into detail but said the more interest she expressed, the more he pulled back. The "incident" with Ben had made her less tolerant of ambivalent men, and yet those were the kind she seemed to attract. She wanted constancy, which Jay did not seem able to provide. "He doesn't seem to care. If I come over, fine; if not, that's fine, too. There's a reason he's never been married, Fran," she said. She told Maureen she was going to break up with him but she never seemed to. "Why not?" I asked. "Because it was so good in the beginning, and because there's no one else." She felt angry then toward all men and resentful of her work. She joked that she and a few of her friends on the magazine's staff were thinking of writing a column for workaholic women: "No Time for Lust."

During the few minutes in which we waited for my baggage, Jay and I talked. He was not handsome, but there was something boyish and distracted about his looks. His hair was brown but there were a few streaks that looked as if they had been spray-painted gold, which added a little sparkle to his looks. He wore Hush-puppies, with the laces untied, and a toggle coat like college students used to wear. I concentrated on him first because I was a little afraid to look at Daisy. This time it had been almost two years.

"Look, worry lines," she said, pointing to the crow's-feet by her eyes, made even more visible by the harsh airport light. The wrinkles in her face deepened when she smiled. She did look older, but your old friends always look like just a bunch of girls to you. There was only one rough spot between us that weekend. I told her she should cut her hair and she said I wore too much makeup. "It makes you look so New York."

We drove to her house, a pretty peach stucco building in a quiet residential neighborhood. It was a comfortable place enlivened by the presence of her roommate, who was a physician. They were not intimate friends but Suzie, who looked like a Playboy bunny who had taken an academic turn (blond and buxom, with killer tortoiseshell glasses), was cheerful and friendly. They did not live like messy college students but like two women making a home. Daisy said it was nice to come home from work and find the house filled with friends and the smells of good cooking.

When I compared this to life in the old apartment, she frowned. The "incident," the apartment, anything she associated with her old life made her ill, she said. She saw herself as having been "deluded" and Ben as "weak." "Fran, he didn't know what he wanted." Her old neighborhood had been occupied by young professional singles. Daisy said she preferred the quiet family neighborhood where she and Suzie now lived.

She was relatively happy, she said, except for her problems with Jay. His affection, or lack of it, seemed to determine how she felt. He loved to be with her at parties (Daisy was wonderful telling stories about the politicians she had photographed), and Jay would shout across the room, "Daisy, come here and tell them what the governor said." But in private he was difficult. He made little comments that Daisy felt were deliberately designed to provoke her. "He just loves the idea that he's a straight single male in a city of so many desperate single women." In the car on the way from the airport, he joked that he and a friend were going to auction themselves off as husbands at a single women's professional club. Daisy nudged me in the ribs. "He's always making cracks like that."

"I just don't kill myself over my assignments anymore," she said while helping me unpack. "I just don't care that much. Ever since Radcliffe, even before, I'd used work as the yardstick. I'd get so nervous about it. It's not the only thing that matters. I see that now. And it's not worth getting so distraught about all the time. There are other things in life that matter more: getting married, raising a family, taking time off. And I'm going to have those things. Balance.

"Now I hear the clock ticking. I feel a sense of resignation. I've lived not just some of my life, but a lot of it. I don't want to fritter away any more time. I don't want to read bad novels, have a fling, spend time with people I'm not interested in. I used to stay up until three in the morning developing pictures and thinking of new ones to take. I'm not doing that anymore. Now when I have to do it, I grunt, groan and gnash my teeth. If I had the drive now that I had when I first came on the staff, I'd be soaring. But I've recently had the realization I've driven hard enough. Once you stop, it's hard to start up again."

Just before we went to sleep, Daisy said: "My mother was 'just a wife' and that didn't work so I thought I'd have a career. Well that doesn't work. Not alone.

"The obsessiveness. The constant working, building monuments to myself. It all seems so pointless in retrospect."

The next day I was sitting in her office when the phone rang. It was five o'clock and she was just finishing her work for the day. A bulletin over the wire reported that the governor had just pardoned a convicted murderer. Someone was sent to interview the prisoner's attorney and Daisy was summoned to shoot. She picked up her camera and started racing. I was not convinced she had lost her enthusiasm for work. Only someone who got as nervous as Daisy could get so excited, too. It was one of the factors that made her such a good photographer.

She told me afterwards that she had been offered and had rejected a job with one of the international photography agencies. At the interview, the personnel director told her, "The job has got to be the most important thing in your life. You have to put it ahead of everything—your personal life, your family, everything." "I realized after that interview that I don't want to be forty and miserable. It can get pretty lonely following that route. I want a husband, a house and a job I care about, but one that doesn't consume me."

Daisy made fun of her interviewer, mocking his self-important tone. "I prefer the more casual attitude here. When I get too wrapped up in a story, an editor will say, 'Oh come on, Daisy. It's only journalism. People look at your pictures and flip the page.' "

Later that day, I asked her about Maureen, whom I had seen in Manhattan about a year ago. She and a tall blond man were walking out of an expensive restaurant in SoHo. I looked quickly at her finger to see if they were married. She was wearing a large emerald ring and a wedding band. Daisy said she had been dating Andrew, who was now her husband, for several years before they became engaged. "He adored her but she kept putting him off." A year after she graduated from business school, she consented to marry him. She was just starting work as an investment banker. Daisy said they had bought a big house in Connecticut that they were busy fixing up. Andrew had renovated the attic so that it could serve as a combination study and gym. "They're really happy, Fran," she said. "Maureen said she was ambivalent at first, but after being married for two years she was falling in love with him. Maybe you don't always have to be sure."

Maureen had been a tremendous help to her, too, Daisy said. She was in San Francisco on business just after Daisy was starting to recover from her depression. Maureen's investment banking firm had paid to have her stay in a luxury hotel. That night she phoned Daisy. "After we got off the phone, she called me back. 'Hey Daisy,' she said. 'Why don't I hop into a cab and spend the night with you?' I thought it was great of her." So in the end, Maureen had been a true friend. When she left she sent Daisy a beautiful set of silver bowls. The bowls easily cost more than any other item in the house. Daisy kept them filled with flowers on the dining room table.

During one of the nights I was there, we went to a party given by one of Jay's friends, a woman lawyer who was "thirty-eight and over the hill." She worked at a major firm in the city and the party was to celebrate the purchase of her new house. It was a beautiful house in the hills of Marin County, large enough for a family of four. "How do you fill such a large place?" someone asked. "With friends," she answered. Daisy and I still didn't understand but the woman told us, "I don't see why not being married should deprive me of buying a house. I have the money and besides, I'm happy living alone."

"Nonsense," Jay said. "She's been trying to marry me for years." He laughed and put his arm around her. Daisy looked annoyed. Jay and his harem of successful old maids.

ON New Year's Eve we had a little Harvard reunion of sorts at the house of an old classmate of ours, Rick. Daisy was afraid that if we didn't go, no one would and she did not want Rick to be alone on New Year's Eve. His wife had recently left him and he was feeling low.

I remembered Rick from college as one of the many who unsuccessfully pursued Maureen. He met Daisy on the rebound, and over the years they had remained friends. After college he married another classmate of ours. Jamie was tall, brunet and extremely rich. Her favorite extracurricular activity was flying her father's plane.

I lost track of them but, according to Daisy, after a couple of years of marriage, Jamie decided to get her doctorate in history. The more interested she became in the Middle Ages, the less interested she became in Rick.

The story reminded me of the those my mother used to tell me about women who lost weight and then suddenly decided they were too good for their husbands. "When you love someone you make compromises," my mother used to say. "Maybe we don't know how to compromise," Daisy said. "Maybe she didn't love him," I said. She had left him a year ago and still he kept pictures of her by his bed.

. . .

DURING my last day with Daisy, we drove to Sausalito to visit a friend of hers who had graduated from Radcliffe in 1962. She was a fair-skinned, red-headed woman with a voice husky from too many cigarettes. She had married right out of college, like most members of her class, had three kids, and left her husband after ten years of marriage. She said she was "super-happy" living alone, but Daisy thought she said it because I was there.

"I was luckier than you girls. I rushed blindly into marriage, which, it seems to me, is the only way anyone can do it. Women your age can't do that. You're older. You've had too much experience to marry unwisely. Which means you'll either have better marriages or more of you won't marry at all. Is it better this way? I don't know. At least I've got my kids."

Loneliness was something she didn't even think about. She was used to it. The house was devoid of heavy furniture but cluttered with possessions that could easily be moved—books, cartons, pots, pans, children's toys—the artifacts of some wandering tribe. She was a sociology instructor at San Francisco State, but the pay was low and she was looking for something better. She had money troubles of a different order from those of her married friends, who complained if they could not take a summer trip to France.

"Men? I'm not sure it's worth it," she said. We talked about the long lonely passages of Anna Wolfe in Don's Lessing's *The Golden Notebook* and discussed a recent article in the *Village Voice,* "Against Marriage," by Vivian Gornick. Daisy's friend agreed: it was not an institution suited to sustain love, only families. "And happiness? That's an American ideal," she said. She had a friend, a Soviet emigré, who thought the trouble with Americans was that they thought about their feelings too much. " 'On a personal level,' my friend says, people in your generation are terribly nice and considerate and kind. Yet as a social group, they're so terribly egotistical, always examining and reexamining their state of happiness. It's such a self-defeating proposition." Daisy and I left feeling guilty, since happiness was all we ever thought about.

NOT long after I returned to New York, I began noticing Daisy's pictures more often in the magazine. I called her once to tell her I liked her recent cover. "Oh really?" she said. She sounded pleased, which seemed like a good sign. Once we talked about all the ex-*Crimson* editors we knew who were already scrambling up the mastheads of major publications. "Do you want to be an editor?" I asked her. "Not yet," she said. "And if I do, I'd rather wait until I have a better sense of my values as a journalist." I admired that. She sounded so wise.

She was traveling a lot and I asked her once if she wasn't lonely, driving up and down the coast, flying to neighboring states. She said she liked the constant motion. And besides, when you were shooting a story, people didn't leave you alone. She told me about pictures she had taken of a group of cattle ranchers who were so angry about some proposed farm legislation that they introduced her and the reporter to every rancher in town. "When do you get any sleep?" I asked. "I don't," she said. "When I'm on assignment, I still get too nervous to sleep." That much hadn't changed since freshman year.

In September the magazine offered her a position in charge of its London bureau. Daisy was excited by the offer but troubled by it, too. Her mother had had surgery that year and she did not want to be so far from home. But more important, her life was too comfortable now for her to disrupt. "I'm not as young as I used to be. It's not so easy to just pick up and go." In our Tenth Year Reunion book, Daisy wrote that her greatest satisfactions did not come from her work but from the things she did outside it—take Spainish lessons, learn to sail and tutor kids in the barrio.

The last time I spoke with Daisy, she had broken up with the woman-torturing Jay and was dating someone else. The calm even tone in which she described the relationship suggested it was much better than her previous one. I asked her if she was still so desperate to get married. "When it's actually a possibility, you don't worry about it so much," she said. She was prospering in her work, too. She was getting bigger assignments, working longer hours and occasionally lasping into the old despair. "I still get so sick about work."

Was it a sickness? I didn't know. I remember her face that night when she was suddenly summoned to work. Perhaps she looked a little nervous but she also looked excited. You could envy a person who had that ability to be so gripped by her work. Was there an equation? Did you have to be that nervous to be that good?

CHAPTER 9

Felicity

He took it all too far
But boy, could he play guitar
—DAVID BOWIE, "Ziggy Stardust"

It was November 1976, just after the Harvard-Yale game and Thanksgiving. I was at the Boston *Globe.* Daisy was in Texas. Paige was in law school at the University of Pennsylvania. David had already left Chile and was heading toward Spain. (We kept in touch only sporadically then.) Of all of them, I probably thought about Felicity the most. Her friends, if they could be called that, were not mine. I knew them only later, when I spoke with them after Felicity's death.

I heard the news from my editor at the *Globe* that night. "This just came over the wire," he said. He could not have known that I knew her, or how much she meant to me, or he would not have been so callous in his remark. "Here, read this. Read about what one of your Cliffie friends went and did."

I read but I really saw only the first and last lines: that she had killed herself and that she had died by a lake, in a car, with carbon monoxide and a hose.

I cried alone in my kitchen that night. I thought about the recent times when I had seen her, how she looked, what she had said, and then I put the article away. I did not want to look at it again but I could not throw it out. And then, seven years later when I was researching an article in Cleveland, the man driving me around asked if I would care to see the Pinegrove School. He was an old Greek immigrant and his daughter had won a scholarship there. But his wife had been reluctant to send her because of rumors that the students there were brilliant but "way-out."

The name Pinegrove held magic for me, if only because Felicity had talked about it so much. I accepted the driver's offer and there, on the two hundred acres of what was supposedly the most beautiful private school in the world, I started gathering details about Felicity's life. I spoke to her friends and read her stories. I realized I had a little collection of Felicity memorabilia I had kept since college, although I had never admitted to myself that I was saving it, or why.

What I found is only a partial truth. People who knew her better may have different or more complete versions. What follows is a brief recounting of a rich and disturbing life.

IT was later, when I talked to the other women, that I realized how much she mattered to the entire class, and that was odd, for she was not a woman who had close women friends. She was catty, bitchy and, finally, disturbed, and she pushed women away. A small handful of men knew her best and she appealed to them not only because she was attractive and brilliant and outrageous, but because she was so frightened. "Let's fuck," she once said, on a dare, to one of them. But when he appeared to want to take her up on it, she backed off and said, "Oh my God, Eric. You mean we're really going to do this?"

She mattered to all of us. I would not have thought it would have touched her to know this, if Daisy hadn't told me a story that suggested it might have. In the middle of senior year, Felicity started to look unusually thin (she had a history of anorexia, but that fall she looked worse than usual). Daisy and her boyfriend, Curt, asked Felicity's closest friend, Sean, if he and Felicity would like to join them for dinner one night; perhaps company and a good meal would cheer her up. You had to know Felicity to know what a ridiculous suggestion this was. Felicity did not do conventional, suburban things like go out to dinner with other couples. She and her friends, Sean and the small group of nocturnal *Crimson* editors who inhabited the same odd hours of the night that she did, went to heavy foreign movies (on beautiful sunny afternoons), or sat up in her room talking until three A.M. And as for dinner, Felicity's standard diet consisted of Kahlua and cream. Or Tab. When Sean told Felicity about Daisy's offer, she howled (God, it was an unpleasant sound, a cross between a scream and a whine): "That's sowwwww nice. That's the nicest thing anyone's ever done for me." She was exaggerating, as always. The point was, she cared that we cared, even if it violated her "code" to admit it.

I saw her middle name used only twice, once in the *Radcliffe Register* her freshman year, where she was listed as Felicity Beth Barrett of Shaker Heights, and once in her obituary, which appeared in the Cleveland newspapers and several others for which she had written. "Beth." It was delicate and prim, nothing like Felicity, who was outrageous and bold. Her death, however, was quiet and efficient, lacking in the dramatic flourish that characterized so much else in her life. And it was painless, which was ironic, for she was more solicitious of her well-being in death than she had ever been in life.

According to the obituary in a Los Angeles paper: "Felicity Beth Barrett, 25, a former staff writer with this paper's Living section, was found dead in her car on an isolated lakefront beach in New York State last Saturday evening in what local authorities said was apparently a suicide.

"Miss Barrett had joined the staff in September as a writer for the Living section and was staying with her parents, Arthur and Kathryn Barrett, in Shaker Heights.

"Born in Boston on March 16, 1951, she attended the Pinegrove School and became a nationally ranked tennis player among girls under 16, winning several major titles.

"Miss Barrett earned her bachelor's degree with honors in 1974 from Harvard University, where she was an editor and feature writer for the Harvard *Crimson* student newspaper and was elected to Phi Beta Kappa, the society of top scholars.

"The sheriff's office of Chautauqua County, N.Y., where her parents had a summer house, said Miss Barrett's body was discovered at 8:45 P.M. Friday in a car parked on a beach with the engine running and a rubber hose carrying fumes from the exhaust pipe to the car's interior.

"Besides her parents, Miss Barrett is survived by a brother, George L., and a sister, Abigail."

It was a skimpy obituary for an extraordinary life, yet the paper's editors may have felt awkward printing anything more. Felicity had worked there until the year before she died, but the circumstances of her leaving were murky. When he heard about her death, the editor walked up to one of his reporters, Molly Quick, a friend of Felicity's who had graduated from Radcliffe in 1971, and said: "You think it's my fault, don't you?" Molly did not answer. She was too shook up, as we all were. But of course it was not the editor's fault. It wasn't anyone's fault. It was Felicity's fault because she was so adept at ruining whatever she did that was good. We were all unhappy and confused in those years. We whined; it was the language of the tribe. So when Felicity complained about the "cold fear"—the fear of success and the worse fear of not having it—who took her seriously?

Jane Beardsley, another of Felicity's acquaintances (she had many more observers than friends because she was so captivating to observe and so maddening to be with), took a more sociological view. "Six graduates of Pinegrove committed suicide in later years. I think it was a combination of youth, affluence and the times. We thought of ourselves as special—we expected fulfillment—and yet we were constantly disappointed. Life wasn't as great as we had been led to believe it should be. By the time we got to college the rules were gone. Relationships between men and women were breaking down. In the years when you had parietals and 'dates' you had the pattern of the predator and prey. It wasn't good but at least you knew the rules. We had the same romantic and sexual urges but we didn't know how to play them out. And then expectations about women were changing rapidly. It was not clear to us how to act. We wanted to be successful, attractive and 'ideologically correct.' They don't have to conflict but they often did. Suddenly we were doing a man's job with a woman's psychology. To that Felicity added problems of her own. She had some problem about growing up. She didn't want to be womanly. She liked the idea of being flat-chested and shapeless. Maybe it was tied up with Catholicism and sex—who knows.

"To me Felicity had everything. I couldn't understand how she couldn't be happy then. But I understand it a little better now."

Molly said Felicity could have been the model for Tom Wolfe's essay on the "Me" decade: narcissistic, completely wrapped up in herself. But Felicity would not have been happy embodying only one stereotype. She strove to embody them all—superman, superwoman, liberated woman, *femme fatale.* She was so talented that she nearly succeeded in being all those things. But as good as she was she was bad, too—mean, lonely, selfish, and brutal to herself. Self-destructive, people said. Was it because she was a woman, or a member of a particular generation, or a particular class? Some said her problem was endemic to places like Harvard, the compulsion to achieve, no matter what the cost.

In death as in life, Felicity was an object of speculation. The only thing Americans love more than a brilliant success is a brilliant failure, a professor of ours once said, and Felicity was both. And she was shockingly original. Ten years later the librarian at the Cleveland paper where Felicity worked for two months recognized the name instantly: "Felicity Barrett? You mean the girl who died? Sure I remember her." People were intrigued about Felicity while she lived and perplexed by her after she died. She was the paradox of our class. All our conflicts were bound up in her.

SHE wrote so much about Cleveland that it was hard to separate the Cleveland of her childhood from the Cleveland in her mind. By Cleveland, of course, she meant Shaker Heights and the affluent suburbs built on industrial wealth. In reality, the city has an active cultural life, but to Felicity home was the place that in crossword puzzles is used as a synonym for wealth. "The whole environment is about money," said her friend Neil Bookman, who grew up near Felicity and knew her at college.

Felicity's aspirations were intellectual, which distinguished her among a more social crowd. "You'd be dating this beautiful girl and all of a sudden she would start talking about *And Quiet Flows the Don,*" Neil said. But in every other way, Felicity embodied the female ideal of her parents' social set. She was beautiful, she was never without a tan, and she had a closet the size of a small room. If at Radcliffe Felicity rejected the debutante side of her upbringing, in high school she rebelled against it in a more characteristic way: she strove to out-jet-set the jet set.

The Barrett house was a twenty-five-room mansion, a grand and imposing old estate. Felicity never was very specific about what her father did; for at least a part of his career he seemed to have been in public relations, although apparently he had made much of his money in oil. Friends said her father was an arresting figure, a tall, dark, craggy man. He had grown up in a small town outside Scranton and had graduated from Princeton after the war, but those were the only facts about his past that Felicity mentioned. In college, she confided to her closest friends that she was disturbed that her father said so little about his past. A few months before she died, it was rumored that she had made a pilgrimage to Scranton in the hope of uncovering more about his background.

"I remember meeting her family," Bookman said. "They were so unemotional, so removed. Her mother was aloof, not personable or warm. Her father was very handsome, very tall. He was fanatically prepped-out with his clear-rimmed glasses. No one ever talked about 'family.' It was as if they didn't have a past. There was no sense of enveloping history. After the suicide I thought about this. I had a roommate at college who was from a similar background. His father was from a poor Jewish family in Brooklyn and his mother was a Southern aristocrat. Martin didn't know who he was. He didn't have roots to draw on. If you grow up like that, you have difficulty nailing down what your spot is. Felicity had no sense of being part of any culture or group."

She was raised a Catholic because her mother was a Catholic, although religion was downplayed in their household. Mrs. Barrett had graduated from Vassar but had never worked. "A lot of the women in that neighborhood had gone to Vassar, Radcliffe or other good schools." His own mother had given up a career as a musician to come with his father to Ohio. It was considered dramatic when one of the women in their neighborhood used her husband's money to open a health-food store. Mrs. Barrett was kept busy raising her children, of whom Felicity was the oldest. Felicity's suicide was hardest on her, said Candace Shine, one of Felicity's classmates at Radcliffe. "I don't think she could possibly understand anything Felicity was going through."

But the person who mattered most to Felicity was her father. People said wonderful and terrible things about him. He was charming, bright and worldly, but his most interesting asset was his energy. Felicity had it, too, although in her it seemed to have turned inward on itself. Mr. Barrett pushed his children, that fact was clear enough. When word of her suicide first reached the press, he asked all his friends not to speak with anyone. He knew what people would say about him. "Art was the kind of father who would withhold affection until one of his children did something wonderful," Molly Quick said. The day after Felicity's funeral, he locked himself in a room with a bottle of bourbon and traded Felicity stories with Molly.

"I remember the first time I saw her," said Jane Beardsley, who also attended Pinegrove. "She was practicing in the gym. She hit fifty forehands and fifty backhands. Then fifty volleys, twenty in a row without a miss. There were two white lines on the wall. Felicity didn't just hit the ball between those two white lines, she hit it in the tiny square inside.

"Felicity could hit fifty perfect backhands, then miss the fifty-first and think she was horrible."

She was more than a good tennis player. At fifteen she was ranked among the top ten tennis players in the nation among girls under sixteen. Her peers were girls like Chris Evert. Tennis, in those years, dominated her life. Every morning she would get up two hours before school to practice, but as in everything else she did, she affected an attitude of nonchalance in public. Her picture frequently appeared in the Cleveland newspapers. Periodically she would fly off to Mexico to play in an event and always return with a tan and tales of the sexual carryings-on at these events. Even then she implied an intimate knowledge of sex. Her high school essays, which she was asked to read aloud in her creative writing class because of their arresting style, suggested that their author led a fairly torrid social life. Felicity had more than her share of dates, but when it came right down to it, she was uncommonly shy.

"She approached me at a party," Neil Bookman remembered. "Why she wanted to have anything to do with me I don't know.

She was this super-preppy tennis star and I was this little wimpy guy. I thought, maybe she has more depth than I give her credit for to be interested in someone like me. We went out for a part of our senior year. It was great for me. That this beautiful famous woman was attracted to me was an incredible boost to my ego. But even then I couldn't figure her out. She was impenetrable. You thought either you must be incredibly stupid or she was deliberately acting to keep you at bay. We went to the movies. We drove around. I had no idea that she was intellectual except that she read an amazing number of books. I hadn't known she was smart. She hid that side of her. I was totally surprised when she got into Radcliffe and Yale. I never knew that was important to her. Instead she cultivated the image of being this very social jock.

"At the end of the year we stopped going out. She simply announced this was the end. I asked, 'Why?' She said she just wasn't going to be available anymore. I didn't see her again until college, my sophomore year, when one night, completely unannounced, she showed up at my door at nine P.M. She said she needed to talk. She must have weighed ninety-five pounds. She looked terrible, anorectic and very pale."

Pinegrove was among the best-endowed schools in the nation. You took a stroll on that campus, two hundred acres of choice suburban real estate, and thought you were in a sylvan wonderland, intruded upon only by the occasional Giacometti or Henry Moore. To anyone harking from that school, Harvard surely must have been a disappointment, with its Puritan brick buildings and sallow lecture halls. Pinegrove was built on the estate of a European expatriate whose goal was to create a community devoted to scholarship and art. He commissioned a team of prize-winning architects to design the buildings. The theory was that being surrounded by beautiful buildings and *objets d'art* would heighten the students' intellectual and emotional awareness and make them better people. Whether it had the intended effect is questionable. "Something was rotten there," Felicity's friend Candace said. Perhaps it was the competition. It was more difficult to be admitted to Pinegrove than to Harvard; only two out of fifty students were let in. And inside, the pressure was fierce. It was not to make money (their fathers had done that) nor to marry well (their mothers had done that). It was not necessarily even to be fulfilled, which was more difficult. "Felicity," said John Swarthington, a former *Crimson* colleague and friend, "wanted to be great."

She cut quite a figure at Radcliffe freshman year. "Radcliffe didn't have too many beautiful, blond tennis-playing types," an acquaintance, Ian Andrews, recalled. "Felicity was besieged by men, tall, athletic, good-looking types." The door of her room in Cabot Hall was plastered with messages: "Felicity, call Ken" or "Felicity, Dinner? Rob." Within weeks she was a center of social activity. The first semester of Felicity's freshman year the dormitories were not yet co-ed. Women who wanted to meet men ate in the Freshman Union, but Felicity could be found with the more racy social set in Lehmann Hall, the nonresident student center. "She was flirty, kooky, daring and bold," Ian said. "She liked to take pills and say outrageous things but you wouldn't say she was crazy. A lot of personal alienation expressed itself in the antiwar movement then but Felicity wasn't a part of that. She seemed straight for that reason. She wore fairly expensive, rather preppy clothes, maybe occasionally a pair of purple bell-bottoms accentuating her little bottom. She was much too stylish to ever really look like a hippie. She did well in her work. Then midway through her freshman year she disappeared, returning sophomore year. She didn't say much about why she had left. You wouldn't have known she'd had a breakdown. Externally she seemed to cope. You wouldn't say her visible life was collapsing around her."

"She seemed happy, well adjusted, beautiful, social but very smart," said Candace Shine, who roomed with Felicity and became a confidante and rival in later years. "She was friendly with me, I suppose, because I seemed exotic, because I had grown up in France, and because my father was an art dealer. Later, I think I was her sidekick, someone she could feel superior to. Felicity did everything I did, although always just a little bit better. She was wealthy, and it was a very showy sort of wealth. At Christmas, when everyone else went home to study, Felicity went off to Morocco on a yacht a friend of her family's owned. Her family was the most competitive group of people I'd ever met. You had to be the best at everything, super smart, the best athlete and the most beautiful. She was hung up on weight. She was always dieting. And she would talk about how insecure she was. 'I'm so fat, I'm so ugly, so stupid,' she would say. But it was hard to take this 'dumb blond' act seriously."

When she came back from her Moroccan vacation, she said something to Candace about having jumped off the yacht and swum out too far. That was the first sign something was really wrong. But there were others. Her father had gotten involved in a business endeavor with a fellow Princeton alumnus that had its ups and downs. One year Felicity's family was richer than they had ever been and the next they were tightening the reins. Felicity did not give the impression that now the family was suddenly poor, although she was candid about problems at home. "It was more like instead of vacationing in Saint-Tropez, her family would have to spend Christmas in Florida next year," Candace said.

But deeper issues troubled her. She admitted even she was not sure of the reason for the nervous breakdown that caused her to leave Radcliffe midway through her freshman year. She felt it was chiefly due to her decision to give up tennis. She had stopped playing, somewhat abruptly, the summer before freshman year. And yet she still walked around with the racket as if it were a natural extension of her arm. "I felt I was becoming too much like a man," she told one friend. According to her psychiatrist, she said the racket represented a phallic symbol, and in wielding it, the strong, fiercely competitive Felicity was striving to turn herself into a man. To her friends there were more obvious causes. It was difficult for her to give up tennis, which had been such an integral part of her life. Perhaps she felt she was disappointing her father; perhaps she was frightened about what would make her "special" now. The "beautiful, wealthy tennis champion," was no longer so "wealthy" or a "tennis champion," and I doubt that for anyone as complicated as Felicity "beautiful" was ever enough. At the same time, the Harvard community placed a premium on being intellectual and aesthetic: tennis players were regarded as "dumb jocks." Felicity, who was especially sensitive to what was valued and what was not (it partly explained her genius for style), must have picked up on this. She tried to move in a new direction, but since that direction pointed away from the social competitive world in which she had been raised, the change could not be made easily or with grace. "Deep in her bones she knew what it was like to come out at a debutante ball," John Swarthington said. "She tried ruthlessly to excise that from herself. Boy! She must have been really strong to do it as abruptly as she did." And so many of us made jagged cuts with our past. "It was an intense time of life for everybody," John continued. "We all did foolish things, cataclysmic things. It's just that Felicity did them with more intensity than most."

Felicity never played tennis again—with one exception. Three years later, at the end of her senior year, she did so on a dare. She was dating Eric Steiner, a member of our class, Felicity seemed genuinely happy with Eric, who convinced her one night to pick up her racket again "just for fun." It was a weeknight during the winter semester and the Palmer Dixon Tennis Courts were closed. She and Eric broke into the courts and after some fumbling, managed to find the lights. There, in the eerily lit tennis bubble, empty except for the two of them, they hacked away at that ball. Felicity was "fantastic, a champion," Eric said. And she seemed to enjoy it, proof that that part of her life was safely in her past.

"I thought she had recovered completely," Eric said. "I thought, Here is a person who has undergone a tremendous hardship, and she proved she could cope." Eric said he was completely unprepared for the news of her suicide. "I'm convinced it was the incident at the newspaper. A series of events drove her to the abyss and then into it. If it weren't for that I think she would've made it. People thought Felicity was a lot more crazy than she was."

FELICITY invited Candace to stay with her the summer after her breakdown freshman year. The mood in the large brick house was somber. Her father was still preoccupied with his business and her mother was distraught over her eldest daughter's collapse. Up until then, the people closest to Felicity had had little idea anything was wrong. Felicity sounded better, though, when she finally returned home. She called Candace and coaxed her to fly out. "My father will find you a job," she told Candace. "Felicity told me she needed me," Candace said.

Candace functioned as a sort of psychological nursemaid and housekeeper that summer. Felicity's father did not find her a job ("Felicity probably never even mentioned it to him"), but Candace's uncle found her a position in an art gallery. As an outsider living so intimately with a family with sudden and severe problems, Candace did not feel welcomed by the rest of the family. "I don't think Felicity's mother liked having this stranger around," she recalled. But Felicity was glad to have her there, if only as a distraction, someone to draw her outside herself.

In later years, they were to have a massive falling-out, which was in keeping with Felicity's bad history with women. Only Molly Quick survived with her affection for Felicity intact. But that was because Felicity and Molly stood on equal ground: there was parity between those two tall pretty women. With Candace, Felicity knew herself to be in charge.

Felicity was also cruel to anyone who adored her too much. She abhorred "slavish devotion" and reserved her worst abuse for Candace, whom she insulted by calling "conventional." But during that summer they were companions. Felicity saw her therapist and read constantly in her room; Candace went to work. Once, the two of them, accompanied by Felicity's younger brother George, drove to the family's summer retreat, a beautiful fifteen-room "cottage" in Chautauqua County, N. Y. "It was Felicity's favorite spot," Caudace said. "She was really happy there."

Either Candace was the first person to notice or Felicity first began her bizarre and destructive behavior with food that summer. Until then she had been healthy, even a little plump. But after her breakdown she started losing weight and forcing herself to throw up. Psychiatrists said it was confusion over gender and sexual identity that caused so many women in our generation to harm themselves with food. Perhaps the problem had simply gone unnoticed before. Or perhaps they were right, and the pressure during those times made it worse. But in Felicity, a previously harmless indulgence in dieting reached obsessional extremes. She, of course, denied it. She hardly spoke to anyone about this, but the evidence was there. In public, she consumed nothing but salads and an endless stream of iced coffees and Tabs. But occasionally, at night, you saw her rushing out of a food store, tearing into the bag of groceries in her arm before she could get it home.

The pattern was established that summer, Candace said. "She would eat and throw up. We'd go into a supermarket and Felicity would take a box of cake off a shelf, eat it and then walk out. She'd steal food." Afterwards, Felicity would go into the bathroom and make herself throw up. Candace said Felicity's psychiatrist theorized that she ate to "feel pregnant" and "fill the void," and then starved herself to get rid of her breasts and other female traits. But even if this was true, knowing it did not seem to help. Within the year Felicity's weight dropped twenty-five to thirty pounds. She never returned to a normal weight again.

At the end of that summer Candace returned to Radcliffe, but Felicity took an additional semester off. When she did return, in the spring of the following year, it was as if she had never been gone. She spoke to very few people about her breakdown, and when she did make mention of it, it was in a vague and offhand way.

It must have been disorienting to be back at school. Her old friends were well into the routine of sophomore year and Felicity was starting out as a freshman again. People who took a year off rarely felt at home with either their new or old classes. She was lonely and frightened but rarely confessed that to anyone. There was a "code" to Felicity's behavior. It was all right to be bored, weary, disgusted, disdainful or mildly amused. It was not all right to be enthusiastic, unhappy, frightened or lonely. And if you were those things, it was in impossibly bad taste to talk about them. There was too much talk in the dining rooms already about "feelings" and Felicity, quick to spot a trend and avoid it, avoided that one. It was also a part of the code: It was "cool," even admirable, to assert one's opinions on public events, but it was foolish to dwell on one's own tiresome moods. In one of their many mock-serious discussions, she and her friend Sean McNally agreed that suicide was a foolish thing to do, not because it was cowardly or evil but because it was "boring." "It was our tough way of saying it was 'bad,' " Sean said. "Basically, we were both sentimental people."

Not long after she returned to school, she showed up unexpectedly at the door of her old friend Neil Bookman. She viewed Neil, a discarded boyfriend, as safe. "I just wanted to talk," Felicity told him. Neil was surprised. He and Felicity had not spoken much since high school. He invited her in for what turned out to be an hour of awkward conversation. Unsolicited, she told him the details of her social life. "I had no idea why she was telling me this, but I listened. I was still interested in her, I was always interested in her, but I felt it would take too much effort to work first on her and then on us so that we could have a relationship." At one point she asked if she could use his bathroom. She dropped her purse onto his bed, causing its contents to spill out. "There were all these pills in there, dozens of them. They weren't prescription drugs, just over-the-counter stuff, water pills, antacids, pills for dehydration—that kind of thing." Felicity lugged around the contents of an anorectic's well-stocked medicine chest. With her various eating disorders, her digestive system was probably a mess.

She and Candace roomed together the second semester of her sophomore year but it was an unfortunate union. Felicity was not an accommodating roommate. She smoked, kept odd hours and was deliberately tactless at times, taking an almost perverse pleasure in her ability to shock. And Candace was such a tempting target with her emphasis on etiquette and protocol. Candace went around making rules and Felicity went around breaking them. At the root of their problem was an imbalance of love. Candace adored Felicity, who seemed to have no interest except to use her. Candace's affection suggested a lack of pride, and when Felicity sniffed out weakness she could be inhumanly cruel.

The great wrong for which Candace never forgave Felicity occurred during the beginning of Felicity's sophomore year. Candace had a friend who lived in Winthrop House, where she and Felicity lived. Douglas was sympathetic and astute and Candace confided Felicity's latest acts of terror to him. What Candace did not know was that Felicity and Douglas were having an affair. "I knew she was having a torrid affair, but she did not say with whom," Candace said. After three months of complaining heartily to Douglas, Candance found out the name of Felicity's mystery man. "I was so humiliated. I couldn't believe they would do that to me. On the other hand, it was just like her. She deliberately copied me, just so that she could do whatever it was I did, but better. She became interested in writing for the *Crimson* just because I did, and she was interested in Douglas because he was originally my friend."

It is true that Felicity and Douglas were an odd pair: Felicity was glamorous and sexy, despite her thinness; Douglas, whose father taught history at Columbia, was more of an intellectual than a lady's man. But Felicity had just recovered from her breakdown and was in desperate need of a friend, and Douglas made himself eternally available to her. On a moment's notice she could run to his room and unload her problems on him. That he was not in the glamorous set maybe even made her feel safer and less inhibited. Douglas had a reputation of being brilliant and Felicity worshipped brains; but Douglas was also a friend, and without him, she might not have survived the year.

Meanwhile, Candace was mortified. The situation was especially unpleasant because all three of them lived in Winthrop House and could not even eat lunch without seeing one, or worse, two of the others there. Eventually, Candace packed her bags and moved up to Radcliffe. She never spoke to Felicity again during their undergraduate years. But Felicity, who never mentioned the incident either, committed the indiscretion of writing about Candace in the *Crimson* at the beginning of senior year. It was Felicity who, in her warning to freshmen, described in lurid detail her former roommate's hair-removal techniques. Not everyone knew who the woman was, but Candace thought they would. She felt she could never forgive Felicity, but she did.

They were in New York. It was a year after graduation. Candace was working for a magazine at the time and Felicity was sitting at an outdoor cafe with Molly Quick and a few other friends. At first Candace did not recognize Felicity, who during that period had stopped frosting her hair. But Candace recognized the voice—"You know that shrill, whine. 'Candace,' she called out, as if nothing had ever been wrong. I tried to be cool and wave but I couldn't. She affected me, I don't know why. I knew I'd never cut free of her," Candace said.

The only time Candace heard of Felicity again was after the newspaper scandal. "I think that incident showed her that she would keep on acting in this self-destructive way. It was her whole way of life—the way she would drive, the bulimia, the drugs. She was very reckless. You knew this woman was either going to be an enormously successful big-time journalist or die."

After Felicity's suicide, Candace cried, too. "She was my nemesis but a part of me, too. We could all see parts of ourselves in her. She was everything the successful Radcliffe woman was, taken to the extreme. She was trying to be the best at so much. She had to be the prettiest girl and the best dressed, too. She had to be the smartest and the thinnest. She had to be an athlete. She was pulled in too many directions."

THE affair with Douglas cooled after a while. As much as Felicity loved analyzing Henry James, she did not feel temperamentally suited for the academic life. Both Candace and Douglas had "comped" for the *Crimson* and Felicity decided to give it a try. As soon as she saw the reaction her articles provoked, she realized her true calling.

Felicity learned fast. She worked all the time, bent on perfecting her skill. She wanted to know who the good journalists were so that she could study them. It was uncanny how quickly she absorbed various styles. She didn't just read the articles of famous writers, she inhaled them, adapting their style so that often it was hard to distinguish theirs from her own. She was serious about her work and therefore atypically humble. Journalists with half her skill would expound upon their work and Felicity would listen patiently. But she was discerning and quickly steered herself toward the people who could teach her the most. Those long hours of serious discussion at the *Crimson* formed the basis of her social life. She was happiest then, sitting up all night, drinking Tabs and arguing about the merits of this or that writer's work. She made her best friends then. You couldn't be Felicity's roommate and like her for very long, but you could be a fellow writer and develop a deep and abiding respect for her. Her otherwise erratic life snapped to military attention when organized around the constraints of her work. Felicity the professional was remarkably sane. Writing gave her a way of being sincere.

One of her favorite partners in these talkathons was Sean McNally, a cartoonist for a Boston paper who prowled about the *Crimson* at night. He was older than most of us, having put off his graduation (apparently indefinitely) and was something of a fixture around Harvard Square. He observed all of us coolly with his artist's eye, but his favorite subject was Felicity. His drawings of her were all oddly formal, lacking the humor his other pictures had. (Perhaps because she was so much a caricature of herself, Sean never made one of her.) Dozens of his sketches of Felicity hung in his studio, black and white and static and intense. And yet none of them looked like her. All her wildness was gone. Perhaps he caught a side of her the rest of us did not see. When he and his longtime girlfriend Brigid had a falling-out that year, he and Felicity became friends.

Their relationship, like most of Felicity's relationships with men, straddled a no-man's-land between friendship and love, with the matter of sex left vague and unresolved. One night they were talking in Sean's room. It was late. Felicity looked at her watch. "Jesus Christ. What am I doing here?" she shrieked. "God, Felicity," Sean said. "I'll walk you home." "She seemed put off," he said. "I couldn't figure out why. I walked her to Winthrop House. That's where she lived. And then I gave her a kiss goodnight. 'Well I've been waiting for that. What took you so long?' she said.

"We pushed it, but both being Catholics, you know, we didn't want it to work out. But she definitely wanted me for a strong friend. Her attitude, after that night, was, 'Well, I guess this means we're going together.' You thought of Felicity as being so sophisticated but she was so awkward sometimes."

They talked, mostly about journalism and about the writer John McPhee, whose book on the U.S. Open at Forest Hills, *Levels of the Game,* they admired. "We talked about how McPhee managed to get all those facts. You couldn't just watch a tennis match and write a book like that. You had to go back and study every point. Felicity was intrigued by that. She wouldn't play serious tennis with me but I did get her to play squash. She'd act real uninterested, you know, so cool, but she couldn't let me win. I said, 'Now Felicity, don't give me points.' 'I wouldn't do that,' she said, in that shrill voice of hers. At that last point, she'd lose herself and really go after it. She was great. Perfect. So matter of fact. God, I loved watching her. We'd be all sweaty and then go back to her room and talk about David Bowie or writing."

He would entertain her with stories about former *Crimson* writers who were now famous. She was hungry for names and details of other writers' lives. One of the writers Sean talked about was a former *Crimson* writer named John Bloom who had had a nervous breakdown the week he was staying with Sean. Felicity never revealed the details of her own breakdown to Sean—she hardly discussed it with anyone—but Sean's recounting of the incident provoked her to discuss the topic in general terms. "We talked about how serious it was being crazy. You forfeited your ability to deal with the real world. It was ugly, we said. It wasn't 'cool.' It was serious, like cancer."

They also talked about tennis, and why Felicity had quit. "She didn't like the ethos. People tried so hard to win that they turned into little monsters, she said, other players and her too. She also thought they were a pretty empty-headed group. She may have picked that up from her father. I think she sensed he had a certain disdain for the bubble-headed tennis player."

Sean was one of the few people who actually met Felicity's

parents. He saw them at graduation and said they were so happy to see Felicity graduate after all she had been through. "Her father was tall, handsome, cool, everything she said he was. And her mother, I really liked her, too. They weren't warm and huggy people, but obviously they were proud of her."

"Did she love them?" "Oh God, yes. She did her little rebellion numbers but she adored them. They were the most important thing. And it was also important that they be there and that they be together. That's what she wanted more than anything else."

At the end of that year, Sean's old girlfriend Brigid reappeared. "She got scared; I was spending too much time with Felicity." He and Felicity did not see as much of each other as before but remained friends; Sean may have been her closest. They wrote to each other and talked long-distance almost every month during the next few years, right up until the time of her death.

The best picture of Felicity isn't one of Sean's. It is a small color photograph, the kind you take with an Instamatic, of Felicity standing in front of a Rolls-Royce. The car just magically appeared in front of the *Crimson* one day. Dean Kalish, a *Crimson* editor, must have seen Felicity walking down the street and said, "Hey, let's get a picture of the Duck in front of that Rolls-Royce."

It was a perfect shot, vintage Felicity. Her skin is a deep brown, tanned and rich. Her eyes, wide and protrusive in their bony sockets. And her smile, half-serious, half-mocking. That's Felicity, slouching against a Rolls-Royce looking silly and cool.

"I get so mad at her," Sean said. "Sometimes, I'll be driving along and I'll think to myself, Goddamn it, Felicity. Why'd you have to do it? Now I can't call you. Why'd you let me down? How bad was it?"

THERE were odd little incidents concerning Felicity throughout her college career. The fall of her junior year, she had a roommate she couldn't abide, not because she resented the woman personally as much as she did not want anyone to be privy to her moods, which were predominantly unpleasant. Her response was to make life as miserable as she could for the woman. She would invite Sean to wander in at all hours of the night. The girl hated smoking so Felicity would smoke in bed. That winter Felicity's room caught on fire. The rumor was that Felicity, depressed, had fallen asleep with a cigarette in her mouth. No one knew whether it was deliberate, but the upshot in any case was that Felicity got her own room.

Senior year she had an affair with Eric Steiner, David's rival and an executive editor of the *Crimson.* Eric had broken up with his girlfriend in the fall. No one was in a mood to be serious that spring and gloomy April, with graduation looming ahead, tempted seniors to do crazy things. One night Felicity, Eric and Felicity's friend Jean Pingry, a strapping girl who later turned out to be gay, attended a party together at the *Advocate,* the literary magazine. Felicity started joking with Jean as to who should sleep with Eric first. Jean excluded herself but offered Felicity as prey. "Eric, ask Felicity first," she coaxed. Having instigated the affair, Felicity could hardly back out now. "Eric," she said later that night, "are we really going to fuck?"

Felicity adhered to her end of the bargain, and the dare led to a small and lovely affair. Felicity was candid with Eric, not because she attributed to him any great gifts of insight or tact. (If anything, Felicity was closer to Sean, John Swarthington and other men she knew. But two people could consider themselves close friends of hers and yet know about entirely different facets of her life.) She spoke to Eric about topics she normally did not discuss, revealing her more tender side. It may have been the strongest admission of need ever attributed to Felicity: Eric said she liked to be held.

"There were times when she could be exceedingly full of feeling. I loved her when she was that way. And other times she'd pull away, put on an act. She'd be talking and someone would start to listen and she would get all animated. I hated when she did that. 'Felicity, why do you do that?' I asked, but she didn't know. She wanted to be different and relished the idea of having a dramatic effect.

"When we broke up it was because of that: I felt she was too inconsiderate, too self-absorbed. It was my birthday. I tend to make a fuss about birthdays, you know. When my wife turned thirty-five last week—it had been a difficult year—I bought her all kinds of presents to cheer her up. I made her a giant scrapbook with photographs and memorabilia about her life. Felicity would never do anything like that. I was feeling especially low the spring of our senior year. I was getting ready to graduate and had no idea what I wanted to do. I dropped some hints about my birthday, which was in April, but Felicity ignored them. She wasn't at all into that. She was too self-involved."

They spoke occasionally over the years. Once, after they had graduated, they bumped into each other in Boston. "Eric, I'm so horny," Felicity crooned. Eric didn't take her seriously. "I knew it was all part of the act."

He did not hear of her again until her death. His reaction, like that of a lot of her former friends, was to ask, "Was there anything I could have done?" But it was at our Tenth Year Reunion that he was really struck by Felicity's suicide:

"Such a gyp, I thought. Here was someone who had so much raw talent, and actually not that much of it was raw. She was so curious. She had such an agile mind. She would talk to me for hours about things. When she was writing that piece about the girl who ran away and killed herself, she was so intent on getting inside that woman's head. She wanted to understand it from a cosmic point of view. And yet there were these weird wrinkles in her life. Felicity told me she hadn't had a period in over two years. The one time she had one was after the first time we made love.

"You know I do a lot of hiring in my job," he said. (Eric is a newspaper editor in California.) "I never hire people who are happy. They don't work out as well. I hire the unhappy people. They have this craving inside of them. It makes them better at what they do."

IN 1983, Molly Quick left her job as a reporter for the newspaper in Los Angeles where she and Felicity had met. Molly was going out with her editor but their relationship had a happier ending than Daisy's, at least from Molly's point of view; she moved to Seattle and her editor followed.

We sat in Molly's small apartment, a makeshift home until she and her lover could find a place to live. Molly was on and off the phone, talking to her friends.

"I don't know one woman my age who hasn't been through an odd, strange time in her romantic life," she said in an aside. But to the woman on the other end, she joked, "What's your problem? You've got the baby, the husband, the career and everybody loves you. What could possibly be wrong?"

MOLLY met Felicity in the spring of 1975. She had just started work at the newspaper. Felicity, who was then a summer intern, simply walked up to Molly and said, "Hi. I was you at the *Crimson.*" What she meant, she explained, was that Pat Sorrento, the typesetter at the *Crimson*, mistook them for each other, which was not hard to do. Both were tall reedy types and although not beautiful, were considered attractive by men. Molly slinked in and out of the *Crimson* in black turtleneck sweaters, leather jackets and tights.

Both she and Felicity were terrified that summer. Watergate had just reached its climax and every young journalist in America wanted a job like theirs. For Felicity, who was hardly twenty-three and had never had a regular job, and for Molly, not much older or more experienced, the pressure was fierce. "Felicity and I would hang out together. After work we would go to the press club, order drinks and talk about the 'cold fear.' " The "cold fear," Molly said, "was when you were scared of being successful but were even more afraid of the reverse. With me it was a game. I cultivated unhappiness. Felicity was more serious. It was part of her aesthetic. She saw the apocalypse as imminent all the time. My fears centered around work. Felicity was more scared of life than work."

Their friendship was intense, tinged with competition and love, a curious combination of life-and-death drama, envy and support (the person you hated was the one you would lay down your life for, too) that so many women at Radcliffe had. Felicity spoke in vaguely contemptuous terms about most women, but she was not contemptuous of Molly, perhaps her only real woman friend. She was as pretty as Felicity, and that established a certain parity between them. Molly was attractive to men and this used to drive Felicity mad. "She couldn't stand the way I flirted," Molly said. Felicity actually admitted to being envious of Molly, and in some warped way this cemented their bond. Felicity cared what Molly thought. Often after work, while Molly ate and Felicity watched—her taste was for expensive and small things, prosciutto and melon, artichokes in white wine, food that teased you but never filled you up—they would talk about writing, people, life and death. Both women were very taken with the drama of their lives, their desire to do well, and their fear and mutual desperation. At the end, it was Molly whom Felicity called. The operator at the newspaper took the message. It was on Molly's desk when she returned from the funeral.

It was frightening but romantic, too, to live on the edge the way Molly and Felicity did. Felicity spoke to Molly of her breakdown, not as a troublesome part of her past, which, in her gloomier moments, was how she might have viewed it, but as a battle scar.

"A badge of honor," Molly said. "We relished talking like that. It was like telling war stories." Molly believed she outgrew her romantic infatuation with fear. "Felicity might have, too. My feelings about Felicity are so mixed up with my own youth. She *was* me."

Very quickly Felicity became a major attraction in the newsroom, Molly said, and provoked a reaction not unlike the one she had aroused at the *Crimson.* "Everyone thought she was brilliant and was in awe of her writing." Felicity worked as a summer intern in the paper's revamped Living section, and at the end of the summer was offered a full-time job. At twenty-three, she was the youngest reporter on staff.

In many ways, the paper was a perfect showcase for Felicity. Watergate had elevated the status of journalism, giving the once shaggy profession an air of glamour and respectability. Felicity liked the ripple that now went through a room when she declared she was a reporter from a newspaper everyone had heard of. The "new journalism" was in vogue and reporters in her section were encouraged to try a more impressionistic style. No one suggested they distort or "embellish" the facts, but they were encouraged to try a more novelistic approach. Felicity, more a writer than a reporter anyway, adapted easily to the changing rules. Had she been forced to adhere to the more rigid constraints of daily journalism, she might not have remained a reporter for long.

At the same time, her editors tolerated her bravura, which they may even have encouraged. More confident now that she was a full-time member of the staff, she took risks that brought her notoriety if not acclaim (Felicity relished both but would settle for either). One of Felicity's assignments was to cover parties. It was an environment she claimed to detest and yet thrived in—showy, flirtatious, and at its core, hollow. It was inevitable that she would do her best writing in an atmosphere in which she felt so torn. She loved the false intimacy of a crowd, yet her reporter's pad gave her the license to stand back and judge. Her pieces fairly smoldered with disdain.

The most famous Felicity story concerned not an article she wrote but an indiscretion she committed at a White House party the newspaper had flown her to Washington to attend. It was an unwritten rule among the White House press corps that you did not ask political questions at certain social events. Felicity, who had not the least interest in politics, marched up to an official at one of these events, and in her shrill whiny voice asked what he thought of President Ford's pardon of Nixon. The White House press corps was banned from social functions for several weeks afterwards, but rather than detract from Felicity's stature as a reporter, the incident only added to it.

Her little adventures in private life, however, were much more serious and cost her friends. Her first summer at the paper, she roomed with Jane Beardsley, a classmate from Radcliffe and Pinegrove. Felicity, Jane and another roommate shared a house. Jane said the rooming situation worked out well at first because "we didn't have a stereo and we did have a maid." It deteriorated, however, when Felicity acquired a stereo, the maid was let go and Felicity's moods grew more erratic because of worsening problems at home.

Jane said she could tolerate Felicity at first. "She was good at getting people to help her. She made you feel good about doing it. She'd flatter you—'You're such a good editor,' she used to say." There were also instances in which Felicity was kind. Jane's father died that summer and Jane said Felicity was genuinely thoughtful. Her mother sent a basket of fruit and vegetables from her garden over to the Beardsley house.

In September, Felicity, Jane and two other women moved to a larger house. As Jane expected to be the first person back after the Labor Day weekend, the housemates gave her the one set of keys. When she pulled up to the house, she saw the windowpane in the door was broken. "Oh God, I thought to myself. Here the people have only been gone a week and already someone has broken into the house." She immediately called the police. At the same time, Felicity arrived, waving a bandaged hand in the air. "Look what I did," she said, laughing, and holding up her bloody wrist. "My God, what happened?" Jane asked. Apparently, Felicity had decided not to spend the weekend with friends and come back early. Not having the keys to the new house, she decided to break in. It was just like Felicity to do that, Jane said. But more distressing, according to Jane, was how she did it. "What possessed her to push her hand through the glass? Even the police suggested it might have been easier had she simply used a rock."

Felicity, of course, was without remorse. "She never even cleaned up, not the blood or the broken glass. And she never remembered to lock the door. 'Why bother?' she said. 'Obviously we know now that anyone can break in.' "

Felicity was insufferable. She played her David Bowie albums "full blast," Jane complained, which antagonized Jane, who was struggling through her first year of law school. Jane had terrible study habits anyway, but Felicity made the situation worse. Jane asked Felicity to keep her door closed when she played her stereo, which was usually at night, after a late round of drinks with Molly and her friends. Felicity usually came home stoned or a little drunk. "She never closed the door."

At times Felicity was simply crude. "She had absolutely no manners. The people who owned the house had lent us their china and woven placemats. Felicity broke dishes and used the placemats as handkerchiefs." And when she did break dishes, either inadvertently or in a fit, she didn't bother to clean them up. "She didn't clean up the broken ones and the ones she hadn't broken she left dirty in the sink." Everyone would have to tiptoe around the kitchen the next morning, to avoid the broken glass.

"She was constantly borrowing my clothing. (I'm four inches shorter than she is and yet she wore a smaller size, that's how thin she was.) I had this one black velvet blazer Felicity loved. She asked if she could borrow it. I said no. She'd borrow it anyway. She never took a bath. She said that like the French, she thought bathing was unhealthy. Instead she wore lots of perfume."

Yet Felicity was not without her vanities. Even in winter she would sunbathe on the roof to maintain her tan. At the same time, she displayed an appalling lack of pride. She still wore her scruffy, seductive uniform of torn blue jeans and a silk shirt. And because she was so thin, and almost flat-chested, she rarely wore a bra. "She used to leave her shirt open down to the navel. Once when we were in the supermarket, this man stared at her because her breasts were practically sticking out. Felicity didn't seem to care. She wasn't embarrassed at all. As soon as we got out of the supermarket, she looked at me and said, 'Doesn't the jerk know women have boobs?' "

At the same time her eating habits were getting more bizarre. Felicity never ate normally, but now "she would deprive herself of food for days at a time and then come home and devour an enormous meal. One night I watched as she devoured part of a whole roast beef, a frozen loaf of bread, a package of frozen vegetables, and a salad, which she ate out of an enormous serving bowl. Then she went and threw the whole thing up."

Her behavior deteriorated all that spring. She would come home from work, swallow a bunch of Quaaludes and smash dishes all over the place. "She'd get drunk and then go out and get in her car."

At the end of the year, her housemates made an appointment to meet a maid at the house and clean it for the owners, who were expected back in June. Everyone showed up but Felicity. At the same time, Jane was studying for final exams. The day before her last exam, she asked Felicity not to play her stereo just that one night. Felicity played the music full blast. "Usually she was just thoughtless. That night she was malicious. I felt sorry for her because I knew she was having problems but I was mad, too. I always thought if you observed people long enough, you could eventually understand them. I never figured out Felicity. She was too smart. She had too many rationalizations for everything."

She ran around with several men, although her taste was growing more disjunctive and extreme. On the one hand, she would spend time with writers and editors with whom she could discuss her work. But these were not the men she had affairs with. Those were a more particular breed—beautiful but empty. Felicity dated one man who was so good-looking that when they walked down the street, it was he who evoked the catcalls.

Her moods did not appear to affect her work until that summer. In July, Frank Green, a features editor at the paper, was put in charge of a new spruced-up section called "Fitness Plus." The intention of the editors was to attract more serious writers to cover leisure and health. One of the first people courted was Felicity. She was asked to write a piece about the city's singles scene as it played itself out around the tennis courts of some of the area's more swinging apartment complexes. One reporter was dispatched to write about, in the words of the paper's headline, "those who rally," and Felicity was assigned to write about "those who score."

What happened after that was vague and confusing, partly because Felicity did not talk about it much and partly because the paper felt remorseful about its own uncertain hand in the event. Molly, who was working in the newsroom at the time, remembers certain circumstances of the case:

Felicity wrote her story, and as usual, her editors were pleased. A few days after the article appeared, Molly received a call from Jim Henderson, Felicity's editor in Living. "Molly," he told her, "please be around for Felicity this evening. She's really upset. She's going to need you to stick by her." A few hours later, Felicity called. "What happened?" Molly asked. Felicity said she did not know except that someone had written letters to the editor alleging that whole lines of dialogue in Felicity's story were lifted straight out of E. M. Forster. "Two English teachers wrote in and demanded her head on a platter, which the paper gave them. I think the publisher later regretted it," Molly commented.

It was a piece that would obviously be identified as Felicity's, even without her byline. It seethed with sexuality and innuendo, and yet at its core it was about loneliness and despair. Anyone familiar with her writing could hear her voice in it. And then, for no reason at all, in the middle of a perfectly fine piece, appear bits of borrowed dialogue. The inarticulate mutterings of a hairdresser, an airline secretary, an airline pilot, are peppered with the Forster quotes. What was most disturbing, however, was that the additions, far from enhancing the piece, detracted from it, interrupting its flow and calling attention to themselves, almost as if Felicity had planned it that way.

Her friends had various theories. Jane Beardsley said it was plagiarism, pure and simple. "Felicity always made up quotes. She used to cover parties that started at seven-thirty and make an eight o'clock deadline. There was no way she could have done that. She had to have made up the whole thing."

"I couldn't believe she was so bad or so stupid as to plagiarize something," said Candace Shine. "Maybe she didn't realize she was doing it. It may have been some form of psychosis. Her mind would identify with whatever attracted it. I doubt if she could even tell the difference between her words and Forster's."

Sean said that whatever she read "stuck hard. She was an imitative stylist." In college, he said, she was working on her own voice, but like any writer, concentrated intensely on the prose style of other writers. "I could see their presence strongly in the pieces she wrote. She was attempting to absorb their style and turn it into her own. When she was reading another writer, she was in the grip of that voice."

"She had a memory for language. She had an ear for it. She could mimic almost any writer's voice," Eric Steiner said. "And Felicity had a desire to enhance reality, to enrich it. This was the part of her that liked to dramatize events."

Jane added, "There were often times when I don't think Felicity could honestly distinguish what was real from what was in her mind."

"She was such a damn good writer," Molly said. "There was no reason for her to do that. It was inconceivable that it was deliberate. She was in such an emotional cauldron at the time she could've done anything."

Sean said Felicity was depressed and in her highly emotional state may have interpolated the quotes with any number of motives in mind. It had been a difficult year. That winter she had been out in a car with a writer from the paper when he was summoned to cover a plane crash nearby. When they arrived at the airport, they were witness to a gruesome scene. Bits of blazing fuselage littered the runaway and charred limbs and other parts of bodies hung from trees. Felicity complained for weeks afterwards that she could not sleep. She talked about a friend of hers who had been killed in a mountain climbing fall earlier that year. Sean said all of these events affected her, but none so much as the instability and loneliness of her own life. It was this, according to Sean, that caused her to act like such a madwoman the previous year. Felicity adored her father, who was working in Paris, where he might have to remain. She was distraught at the thought that the family might not be together and the news evoked a kind of backlash in her. She no longer wanted to hear about transient people's lives. Divorce, the singles scene—all of it disgusted her. It was at about this time that the paper approached her to write the tennis club piece. Sean said Felicity bristled at the idea. "She said the idea sickened her. She did not want to write about swinging singles at a time when her own life was in disarray."

According to Sean, Felicity made her reluctance known at the newspaper, but her editors prevailed upon her. "They said, 'You've got to. Be a professional. Don't be so soft,' " Sean said. There was also some discussion about how she would present herself at the complex. The newspaper did not want her to reveal her identity as a reporter. Felicity wondered how she would be able to take notes. An editor suggested she duck into the bathroom and write on pieces of toilet paper every time she had to jot down some quotes. "No one at the paper told her to lie and say she wasn't a reporter," Sean said. "But then she was told not to volunteer that information either. Felicity said she couldn't do that. They encouraged her to try."

The weekend before she wrote the piece, she flew back to Cleveland. According to Sean, "She was just too overcome by everything going on. Sure she was flamboyant, but the core of her was a little girl who only wanted stability in her life." She spent most of the weekend in her room, where she sat up all night reading E. M. Forster and Virginia Woolf. Molly said she read "until she couldn't think straight." When she came back, she wrote the tennis club piece.

She was fired a day after the two English teachers called to complain. Perhaps "fired" is too strong a word. The editors, many of whom cared about Felicity and considered her a friend, were troubled. Her crime seemed so pointless. They were reluctant to let so much talent go to waste but were also baffled by what seemed like such a self-destructive act. Yet the subtleties of Felicity's mental state were irrelevant from the newspaper's point of view, and perhaps even from an ethical one. Plagiarism was a serious charge. After much deliberation, the editor of the newspaper asked Felicity to leave. The editors were as helpful as they could be. They assured Felicity that they would help her find another job and even suggested that it would be possible for her to return to the paper some day. But her departure remained unnerving, because it was really Felicity who had forced their hand.

Just a month before the incident, the paper had come out with a handbook on style in which Felicity's work was singled out for praise. She was held up as an example of what a successful writer ought to be. "She was on top of the world, then," Molly Quick said. "It was great. The handbook talked about this young reporter and how well she wrote."

But in a way perhaps Felicity was relieved to go. Too many pressures were bearing down upon her. Her success made it harder to leave and yet the pressure to maintain it was unbearable. But you could not imagine Felicity standing up and calling, "Time out." Her method of change was more jagged: she didn't quit, she broke down. Perhaps it was the only way she knew of taking herself out of the race.

She returned to Boston then. In some sense it had become home. The surroundings were familiar, and Felicity had friends in town, one of whom persuaded her to join the staff of his news weekly. "I encouraged her to come," John Swarthington said. "I knew it was important for Felicity to work with people with whom she had a deep bond, people she could trust. Felicity could throw herself into things with great intensity, and I felt it was important for her to be working for people who could tell her, 'Okay, Felicity. Knock it off for a while. Go home and get some rest.' "

It was Felicity's great fortune to have a friend like John, who had been an editor on the *Crimson* at the time we were there. He considered himself a friend but not as close a friend as he became in the next six months. He rescued her from what otherwise would have been a difficult position. If Felicity wanted to work again, she would have to explain the circumstances under which she left her previous job. That prospect could not have been too appealing, yet it was essential that Felicity get right back to work. John made it easy for her by introducing her to his editor, who was also his mentor and friend. When the editor, Louis Rayburn, interviewed her for the job, he said, "You've got to tell me the circumstances so that I know and I can answer any questions I may get." And Felicity did. He was probably the only person to whom she gave a complete accounting of why she left. Rayburn was satisfied with her explanation and hired her.

I saw her, too, that summer. It was in a restaurant in Harvard Square, Iruña, an odd little Spanish place tucked out of the way in an alley off Boylston Street. The food was simple but expensive. Felicity announced she was "famished" and then proceeded to pick at her dinner of hearts of palm and wine. It must have been awkward for Felicity. She assumed I knew she had been fired, which I did not. I thought she had left because she did not like the atmosphere. I remember how critical she was of the newspaper and what she called its sensationalist approach. "They're so superficial," she said in that howling whine. "All they care about is style. God, I can't stand it." She leveled the same criticisms against the country clubs of Shaker Heights. I thought it was admirable that she was moving away from that.

I wanted to talk frankly to her. I had just left my second newspaper job and and I, too, was feeling worried and confused. But I still did not feel comfortable talking personally with Felicity. Ever since I had broached the subject of our mutual eating disorder that night at the *Crimson,* and she had looked at me, admitting with her broad grin and expression of shock that she was about to lie, I had felt that honest conversation with Felicity was impossible. So she railed on about how she hated her old paper and I muttered something about how interesting it was to work down South. I left the dinner feeling confused and bored. I assumed she must have felt the same way. I never saw her again, though I always hoped to.

John Swarthington cared for Felicity in a way that brought out her best side, which not everyone saw. Felicity often spent the evening with him and his wife, Linda, a writer whom Felicity admired. As her editor at the weekly, John was privileged to know Felicity's more stable side. "She was very genuine with me. I knew she looked forward to working and was hoping to find the kind of work that she could do and that could help stabilize the rest of her life. I think she saw me as someone who could help her and therefore was more considerate with me than she might have been with other people."

Felicity seemed to take a grip on her life during that interlude in Boston. Some people even said she was happy there. "Every day she'd bring her lunch to work"—John laughed—"lettuce or cottage cheese," and then be out all day on the road with her sources. She worked hard but was not under as much pressure as she had been. The weekly was a much more informal place, somewhat like the *Crimson.* Deadlines were looser, and she was working with people who understood and appreciated her, John said. "Rayburn and I didn't care how she dressed or what time she came in. Her outrageous comments didn't upset us or provoke us." She was able to discuss her work seriously and frankly with John, and was not difficult to work with. "Felicity had reasons for everything she did, so naturally there was a certain amount of debate. But if I was able to convince her about something, she would change it without any problem. She was responsive and responsible as a journalist," John added. "She wasn't imperious with me."

She was productive during those months. She wrote as well as she ever had, on subjects that were not her usual fare: a congressman from Massachusetts, an anchorwoman on the television news, a pitcher from South Boston. I saved the piece about the pitcher. It was not about baseball so much as about winning and losing. As always when I read Felicity's pieces, I was in awe of her talent. Did the piece have the same impact on everyone who read it? I think it must have. Years after Felicity's suicide, I came across a piece about a pitcher in a national magazine. The byline was "Molly Quick." What else would have provoked Molly, who cared nothing about sports, to write about pitching except that Felicity had?

Felicity steered clear of her former subjects, singles bars, parties, sex. Instead she wrote about issues from which she was more detached, and the fresh perspective strengthened her prose. She concentrated on reporting as well. As penitence? Perhaps. She never admitted to anyone how much she was troubled by the plagiarism charge, but it was apparent now from her new approach. To say that Felicity never cared about "the facts" would be as wrong as to say that she never changed them. She had spoken of a larger truth, the truth a novelist conveys when he makes up the facts, which was not quite the same as a journalist's "truth." Now she concentrated more on the journalist's truth —quotes, dates, facts, exact details. She called back sources dozens of times and corroborated everything. Her new attitude proved that she, too, had the capacity to change. Who knows in what other ways she might have changed?

Yet she was by no means "reformed." Her social life was still erratic and she was so thin it was hard to imagine her having any kind of normal sex life. Her best relationships were still largely with male friends. She kept in touch with Sean, whom she spoke to almost daily. He said she was seeing a psychiatrist and that she continued to receive troubled bulletins from home. But she had her work and that steadied her. Other women made work the focal point of all their neuroses. They got nervous about it, procrastinated and shied away from doing the thing they loved best. Felicity had doubts about her ability but did not let them paralyze her. "I think what was true of Felicity was true of many fine writers. Deep, deep down, she knew she had talent, she knew she was good. But she set very high standards for herself and tortured herself in trying to meet those standards."

She continued to prosper under a regimen of work and a steady routine until the structure that brought her stability collapsed. The publishers decided to produce a more "slick" product and Rayburn was fired. In a show of loyalty for his friend, John resigned. Felicity was not a member of management and so technically her job was secure, but it made no sense for her to stay.

The new editors were less concerned about any individual writer and her talent, and without John and Rayburn, the mainstay of her emotional support was gone. Felicity remained on staff another few months and then decided to leave. In April she told John she wanted to go home.

"For Felicity to go back to her parents' house was the worst thing she could possibly have done," Candace Shine said. "When I heard Felicity was living at home, I knew that something was wrong." Yet she had no choice. She had no source of income and her funds were running low. And Felicity was frugal. As eccentric as she was, when it came to money, "she had the mentality of a banker," according to one of her friends. She could have looked for another newspaper job, but the fear of having to explain the incident at her previous job may have deterred her. And she had worked for two publications in two years and may have felt she needed to rest.

"I think she had been through a lot in a short time," John said. "She spoke wistfully of staying in her own room, walking to the library and taking out good books." He did not feel there was any special cause for worry.

"You didn't have to know Felicity too well to know that there was a lot that was crazy that was going on there and yet I never would have predicted her suicide," John added. "I thought she was really doing well. I felt that if she could somehow continue with her work, that would be a source of strength that she could then use to stabilize the rest of her life.

"I guess I was one of the few people who did not think Felicity was basically crazy. People would look at her and think, How could this woman hold down a job? But she was perfectly respectable, enough so that you could take her home to meet your parents. In fact, I did, and it was perfectly easy for me to introduce her to my mother and father as my buddy.

"She was very genuine with me. The proof of how sincere she could be was that she did turn a number of people into devoted friends. I'm feeling it now. I just was always rooting for Felicity. Deep down I had a lot of sympathy for her. I wanted her to be happy."

THE letters people received bearing the postmark Shaker Heights in the spring sounded hopeful. "She said she wanted to settle down and relax. She had been running constantly since high school, to Radcliffe and then from Radcliffe to her first newspaper job. She said she wanted to take time to size things up," John Swarthington said. But at home the situation was rapidly deteriorating. Her father was in Paris, where it looked as if he might have to remain. And the behavior of her brother and sister depressed her. Abigail had taken a serious fall off a horse and the next month insisted on going out riding again. And her brother George, she complained, was acting listless. She was the responsible oldest child and it bothered her to see all the people she loved around her unhappy.

She waited a period of months and then began looking for jobs. She knew how important it was for her to be back at work. She wrote to a group of ex-*Crimson* editors who had started their own weekly in Vermont, but their initial response was that they were "overstaffed." A year before, any writer on the *Crimson* would have been delighted to have Felicity join his staff. Now one of the editors at the paper complained that her writing was "too sophisticated" for their readers. Felicity sensed the coolness of the reply and did not try to get them to change their minds.

She eventually took a job with a newspaper near home. It was not of the caliber of the other places where she'd worked, but she was not in a position to be choosy. She was glad to be back at work, she told Sean. She worried about her stories as she had always done, which Sean took as a healthy sign. She discussed with him her concern about a story she had written and wondered whether she had not been too hard on the piece's subject, a "tennis mother" she had portrayed in an unflattering light. "She was worried that the mother would come across looking very stupid," Sean said. " 'Should I have done it?' she asked. 'Gosh, yes, Felicity,' I told her. 'It's good. It'll benefit other people.' She worried that she was a 'bad person' for exposing the woman, but I told her I didn't think she was. 'The fact that you're discussing it with me shows you have a conscience,' I told her," Sean said.

She talked with Molly about the anguish of writing and "the joy of writing a perfect sentence," Molly said. And then, too, there were their nightly outpourings concerning the "cold fear." During these phone calls Felicity sat in her room, usually with her glass of Kahlua and cream. Occasionally she spoke about her family but not in a way that alarmed Molly. "She'd say, 'I'm miserable,' and I'd say, 'Me too.' She'd say, 'My father's terrible.' And I'd say, 'Mine too.' "

But Molly was worried that she spent too much time at home. " 'Get the hell out of that house,' I'd tell her. 'You need to be away from home.' " But it did not seem to make an impact on her. She spent most of her time either working or at home. Occasionally, she accepted a casual date.

So a Felicity who emitted no outward signs that anything was wrong, any more wrong than usual, got into her Pinto one Friday and drove the three hundred miles to her parents' summer house in western New York. It was Thanksgiving weekend. Her father had just returned from abroad. Earlier in the day she had telephoned Molly at the newspaper. It was "urgent" she told the operator who took the call. She had canceled a date she was supposed to have that night.

A reporter in Cleveland who had recently written a story about suicide said that earlier in the month Felicity approached her and casually inquired about the least painful method of committing suicide. The reporter advised hooking up a hose in a car and leaving the engine running, which, according to the sheriff's office in Chautauqua County, is what Felicity did.

. . .

"THAT she died where she did says a lot," Molly said. "She had retreated. She was trying to find something that wasn't there. First in Boston, where we had been at school, and then in Cleveland.

"Damn it, Felicity, if only you'd have hung on. It got better, so much better," Molly said.

Our Fifth Year Reunion book was dedicated to Felicity and two other members of the Class of '74 who took their lives.

CHAPTER 10

Fran

Misery is no guarantee of happiness.
—ELLIS RATNER, vice-president,
Mercer Group, Ltd.

It was August when I received the notice about our Tenth Reunion. I was living with my boyfriend Philip at the time and contemplating marriage if only to be able to check off one "yes" box on the alumni questionnaire. No, I was not married; no, I had no advanced degrees. No, my Radcliffe education had not helped me in later life. I remembered what a classmate of mine had written for the Fifth Year Reunion book, which basically boiled down to: I hated the place. I have no interest in going back. And leave me alone.

I felt the same way, though I could hardly blame Radcliffe. I was sixteen when I left home with a trunkload of clothes from Saks and Bergdorf's and disastrous misconceptions about myself and the world (799 on your SAT scores meant you were smart; 798 meant you were less smart). Radcliffe was only one stage in rooting them out, but it was the first and therefore the most painful. When I was fifteen and a junior in high school, I told God that I would gladly be miserable for the next ten years if only he would let me get into Radcliffe. He kept his end of the bargain and I kept mine.

My mother was a housewife and so efficient that my father, repeating a joke that was already stale when he heard it from Alan King, said that when he got up to go to the bathroom at night, he came back to find the bed already made. She used to pack a whole week of school lunches on Sunday night so that by Friday, my two brothers and I faced cream cheese and jelly sandwiches on purple bread. IBM might have been better off with my mother at the helm, but we would have missed her. My mother told my brothers and me stories about the Greek myths, she washed and brushed our hair at night. She taught us a book was our best friend and tirelessly reviewed our multiplication tables with us, not because she wanted us to do well in school but more because she did not wish us to suffer the pain of being unprepared. I went through life preparing for disasters that never came.

When I was ten and in seventh grade, she heard Mary Bunting, a pioneer feminist and the president of Radcliffe College in the early sixties, declare that any woman with a college education who was not working outside the home ought to be ashamed of herself. "The nerve," my mother hollered back at the radio. "I'm only a housewife and I feel perfectly fulfilled." This was not a defensive reaction but the truth. My mother led a charmed life. She loved my father, my father loved her, and although she never made it to the suburbs of Long Island like most of her friends, she was just as content to re-create Great Neck on East Twenty-sixth Street in Brooklyn. She hired a decorator to do The First Family of Flatbush's house in French Provincial. I came back from camp one summer to find the place filled with plastic ferns and candelabras with simulated dripping wax. We could not afford real antiques so she and her decorator bought fake ones, an oak table with holes put in it to make it look old. "For this you pay good money?" my immigrant grandmother asked. She called her daughters-in-law the three *s*'s: the shiksa (my Uncle Harry's wife), the shlumpf (my Uncle Shelly's wife) and the squanderer (my mother, who felt she got off easy compared to the other two).

But while my mother enjoyed her daily activities (cooking, shopping and reading *The New York Times,* which she did so diligently that if we went on vacation she made herself go back over the issues she had missed), the women she admired were those with a more pronounced artistic or intellectual side, even if it didn't express itself in a career. Ruth, my friend Miranda's mother, was one. ("I'm just a housewife. But Ruth has a Ph.D.") So the message she gave me was mixed: "Grow up and do what I did" and "Grow up and do something more."

When she was thirty-five my mother joined Weight Watchers. All our lives changed after that. The Pepperidge Farm cookies were exiled to a cabinet no one could reach; starch was served so infrequently that my younger brother once asked my mother the name of "those round things wrapped in foil we used to eat." ("Oh my God. The poor boy has forgotten what a baked potato is!") But my mother was serious about her mission. As a child, she never had a very good image of herself ("I was a big nothing, a zero") and in losing weight, shed the last vestige of girlhood unhappiness. My mother is probably the only nonrecidivist Weight Watcher in America. She still returns for her weigh-ins every month. She used to joke: "There's justice in the world. I was a fat dumpy girl and I've been blessed with a thin daughter." Needless to say when adolescence hit, I, too, began to focus on my weight.

Up until my sophomore year in high school, I considered myself a lucky girl. My mother loved all of us equally but as her only daughter, perhaps she loved me in a different way. She bought her own clothes at Loehmann's or other discount stores, but I was given carte blanche in Bergdorf's and Saks and must have impressed more than a few saleswomen with my snotty ways. Sometimes I think I spent half my youth in these stores. The other half I spent in B. Altman's Charleston Gardens, the cafeteria designed to look like a Southern plantation because even better than shopping I liked having lunch. It was partly the food. My mother had bred into me her lust for eating and we were especially fond of what my older brother called "ladies-for-ladies" food, chicken salad sandwiches with the crusts cut off, cakes and cookies arranged daintily on the plate. (What all this food had in common was that it was sticky, trivial, insubstantial and sweet as opposed to roast beef, my older brother's favorite, or even cold cereal, which my father resorted to once my mother stopped cooking fattening meals for anyone.) But it was also the company. At age thirteen I was my mother's confidante. Over date-nut sandwiches and banana cream pie (in her pre–Weight Watchers days), she would captivate me with stories about her childhood (unhappy), her father (she adored him, although he preferred his only son) and her unexpressed desires. It was a world my brothers knew nothing about. In later years, when we compared notes about our mother, they would look at me as if I were describing an absolute stranger.

In high school, everything changed. My older brother had gone to Harvard the previous year with such fanfare that I decided perhaps I ought to do the same. My decision came in spite of my mother's protestations ("You're a girl. It's not so important where you go to school. I went to Brooklyn College and was perfectly happy"). At the same time, I decided I was too fat (I was too thin) and that I ought to take off a few pounds. "Who do you want to be," my Grandma Minnie asked, "Tviggy?"

Somewhere in the midst of all this craziness, I stumbled across the Radcliffe Girl. She was pale and had long brown hair, neat but very plain. She was walking up the steps of Widener Library and carrying a green book bag over her shoulder. She appeared to me, magnificently, on a catalogue mailed by the college to my older brother, who was sending home exuberant bulletins from school. This was what I had been groping toward. Out went the Villager skirts and sweaters from Saks. In came the dark skirts and turtlenecks and Fred Braun shoes. (He was a shoemaker in Greenwich Village discovered by the black girls in my high school.) I strove for an ascetic-hippie look, black skirts, black tights, preferably with holes. My mother was beside herself. The beautiful frilly pink room she and her decorator had gone to great lengths to create was now a black and white morgue. Her happy well-dressed daughter was growing thin and pale. In addition to dying of malnutrition, my goals were to be a genius at stoichiometry and of course, first and foremost, to get into Radcliffe.

That I had an unhealthy obsession with weight and food could easily be traced to my Trident-gum-chewing mother, but my obsession with grades had a more general root. The emphasis on achievement was strong in my neighborhood. Few of my friends' parents had college degrees and even fewer had professional jobs. But prosperity made it possible for them to give their children what they were denied, and the race was on. The biggest status symbol in our neighborhood was not the kind of car you drove but the college stickers on the rear windshield. (My mother steered that Oldsmobile with its Harvard sticker through Brooklyn like a parade float.)

Nowhere was the mania for getting into Ivy League schools better illustrated than in the offices of Sidney Parker, Ed.D. Mr. Parker was a former schoolteacher who specialized in coaching students for the SAT's. Parents who could barely afford the steep fees Mr. Parker imposed trudged the narrow flight of stairs to his office and asked him to boost their children's scores. To people in our neighborhood, the scholastic aptitude tests were the great equalizer, the democratic escalator that one rode to improve one's social class. (Mr. Parker's modest enterprise eventually turned into no less of a money-maker than Jean Nidetch's Weight Watchers. Like Young Luther, my mother had lived to see her private psychodrama played out in society.)

Few people were immune to the SAT hysteria, including me. Months before the start of my junior year, I began enlisting my mother in a marathon studyfest that was to consume most of the next two years. When I was in eighth grade, a question on the math section of the Iowa tests threw me into such a panic that I had to wait out the rest of the test by an open window in the girls' bathroom. I received a fortieth percentile on the math test, a stigma I felt I would never live down. On the next test, I assiduously filled in the tiny boxes on the grid but at question number 96 discovered that I was on answer number 97. I erased so furiously that I tore the page, and finally gave up. In order to avoid a similar catastrophe on the PSAT's, I studied in advance. "Contumacious," my mother, whom I had enlisted in my cause, would read off one of my lists. "Factious, insurgent, mutinous, rebellious, froward." Or, "laconic is to terse as dastardly is to ——" During those days I walked around with a list of vocabulary words imprinted on my brain (piebald, motley, variegated, pied, particolored . . .). I knew thirty-seven synonyms for the word "varied."

My labors were not in vain. I received the highest PSAT scores in my high school, but was so worried they would drop that I enrolled in Mr. Parker's course. Through no fault of Mr. Parker, my grades went down until through massive amounts of prayer and elaborate rituals (I had to touch certain lampposts a certain number of times) I managed to boost them again. But I couldn't win. I felt my high scores were a result of my studying, my low scores a result of my fear and my true scores, whatever they might be, not good enough. Although my older brother had done little more than run the mimeograph machine, in golden memory he became Mr. Parker's star pupil. "Four eight hundreds and one seven hundred and sixty-five!" Mr. Parker would sigh. I viewed these tests not only as a measure of intelligence but of one's moral position in the universe. Eight hundred meant you were perfect. Seven-hundred and fifty-three meant you were contumacious, opprobrious, heinous, contemptible, which is not to say contemporary or contemptuous. . . .

I thought I would think better of myself for having gotten into Radcliffe, but the irony, and it was lost upon me at the time, was that the day I received my admissions notices in the mail was the beginning of the worst period of my life. My grandfather (who had gotten his education attending free lectures at Cooper Union after work) told me he felt much more joy the day I got into Radcliffe than when my older brother had got into Harvard. "You seemed to want it so much." But I felt like a fraud at graduation, a little angel in a white linen frock floating across the stage to receive her diploma.

Meanwhile, I started to diet with a vengeance. The goal that had preoccupied me for the better part of two years had been accomplished and in its absence I began focusing on my weight. The needle on the scale hit one hundred, then ninety-nine. "Abe, do something. Make her stop," my mother shouted. But there was nothing anyone could do. I developed the habit of starving all week and bingeing on the weekends. Fantasies about sex were replaced with fantasies about food. Chemically my body was accustomed to long periods of starvation, punctuated by periodic "kicks" of sugar and caffeine. Even if I had wanted to, I don't believe I could have eaten normally again. I ate one doughnut a day. I stopped getting my period. My hair fell out. No one in my family had ever seen a psychiatrist, so it did not occur to my parents to send me to one. Besides, I was their happy healthy daughter. It took a long time for any of us realize this wasn't the case.

Leaving home often precipitates anorexia, which psychiatrists say is an expression of anger, immaturity, anxiety and fear. But enough women in my generation had eating disorders to suggest a more sociological cause. We grew up at a time when it meant one thing to be a woman and went to college when it meant quite something else. Anorexia is often spoken of as an expression of gender confusion: You starve yourself to such a weight that you "lose" your breasts and begin to look like a man. Just before I left, my mother, my grandmother and a cousin went to buy me a winter coat as part of my college trousseau. When she saw the price of the coat, my cousin asked how my mother could spend so much. "Don't worry," my mother said. "She'll be wheeling baby carriages in that coat." But even then I knew the life she envisioned for me was not the one I would lead.

The summer before I left for Radcliffe, I worked as a secretary to Mr. Parker and served as an advertisement for his course. "And where are you going to college?" he would ask in a roomful of parents. "Radcliffe," I would answer. "And her brother goes to Harvard!" (By now my mother had both a Harvard and Radcliffe sticker on the car.) I was miserable in that office. I worked with two overweight secretaries who were always ordering up Chinese food and turning the air conditioner on high, while I was starving and my fingers were turning blue. "If you'd eat you wouldn't be so cold," Sylvia, the larger one, said. Her daughter had fallen in love with my older brother while he tutored her for her SAT's, but since the love was unrequited (secretary is to office assistant as jilted daughter is to ——) she took out her vengeance on me. But I could not eat except for the one elaborate treat I'd give myself precisely at noon, when I'd run down to the bakery and with all the fanfare of preparing for an elaborate feast, select the one magnificent pastry that was to last me the rest of the day. And if the kindly woman behind the counter accidentally picked the wrong one, I'd scream. She was tampering not only with my sucrose supply but my entertainment and social life. I cared about nothing now but my food.

At the end of that summer, I was so thin that it was no longer possible for me to wear a girl's size three or four. My mother was alarmed, but she hoped that whatever problems I had would disappear at Radcliffe.

So I arrived at Radcliffe pretty much a basket case. Whatever problems I had managed to suppress at home blossomed in the insalubrious environment at Harvard. One nervous person is a problem; five thousand are a nuthouse. If you were sane to begin with it was not likely to last, but if you were sane it wasn't likely that you'd be at Radcliffe. I was at Radcliffe.

I was sixteen and emotionally immature when I arrived at Radcliffe, but it was a difficult time to be at school. So much was changing. Some people thrived in that anarchistic atmosphere but I did not. I remember coming home to Brooklyn the week after I had slept with Marshall. "Tell the gynecologist that you're a virgin so he doesn't hurt you," my mother said. Out of a combination of malice and the pure pleasure I took in shocking her, I told her I wasn't. She was so upset that she sent my father downstairs to talk to me. My father, whose attitude toward sex was more casual, had trouble feigning distress. (He looked more like he wanted to hand me a cigar.) His only question, and it made me feel worse, was, "Did you at least care for the man?" It was one thing to break rules if you believed in what you were doing. But like Eleanor, I often had the sense in those years that I did not know what I was doing and was being pushed.

It was during this period that I made my conversion from dutiful daughter to family black sheep. First, I stopped caring about my work. Then I stopped caring about my weight. The world was falling apart and I no longer entertained the hope that a needle on a scale or a number on a report card could fix it. Only now I couldn't eat like a normal human being even if I wanted to. Who knows what kind of hormonal development I had screwed up with my crazy dieting in high school but by now it was a way of life. I binged when I was happy. I binged when I was sad. I never ate for fear of gaining weight but once I put that first tantalizing morsel in my mouth (and at Harvard, the food was so bad you had to be crazy to extract pleasure from it), I was off and running to procure the rest of my fix, usually from Cahaly's, the small grocery near our dorm that could be relied upon for condoms, No-Doz, Coke and Häagen-Dazs. A binge could strike at any time. Often I came into breakfast sick from having consumed a pint of Häagen-Dazs. I did not throw up, which is what other women did, but starved even more strenuously the next week so that I became even more incapable of forestalling a binge. Which was why the psychologists I saw, Franklin, and eventually Johanna, were unable to help. They assumed the problem was purely emotional. "Stop eating and you'll figure out what is wrong," they said, but I was as incapable of stopping as I was of telling my heart not to beat. I bought so much junk food that my checks began to bounce.

But I knew there were others like me. Even as a freshman it was clear to me that college women were obsessed by food. Nothing could reduce a table of otherwise intelligent women to a bunch of nattering lunatics so much as the mere mention of the words "diet" and "weight." By sophomore or junior year, the media were starting to give some coverage, though not much, to "the Starving Disease." And by the time I saw Felicity Barrett running through the dark, gobbling down a bag of M&M's, I recognized in her my own drug-frenzied state. My mother, who never knew how I was going to look when I stepped off the Eastern shuttle when I came home from school, realized that I had a problem. She thought it was my weight. My therapist thought it was my mother. And I naturally thought it was my therapist. After years of searching for answers, I'm not sure that understanding would have helped.

IN the meantime, I continued to rebel in more conventional ways. The summer after I returned from Winston-Salem, my older brother, catching me smoking in our basement, said, "I guess I always knew you'd be the one in our family to smoke." In not being happy, I was violating the family code. My older brother in particular saw himself as the embodiment of the American dream: from Flatbush to Harvard. The system worked because he did. Only I didn't. During the next four years I tried to figure out why and convince my family that they were to blame. Usually, the chief culprits were my mother or my older brother, depending on which therapist I saw. My father and little brother were usually exempt from blame, but we could conjure up evil things to say about them, too. "Didn't you resent that your father was never around?" (The sad thing was that when I told this to my father, he wondered if perhaps I was right and worried about this for the next ten years.) But these sessions never helped. I was an angry person; I did not need anyone telling me to be more angry. I was a negative person; I did not need anyone showing me more reasons why I ought to be upset. But I was also desperate to revert to the happy little girl I thought I had been and staged a violent battle against anyone (including Dr. Paige) who said it wasn't so.

For four years I continued to careen through Harvard and yet, through it all, I managed to look and act reasonably sane. ("You were this tough wily New Yorker who knew her way around"—Paige's observation.) It is important for me to make this distinction because part of my problem was that I rarely acted or looked as crazy as I felt: I managed to receive good grades, write for the *Crimson* and have a reasonable relationship with David (and for the part of it that wasn't so reasonable, I was not entirely to blame). I cannot say I benefited academically; the last serious textbook learning I had done was during my senior year at James Madison High School. But I did manage to get things—awards, jobs, placement in seminars on subjects in which I had no interest (most memorably, an entire fall semester devoted to "the camel"). I applied for the sheer pleasure of "getting in"; being in was never as interesting. Freshman year, to the astonishment of my classmates, I was admitted to all four freshman seminars to which I applied. I had told each professor his was the seminar I was most eager to take. Unfortunately, two of them were married to each other and compared notes. Fortunately, they were getting divorced and competed over everything, including me. I managed during my undergraduate studies to pick up a few new names:

Marx, Freud and Weber. I was especially fond of the last, whose *Gemeinschaft* and *Geselleschaft* were certain to impress anyone you nagged for a job. I learned more from the people I met, which for most of us was the real advantage of going away to school. It broadened your horizons, for better and for worse: for better in that you finally understood your position in the universe (middle-class, ethnic, public school girl) and the limits that implied (you could live in a townhouse on Beacon Hill; you'd just have to buy your heirlooms). I met people whose parents were divorced (none of my parents' friends were) and daughters and sons of professors from MIT. I picked up a general rule of thumb: The classier, the richer, the more well known the parents, the more screwed up the kids. I learned Maslow's hierarchy of needs: food, clothing, shelter and then the tough one, fulfillment. A thousand sons of doctors and lawyers were walking around looking for fulfillment, a bad goal. But the rule applied with less consistency to the women. Regardless of parents' occupation, the women tended to bunch at the screwier end of the scale. Perhaps my friends were a skewed sample. Misery was a prerequisite; we thought happy girls were the kind you saw reading *Seventeen* magazine. But at Radcliffe I met women who were like me: "nervous, neurotic and generally nuts," my older brother said.

The same strong drive that brought me to Radcliffe had brought them, and our anxiety and constant restlessness heightened the intensity of the relationships we had. True we were jealous maniacs and looked at each other's accomplishments as part of a zero-sum game: You win, I lose. But it was because of the turmoil we were in that our friendships during that period were so rich and so intense. So Paige and Daisy and Miranda and I would sit up all night and try to trace a thread back through our lives and figure out "Why?" I have made many friends in the years since college and still have friends from the years before, but no women will ever mean as much to me as those I met during my college years.

By the end of college, I had a pretty good idea that I was better suited for the rigors of daily working life than any free-floating existence as a student or scholar. Higher education was out; even if I'd wanted to be a lawyer, which seemed the occupation of choice (women who twenty years ago might have been schoolteachers now set off in a herd to law school), I did not think I could sustain three more years of school. So I aimed for what was then the less reputable profession of journalism; newspaper work still seemed grimy enough to be interesting. But the first place I went after graduation was Brooklyn.

Ever since he was eight, my older brother has wanted to recreate in the world his position in our family—President of the Schumers, favorite son of the United States. His first bid for higher office, to be president of our junior high school, failed. It wasn't until my own campaign that my mother came up with the winning slogan, "Good Humor with Fran Schumer," printed on ersatz ice cream pops made of tongue depressors and oak tag. But he beefed up his act so it would never happen again. Even before he got out of law school, he started running for office. Planeloads of ex–Adams House residents descended upon Flatbush and helped plaster the neighborhood with pro-Chucky signs. In exchange, my mother provided tuna fish sandwiches and comfortable beds (often mine). My jobs ranged from licking envelopes to trying to get rid of the plush orange velvet sofa my mother's friend had donated to campaign headquarters but that couldn't fit through the door. "Now make sure you're careful with Geraldine's couch. It's expensive." (We ended up dumping it in a vacant lot in the middle of the night.) It was the summer of 1974 and Richard Nixon had just resigned. I stood on subway platforms and exhorted voters to give a new generation a chance. All the while I worried that this would be my role in life, to be the troubled younger sibling of a very great man. I wore a big pink button that said, "Hi, I'm Chuck Schumer's sister," and felt like a fool. (This would later be known as the Billy Carter syndrome.)

Twenty-five hundred miles later I was in Wyoming, about to be fired from my first newspaper job. The managing editor, a Yale alumnus, had a habit of hiring inexperienced Ivy League journalists and dumping them in the hands of the city editor for training. The city editor, an army alumnus, held blacks, women, Chicanos and Ivy Leaguers in equal contempt. Unfortunately, the managing editor had a cocaine habit that kept him generally unavailable to the inexperienced recruits he lured out west. So after two months of seeing geysers, grizzlies and all the big attractions, I packed up the Plymouth Duster my parents had helped me buy as a graduation present and began scouting out other jobs. My brother, who had just won his election, came to keep me company. In Limon, we ate steak 'n' eggs because Chucky wanted to taste real Colorado beef; in Kansas, we stopped the car because Chucky wanted to touch real Kansas wheat; and in Missouri, we drove hours out of our way off the expressway because Chucky wanted to see the source of the Mighty Miss (a brackish mudhole barely twenty feet wide). I spent the night throwing up in St. Luke's Hospital in Kansas City because apparently real beef and real wheat didn't agree with me. By the time I arrived in Charlotte, North Carolina, I was eager to work.

The Charlotte *Observer* was an excellent paper. Never in my three-month history as a journalist had I worked with editors I liked more: Rocco, the ex-hipster from St. Louis who liked me for what he called my "instant outrage—give Schumer a whiff of a story and she's flying out the door before she even hears the facts"; Barney Gold, who saved me from being the only reporter in the newsroom so obviously from New York; and Howell Johnson, a Southern gentleman who ran the paper with dignity and tact in spite of us. At first, I labored valiantly to prove what an enterprising reporter I was. I wrote stories such as "Spring," "The First Day of School," "Charlotteans Fear New Sculpture Downtown." But after three months, I lost steam. The city was headquarters for middle management U.S.A. and filled with housing developments to accommodate them—WillowWay, Sunnybrook Farms and Home-on-the-Hill. My own apartment complex, Mount Vernon, had white cardboard columns, portraits of Martha and George, and a swimming pool shaped like the Liberty Bell around which one could meet salesmen named Duane. Still, Mount Vernon was preferable to El Flamingo (plastic flamingos on the lawn) and Rebel Yell (no blacks, no Jews allowed). Most of the reporters I worked with were older, male and married, and it wasn't much fun being invited over to their houses for dinner on Friday night. My alternatives were quiet evenings at home with Martha and George. Or Duane. A handful of single women worked for the newspaper but the dress-for-success crowd had not yet arrived and, like most of the older women I met in my early days of journalism, these were either alcoholic, divorced or otherwise alone. Many were bright and interesting, but I'd rather have died than have led the lives they did.

When I had written enough "spring" stories to earn me the reputation of being the newsroom wimp, I became involved in a more serious story. It was about the head of a home for emotionally disturbed children who had killed himself. The man had talent and an overabundance of drive, but after a lifetime of asking himself "what next?" after each new goal, finally answered by putting a bullet in his head. I threw myself into that story with an intensity I had not felt in years. "Great job, take the rest of the day off," my editor said when the story appeared. But I felt depressed and drove from shopping mall to shopping mall in a Didionesque fog.

Now when editors approached me with stories I brushed them away. I had elevated my status in the newsroom so that I no longer had to write daily features and had convinced my editors to let me work from my home, which was a big mistake: it made me further isolated and cut me off from the newsroom antics that kept other reporters sane. My spirits were sinking fast. I don't know what I had expected of a career, but this wasn't it. Compared to my mother's life, it seemed I had a raw deal. She went off to college, which she treated as if it were summer camp, married my father and had three kids on whom to unload her various psychological ills. At forty-four she had still never been to a movie by herself. I had few friends, an apartment that consisted of three empty rooms and was usually too agitated to even spend an evening alone reading. Psychologically, it seemed that we had switched places. My mother was the thin, happy, confident daughter she had wanted me to become and I, bingeing all the time, had acquired her old fat self.

Not long after the story about the suicide, I started working on a piece about a unionization drive. The only things people in North Carolina hate worse than the surgeon general's report on smoking are unions. I wanted to write the story because it was controversial and because, like any good reporter, I was intrigued by stories that no one wanted me to write. The other obvious attraction was that this story's heroes were underdogs. I had a lifelong empathy with losers, partly out of compassion and partly in opposition to my older brother, who always rooted for the winning team. (He loved the Yankees; I loved the Mets. He loved America; I hated it. He was for the war in Vietnam, at least in the beginning; I was against it. Once we caused an entire waiting room at Kennedy Airport to break out into a raging argument over the merits of Marshal Ky. "I'll never take you children anywhere again," my mother vowed.)

But I also tried to be fair. My father, in reaction to his father, a hotheaded socialist, had always urged us to see all points of view, so many, in fact, that they would justify his own fatalistic inertia. Trying to please them all, my older brother, my father, all those voices in my head, I sat down to write. But I got much too carried away. I had a tendency to exaggerate the power of the press, particularly when it was in my hands, and tormented myself with the urgency of writing the article. Like Paige, I too suffered from a combination of perfectionism, fear and laziness.

If the A. J. Liebling version of this union piece did not roll right off my fingertips, I headed for the nearest junk-food emporium and buried myself in a sugar-saturated oblivion of chocolate ice cream, English muffins and, for the sheer torture of watching the calories mount, a couple of sticks of butter. The next day it was back to the typewriter and back on the telephone to my mother who, long distance, tried to give me moral support.

"Just write the damn piece."

"I can't."

"It doesn't have to be perfect. Just write."

I tried. How I tried. But after thirty-eight paragraphs, none of which made any sense, I gave up.

It was only at these times that I reached out to other people for help. In Charlotte, I turned to the least likely source, the most cocky of my editors and the one I thought would have the least patience in dealing with a solipsistic female from the Ivy League. He was cynical, hard-boiled and had a reputation for standing by his reporters to the end. It was Rocco who first tried to cure me of my tendency to exaggerate. "Did you really see any tears falling into the fried chicken?" "No," I said. "Well if you print that, then not one of the two hundred Rotarians who were at that Christmas benefit is ever going to believe anything this paper prints again." He took me into the warmth of his comfortably furnished split-level home and in between quarters of the Miami Dolphins game, said some rather touching things. "You're worthwhile and lovable. I know you don't think so, but it's true. No matter what you write."

After several tête-à-têtes with Rocco, we decided that I should pack up and head back home, which, for lack of a better place, was now Cambridge. I decided to reenroll in therapy. "Jewish graduate school," a friend of mine called it, and he was right. Like graduate school, its appeal was spending four years thinking about a subject that you would never grow tired of—yourself. Its other advantages were that you could forestall any decision regarding a career and for a reasonable investment—small when you think about it—procure for yourself an endless source of hope. I called Johanna, who said she'd had a feeling I would call. "We never really finished, you know." She expected me to wait out the year in Charlotte, but I showed up promptly in her office by early that September.

Just before I drove out of Charlotte, I looked back toward the foundry whose union campaign I had hoped to put up in lights. I remembered talking to one of the workers' wives who had agreed to meet with me, despite her husband's warning that it could cost him his job. Just before I left, she grabbed my arm and asked, "Hon, do you think this union really can help us?" No amount of therapy could ever make up for how bad I felt at not finishing that piece. One thing you learn after years of screwing up: Screwing up makes you feel worse than whatever drove you to be such a screw-up in the first place. There were times when I thought I would have been better off had a less sympathetic editor than Rocco said, "I'll give you a day to type up what you have. That's it."

During a brief detour through Atlanta on my way north, I stopped for coffee at a roadside cafe. The woman in the neighboring booth was bubbling to her companion about her job as a reporter for a local TV station. I felt wretched. The world was full of interesting possibilities, especially for women, and although I gave up easily, I was too competitive to give up without regrets. As soon as I finished my coffee, I went to the phone booth and called one of my editors to see if I could come back. "Why don't you think about it for another week," she said.

IT was then that I wrote a long letter to Daisy, who had just gotten back from Moscow. Having left my job in Charlotte, I tried to make sense of why I had left. I said we were always trying too hard. Where were our priorities? Didn't we know how to have fun? It was a long and whiny letter, the kind you can only send to a close friend.

Daisy responded, saying she was moved by my letter, which expressed sentiments that she often felt but was not feeling then. We were at opposite junctures of our "careers" (although we never used the term; we thought of them, more happily, as adventures): I had spent three months trying to finish a story and felt completely burnt out; Daisy had postponed getting her career under way and was eager to jump in.

Cambridge the second time around was a pleasure. I arrived back in Boston in the summer of 1975, just as the Joann Little case was coming to a head. (Joann Little was a black woman in North Carolina who was accused of stabbing her jailer, who she claimed had tried to rape her.) The disc jockey read the news brief in an obviously partisan way. It was good to be home where everyone's prejudices reconfirmed your own. I put an ad in the *Phoenix* and quickly found a place to live on Ellery Street, right in the heart of the student ghetto. My roommate was a skinny biologist who was desperately short of money. The day I moved in she cashed my security deposit and the two of us hopped in her battle-scarred VW and bought fancy coffee beans in Porter Square.

It was about this time that Eleanor, Tess and I had our mini-breakfast reunion. Eleanor had just broken up with Reuben and was struggling through her first year of medical school and Tess walked around in her newlywed glow. I felt scattered, unfocused and generally disgruntled compared to them, but I pushed all those and other negative thoughts aside in the hopes that Johanna would make me well.

Once I had my schedule squared with Johanna (I would see her three times a week in her fancy new digs on Brattle Street; she had completed her doctorate and was now Johanna S. Hanson, Ph.D.). I concentrated on my two other goals, to meet men and to get the kind of easy but respectable job that would pay the therapy bills without taking too much out of me. Anyone who has ever worked for a newspaper knows that such jobs are to be found on copy desks. I went to work on the copy desk of the Boston *Globe.*

In those days the *Globe* did not yet have a professional editing staff and in addition to a handful of old-timers (put out to pasture on the desk) the desk employed spares—the title by which a dubious crew of real estate salesmen, retired reporters or graduate students picked up a supplementary income for working two or three nights a week. It helped if you knew someone (I did) or if you had a nice figure (mine varied from week to week). Sexism, even as late as 1975, was still rampant on the desk. Our most attractive member was a graduate student, reportedly so scatter-brained that she mixed up paragraphs of a story involving Jesus and a Christmas crèche with one about strippers in the Combat Zone. But I enjoyed my leisurely evenings at the *Globe.* The six P.M. to two A.M. hours attracted misfits or people who were otherwise taking time off from life. Every night we would write headlines that, in their way, were as unstressful and absorbing as solving crossword puzzles. We drank coffee and smoked lots of cigarettes. In those days I was smoking two packs a day, which made me a light smoker compared to my hacking desk mates. Copy editing wasn't as demanding as reporting and the pressure of a nightly deadline curbed whatever perfectionist tendencies you had. You weren't struggling to write the best headline in the world. You were struggling to write the best headline you could by eleven P.M. But social life came first. Except for the poor soul whose job it was to keep checking on the fire in Malden, by one A.M. the rest of us were seated around our big copy desk away from home, a round, sawdust-covered table at the Wharf. The Wharf was one of the few bars in Boston that stayed open late enough for us. There our crowd of would-be poets and frustrated writers would make cynical comments about the reporters whose copy we had joyously massacred earlier in the night. I was not the only copy editor who exacted vengeance for not having a byline.

It was at one of these nightly gripe sessions that I met Billy, a reporter for the Associated Press. A widower, Billy was overcome by the task of raising six kids. I spent most of my evenings in Billy's ramshackle house in Chelsea, which mirrored the state of his soul. The ceilings in some of the rooms had been stripped so that looking up at night one could see the innards of a house on the verge of collapse—dangling wires, decaying wood and a bare suspended light bulb. I often wondered, What am I doing here? but looking into Billy's tired eyes, I knew. Billy, like the Irish of his city, had passed his golden age. Once the star of the bureau's State House corps, he was being replaced with a slicker, more professional newsman in the Woodward-Bernstein style. (They had M.A.'s in journalism but Billy could recite Yeats.) And although I was young enough to be his daughter, I felt more comfortable with Billy than with the health-conscious, bike-riding graduate students in Harvard Square. Up in his room, with the kids crying and the house collapsing all around us, we hid from the world. Billy had a friend, a high school teacher who, at the end of a bad drinking spree, went into a mental hospital to complete the rest of a nervous breakdown. His wife and children had left him, so on Christmas day it was just me, Billy and Jim in the hospital room. He looked terrible. His hair was matted and his face was covered with three-day growth that was prematurely white. The next morning as we were falling into bed (this usually coincided with the sun coming up), I shook with the thought of what could happen to people's lives. I looked at Billy and thought, Whatever his faults, at least I'm not alone.

Billy's was a hiding place, and after a spell I felt strong enough to rouse before noon and apply myself to work. Ambition was something Billy did not understand. "Don't you get any pleasure out of doing the job itself?" he asked. "Not unless it counts," I replied. At the same time, a new breed of woman was taking over the newsroom. Almost overnight it seemed that a hodgepodge of former ballerinas, schoolteachers, and young women fresh from journalism school had replaced a desk full of melancholy old men. Although at first the men resented the intrusion, eventually they accepted it with weariness and grace. It was just one more defeat, this time at the hands of women with polished nails and carefully tailored suits. Yet despite their "looking out for Number One," I liked them. They were old enough to have been dumped on in previous jobs and determined not to let it happen again. Although their lives were stable, they were not dull women. They read novels on their lunch break, and had what used to be called "interests." One studied dance. One played the flute. How different they were from the alcoholics and divorcées I had known in my early newspaper days. Even I improved, a little. I learned not to badmouth reporters and to behave in a more professional and diplomatic way. "It's very close to deadline time" replaced "What do you think this is, a fuckin' country club?" Now, we put out a much better paper and had a lot less fun.

One by one these women were making advances in their personal lives that I was not. They were buying houses, getting married or settling down. Even the single ones were talking about condominiums and mortgages. I had moved out of my student ghetto on Ellery Street but only into another, slightly more expensive one. I could not conceive of buying a house, alone or with someone; even furnishing one seemed exotic. I did, however, advance to the stage of acquiring a younger, more suitable boyfriend. He was a handsome law school student and a more appropriate companion at the dinner parties given by my new copy desk friends. (Dinner parties replaced beer and cigarettes once the women arrived. In fact, some people on the copy desk now considered it dangerous to smoke.) Martin's family knew mine and both our families approved. We hoped that in one stroke we could make two sets of parents happy and return two black sheep to the fold. It was not to be, however. We were both in the midst of therapy, and although I admitted to still being neurotic Martin claimed to be reformed. He tried to cure me of my grandiosity (as expressed by jaywalking, etc.), which he felt his therapist, Fritz, had helped him outgrow. I was so sick of hearing Fritz's analysis of my various ills that I finally retaliated and made Martin come with me to see Johanna. "He seemed very uncomfortable," Johanna observed. Martin said that Fritz thought Johanna was probably projecting. And so on, till we broke up.

I was not making headway at all with Johanna in those days. We were still trying various remedies for my eating disease. I tried: to love my food, to practice feeling "entitled" to what I ate, to believe fat was a feminist issue, to believe fat was beautiful. With Johanna's approval, I attended a workshop for women on food in which we touched a turnip and were told to regard it as our friend. None of these remedies felt as satisfying as a good old-fashioned binge. In February, I decided to take a vacation to the farthest away place I could afford. "What? You're going to South America alone?" I regarded it as a triumph of modern psychotherapy that I could hang up on my mother, go, and be miserable, in spite of her disapproval. In a demonstration of self-realization, I flew to Cartagena, Colombia, developed sun poisoning, binged my way down the coast and somehow managed to avoid dysentery. I came home feeling thoroughly depressed. For four months I didn't talk to my family. I even refused to attend my mother's surprise fiftieth birthday party, despite the intervention of my brothers and father. I didn't want to know anything about it, but in later years, when my mother and I were reconciled, she told me how awful she had felt. On the day of the party, my older brother walked to the microphone and told the assembled guests, "I'm sorry my sister couldn't be here. She has other business to attend to." A few months later, my younger brother was sent as emissary to Amherst, where I was staying with a favorite uncle and aunt. He alone of the members of my family had experienced a brief adolescent rebellion at an appropriate age (in high school, he took up the drums and grew long hair). "Don't worry. It'll pass," he said. "I went through this when I was thirteen."

"It's not helping," I said one day, sitting in the increasingly plush interior of Johanna's office. When I first met her she was a struggling graduate student with long hair and hippie clothes. Now she was wearing $200 boots (I knew what they cost because I passed them every day on my way through Harvard Square to her office). "My good money," I muttered miserably to myself. I would have spent it gladly had I felt she was doing me any good. But even Johanna was feeling frustrated. "You're not letting me help you," she said. "So tell me how to let you." "You have to want it." Silence. We could never take it past that point.

After four years and enough money to outfit an army in boots, I "terminated" therapy by just stopping going. At the same time, I started floundering at my job. For a year I had behaved like a professional on the desk but now my real self was starting to ooze out. I showed up late at work, in a pair of jeans that still had holes in them from a traffic accident I had survived in 1975. Even the printers, whose attitude toward women had softened now that they had computers to hate, seemed concerned. Although my sister copy editors made history at the *Globe* by filling dozens of management positions, I could not make the leap with them. The truth was that my heart wasn't in editing. For diversion, I took a short-story writing seminar at Boston University. Once a week we met in the disheveled living room of a famous writer who collected our journals each week. Through her intercession, I became involved with an older man (Harvard, Class of '51). ("He's obsessed with you. He calls you The Slattern.") Each week Wilson and I would meet for two-martini lunches in Harvard Square; in between we would write about each other in the stories we read aloud to the class. I was not embarrassed to appear as a struggling writer in his stories but he did not enjoy appearing in mine as a conservative banker drinking away his lunch hour and chasing after "slatterns."

In the meantime, I kept bingeing and putting on weight. I attended a fiction writing workshop at Saranac Lake, where I sold my first short story. Even so, on the way home I parked my car at the side of the road and decided I didn't want to live. The aftermath of a binge was always depressing. A thousand times I woke up the next morning and asked myself, How could you have done it again? I felt logy from all the sugar. All I wanted to do was binge again, but the thought of it made me sick. At least therapy had given me hope. Now where was there to turn?

It was about this time that David reappeared. We had seen each other sporadically over the years but never as anything more than old friends. In pursuit of his political goals, David had long ago pushed everything else to the side. We were friends, even better ones, now that he was no longer trying to make me into Mrs. Mao Zedung. For years I had seen little of him except the blue, crinkly air mail packets from the foreign cities where he was tracking one or another worthy cause. On that morning when he rapped on my screen door, I was glad to see his tall malnourished body and hear his jarring obnoxious voice. "Hey man, anyone home?" I honestly couldn't say.

WE had last left each other, tearlessly, at the time of graduation. Even before he left the country, which was the following year, he had other girlfriends. He came to my parents' house in Brooklyn one night feeling particularly low. I don't recall ever seeing him like that. He was always exuberant or angry, rarely sad. Even the night of a *Crimson* dinner our junior year, when he heard of his grandfather's death, I do not recall seeing him so much as wince. He only recalled what a coincidence it was that the person who had been president of the *Crimson* the previous year had also, on that night, gotten a similar call. He was always thinking of himself in terms of history; he could acknowledge nothing as personal. But that brief stopover in Brooklyn was different. A woman he had been dating told him she wanted to break up. David seemed shattered and I was both surprised and perplexed that he would confess this to me. Clearly my tenure as the reigning obsession of his life was over.

After graduation he had gone back to Chicago, where he earned some money driving a bus, and then spent a summer working in the giant U.S. Steel plant in his neighborhood. He had taken me to see it the summer I went to visit him on my way to Orlando. I remember his pointing out the squalor of the neighborhood adjacent to one of the largest money-making factories in the world. "Capitalism," he said. His goal, then, was to earn enough money so that he could travel through Latin America the following year. Unlike so many of us at school, David was certain about what he wanted to do and his goals gave him purpose. He did not waste his senior year but spent it writing his thesis and studying Spanish, which he knew he would need for his Latin American trip. It was interesting, too, that his thesis, which was about unions in America, did not toe the usual Marxist line. He argued that the capitalists in America who opposed the closed shop did so not only because they were opposed to unions but because they felt it violated their rights. In a certain sense, they believed in freedom, David wrote.

His destination that spring was Chile. President Allende had been assassinated the previous fall and there were few more sympathetic heroes for the left. David felt almost a biological compulsion to seek the heat, wherever there was a revolution or a moment in history where "right" appeared to be on one side. My instructions that June were that if he should write to me about the Chicago White Sox I would know something was wrong and I should contact some of his friends. I never got any mail referring to the White Sox, although I found out afterwards David did spend some time in jail. He may have been detained merely for routine questioning. David was very dramatic and inclined to exaggerate, so it was hard to tell.

At Christmastime, David made a detour to come visit me in Charlotte on his way further south. We were invited to a party at Rocco's house at which guests were asked to bring "Toys for Tots," but we forgot and brought a bottle of wine instead. He was on his way to Mexico. He planned to travel to Latin America by an overland route, hitchhiking most of the way. It was how you picked up stories, he said. He sent me postcards from various points and at the end of that year, on my twenty-first birthday, I received a card from Tierra del Fuego. No one would ever send me a birthday card from any place farther south, he bragged. (On my thirtieth birthday, he sent me a postcard from the Cape of Good Hope. "One more birthday and I'll have known you for more than half your life.") David was always setting up "records" like these. He vowed to send me a birthday card every year no matter where he was, and so far, he has.

David spent most of the next four years in Latin America, Portugal and Spain. He felt that those countries were most ripe for his brand of democratic socialism and did not feel comfortable in America. David was ambitious, but he was not interested in going to medical school or law school, and disdained the rest of our classmates who did. After graduation, my older brother made a bet with him. He proposed that like other young idealists he knew in our class, David, too, would grow more practical in later years and join the stampede back into professional careers. David swore this wasn't true. They made a twenty-dollar bet, payable in five years. (David never went to law school and my brother never paid.)

He earned his living writing articles for respectable magazines, none of which paid very well. He lived on the road and was often broke. Every few years he would return to America and save some more money. During one of these pit stops in New York, he worked in a bookstore and roomed with a compulsive gambler who liked to read. There was a bathtub in the kitchen that was filled with books. He and David would spend their time sitting in the McDonald's on the then seedy corner of Ninety-sixth Street and Broadway, listening to the old men talk. "I heard these two old guys rappin' about Spinoza and Bellow [Saul Bellow, being a fellow Chicagoan, was an idol of David's]—it was great." Only David would discover literary conversations among the proletariat. Whenever I went into that McDonald's, all I heard were teenagers talking about dates and jeans. I wondered if, like Joan of Arc, he heard things because he believed them.

America made David uncomfortable, so he gravitated to places like McDonald's that attracted the young and the poor. If a person we knew from college lived in an apartment building with a doorman, David wanted to run. He could not stand having someone open a door for him, and when someone did, it often launched him into one of his eloquent fits about the warped values our classmates now had.

He frequently borrowed money because he was often broke, though he borrowed only enough to eat or take a train somewhere or pay the rent. But although he was never prompt in his repayments, they always arrived. His most long-standing debt was for the two hundred dollars he had borrowed to track me down in Orlando the summer before our senior year. Twelve years after he had borrowed the money, his creditor, also my friend, called to say, "Surprise. Guess who sent me a check?"

David ate Chef Boyardee Spaghetti-O's out of a can and wore torn jeans. He hated winter because he was always cold. (His ancient ski jacket was torn and thin. His socks smelled so bad that on the few occasions when he stayed over with me, and we were not often on intimate terms, I'd make him leave his socks outside the door, in a plastic bag, and wash his feet first.) The cold was one of his reasons for traveling south. It was summer in Chile in January, he said.

After two years of traveling he returned. He lived with the

woman who had been his instructor in the Spanish Department at Harvard. She was ambitious, like David, and politically on the left. They were a much more suitable pair than he and I had ever been. Her father was a professor who had taught in Latin America for years, so she and David had that interest in common. She had grown up in a house that was dominated by politics and books. I presumed Luisita was strong enough to withstand him but I was wrong. Once, he confessed to me that she was intimidated by him. Did he do that to women? he asked. I told him I didn't know, but I thought, Of course you do. You're a bully and no one can talk to you about your goddamn politics. But I didn't say it; I didn't even know if it was still true.

He and Luisita were planning to go to South Africa that fall. Anyone who knew David knew he would end up there. His two major issues, race and politics, came together in an ugly and fascinating way there. I envied him in a way. He had purpose, and his purpose was rooted in something more substantial than just a desire to "do well." If he was often angry at the state of the world, at least he had a place in it.

When he came to me that afternoon in Cambridge, I was lying on my bed, in one of my worse states. "C'mon. Let's go to the movies," he said. We went to see Jane Fonda and Jon Voight in *Coming Home.* It was the most fun we ever had. David was good that way, a real booster when other people were sad. Even if your politics didn't agree with his, David would march you out for a beer.

He spent a few more days in Cambridge, though only one of them with me. David did not have a car and he asked me to drive him to Walpole State Prison so that he could say goodbye to a friend before leaving. I had nothing better to do so I agreed.

On the way, David told me about his friend Jonas. He was a local celebrity, an underground hero who had attracted a following among professors and philanthropists in the Boston area. His name had first become well known because of a suit he had brought against the Commonwealth of Massachusetts charging the guards with prison brutality. Jonas won the suit and was awarded $21,000 in damages. Then, in a second suit, a federal judge ordered him released from a punishment cellblock where he had been placed without a hearing. It was during the time he spent in solitary confinement that he began to rehabilitate himself. He looked around the cell, covered with layers of seepage and excrement, and said to himself, I'm better than this.

In the next several years, Jonas taught himself the law and saved a guard's life in a prison riot. His goal when I met him was to petition the governor to grant him a pardon. He had been in prison since he was seventeen, sentenced for life for participating in an armed robbery in which his accomplice killed a middle-aged jeweler.

It was awkward. In front of David, I felt embarrassed for being middle class, for being educated, for being a girl. Something about being around a prisoner made you feel you were the one who had committed the crime. I kept looking at the tattoos on Jonas's arms and the one gold earring in his ear. He looked a little like a pirate, too, with his spiky black hair, almost gray in parts, pulled back into a bushy bob at the nape of his short thick neck. He directed most of his questions to David but frequently turned to me, staring at me in a way that made me squirm.

I went first out of a sense of duty but soon began to look forward to my weekly visits to the jail. It was a hideous spectacle of concrete and barbed wire, reminiscent of scenes of World War II. At night, searchlights lit up the whole of that barren field in which a prisoner would be set upon by guards and dogs if he tried to escape. What impelled me to go, more than the man, was the strength he conveyed. He had changed his life and the totality of that change was inspiring in almost a religious sense. I knew him later, when the governor pardoned him and he began teaching at a college in the state. Then I saw him more realistically. He was not the hero he was set up to be but if I was unreasonably captivated by him, I'm glad. He was a rebel and I could take from him what I could not accept from anyone else. It was his example that made me feel I could change.

In the late summer of 1978, I went to a psychiatrist who specialized in eating disorders. I had all but given up on psychiatrists, but my parents, of all people, urged me to give it one more try. This one gave up on me even before I walked into his office. "Get your feet off my desk. And stop trying to flirt with me." Egocentric asshole. They all think they're Montgomery Clift as Freud. "Former anorectics almost never get well" was his first cheery news. "But if you don't do something about your eating problem, nothing will change. You will just get old." That was upsetting, that I would not change; I would only grow old. Even my parents, who had one session with him, agreed he was mean. He recommended I do one of three things: take antidepressants (too frightening even to contemplate), join group therapy (I hated anything having to do with either therapy or groups) or join a small informal organization run by people who were anorectic, bulimic or ate in a generally compulsive way. The last sounded the least distasteful (no fees, no shrinks), although I had my doubts. I had seen an article about the group in the *Globe,* illustrated by a picture of a very fat woman. It said something about the organization having quasi-religious roots. As a friend of mine once joked, "God is for people who didn't go to college." I furtively walked into my first meeting, hoping that no one from the *Globe* would be there. I could just see the headlines. RADCLIFFE GRAD HOOKS UP WITH MOON-LIKE CULT. Inside, a small group of women listened to one describe a binge in gory detail. I had never heard anyone talk about a binge publicly. "If I do nothing else but stay abstinent in a day [her term for neither starving nor bingeing but eating three meals a day], then I consider I've had a good day," she said. ("Radcliffe grad abandons all hope of worldly success: Swears total obedience to diet club.") Someone mentioned the term "higher power," which was the group's sneaky way of referring to God. The term was also used in Alcoholics Anonymous, on which this organization was based. I tried a second meeting in Cambridge where I saw younger women more like me. Here was a roomful of women who were different in every way, except one: underneath they all described themselves as not terribly happy. And yet the room seemed incredibly full of hope. Perhaps I was just so low that I was willing to surrender to anyone's advice, but I felt in my gut, after twelve years of feeling out of sorts with myself and the world, that something important was going on here. At the end of the meeting, a woman sitting in front of me turned to make conversation. Had she been anything but a dead ringer for Lauren Bacall, I would have fled from the room to dissociate myself from these strange, desperate girls. But God had put her there, this flawless cynical blonde. "It really works," she said.

During the next eight months I was told what no psychiatrist had ever said but what I had long suspected was true: Although psychological problems might have kicked off my binges, they had a physical root. To stop them required the same intense concentration needed to give up alcohol or any addictive drug. Analyzing was held in low repute. ("You don't sit in a burning movie theater and analyze what caused the fire. You put the fire out.") I was also told, ungently, that I was a mess, something Johanna had never dared say. But it did not bother me, coming from these women, who, at least in that department, were obviously my peers. My illness wasn't buying anyone's expensive boots. This nuthouse was run by its inmates, wise to the ways of their fellows. I could fool Johanna, whom I now saw in a more sympathetic light, but I could not fool these women, all of whom were great rationalizers like me. A roomful of bullshitters. They had the perfect approach for rebels like me: no leaders, no rules. I could take their advice or ignore it. No one cared if I listened or not. Naturally, I listened.

The first thing I had to do was learn how to eat normally. This was not as easy as it sounds. When I first stopped bingeing, it was suggested that I weigh and measure my food just to make sure I did not overeat or undereat. Even in a restaurant, I carried a measuring cup and scale. For a person who was self-conscious to begin with, it was not a little humiliating. To this day, I am sure I am remembered by the Ritz-Carlton staff as the young lady who whipped out her measuring cup and scale the minute her meal was served. My "sponsor" (sponsors played alter ego to your id) had told me to eat a cup of salad a meal. Unfortunately, it took six *nouvelle cuisine* servings of endive to fill one Pyrex cup. Dates and newspaper editors could not help inquiring why I was doing this, and I was foolish enough to tell them. Most people were sorry they had asked. Even when I grew thin, which happened fairly rapidly, people wanted to know why I still used my cup and my scale. It was hard to explain to anyone that the problem was in my head. Fat wasn't beautiful but thin wasn't necessarily well.

I saw then for how many years my eating habits had interfered with my moods. If I was unhappy, a sugar binge would make me feel high. I had never really known what I liked to do. But now I knew. Nothing. At that point, I was tempted to go back to my drug, but that's where other forms of help came in. Soon I began going to those meetings in the same compulsive, addictive way in which I used to binge. I received help from women who were recovering from eating disorders and helped others who wished to. The friendships I made in these groups were long-lasting; the group acted like a womb from which I could emerge and reenter when I felt I needed more support. A lot of it was kind of tacky by Harvard standards but that wasn't the point, or maybe it was. It was humbling to put aside your self-consciousness and accept help in a form that would make your sophisticated friends cringe. I do not know whether the advice I received was any better than the advice a therapist might have offered (although I think it was, on the principle that it takes one to know one), but I know how strong a bond I felt in those rooms.

If I wanted to complain, as I often did, the women would ask me, "Are you abstinent?" I would say "Yes." "Then you have nothing to complain about." I wanted to murder them for their lack of empathy, but it proved to be an appropriate response. I had always tried to be the best, the smartest, the greatest. Here the emphasis was on being middle-of-the-road. I had always assumed that believing the worst would happen would prevent it from happening. Here the emphasis was on inner faith. Success was not irrelevant, but it wasn't the goal. When I started attending these meetings, I smoked three packs of cigarettes a day, drank gallons of coffee and used enough artificial sweetener to ensure a generation of three-eyed kids. Within a month, I had stopped doing all of it. And yet I was told not to think it was I who was doing it but the group, and therefore not to "binge" on success.

I was working days now at the *Globe,* and lived a more puritan life. Every day I got up to swim my fifty laps at the "Y." I remained a normal weight, cut my hair and started taking care of my looks, even—especially—when I did not feel like it. I threw out all my old jeans and bought skirts and blouses. For the first time in my life, I ate three meals a day and if I wanted to eat more or less, I reminded myself of the doctor's words. I wouldn't change, I would only get old. I squeezed out of Jonas all the help I could get. He had time, sitting around that prison all day to write me letters. When I came home from work to my large empty apartment, cold because I could not pay for much heat, I pulled my couch up to the fire and read. He wrote to me every day, sometimes twice a day. I pulled his letters out of their thin white envelopes on which he always used the same stamps, with pink and green roses, as if to defy the bleakness of prison life, and prayed that, like Jonas, I would change.

I started testing the waters at home. Weight had always been my personal badge of failure but now I felt I could show my face. Also, my program emphasized forgiving people at whom I had been angry and making it up to people I had hurt. The day before Passover, I woke up with an incredible urge to go home. (Now that I was no longer bingeing, I had "incredible urges" for everything, not just for food. Psychiatrists called it a compulsive-obsessive disorder, which they concede therapy is slow to cure. The people in my program called it being "spoiled.") I didn't even wait to see my editor at work; I drove to his house and asked if I could take the next two days off. At the end of our seder (my family with their ritual Passover objects; I with my cup and scale), my mother took me in her arms and cried.

Still I had to confess I felt pretty lousy about everything. I woke up every morning terrified. My body hurt as if my organs were readjusting. I didn't feel that I didn't want to live. I just felt I didn't know how. The littlest things made me angry. An argument at work would make me burst into tears. In the past I never cried, I binged.

About eight months after I had started going to meetings, I paid a return visit to the psychiatrist who had told me that nothing would change. "Extraordinary," he said when I walked into his office. My hair was neat, I was wearing a skirt and clean fresh shirt, and for the first time since high school, I was at a reasonably normal weight. I told him I hadn't had a binge in the last eight months. "I'm impressed," he said. "But I still don't feel happy," I replied. He looked at me in that same cool appraising way he used when I had first gone to see him. "Now that you've taken care of your mouth," he said, "there's only your mind, your heart and your genitals left."

IT was not that simple. After years of floundering, I felt a surge of ambition, but where to direct it was tougher to figure out. In one blitzkrieg week, I had mailed out applications to law school, medical school and various newspapers around New York but was quickly cured of those fantasies, especially the last. By the time the secretary at *Newsday* came out into the anteroom to get me, I had already left. The truth is, I didn't want to work for anyone. I was as bad at taking orders as I was at giving them. I wanted to apply myself seriously toward a career but was afraid to. It was Miranda who gave me the answer. Once I had sat in the Radcliffe Quadrangle and watched her break down. I couldn't give her the help she needed then. Now she was strong enough to give it to me.

I had seen her during my trips to New York, which were becoming more frequent then. We were at the Cloisters one weekend, when Miranda came up with the answer that had eluded me all along. "Go home," she said. "It's what you want to do, isn't it? Then why not go?"

SHE was going to graduate school and struggling to support herself through her last year. I once had a discussion with her about a mutual friend. Miranda told me she didn't want to see him unless he began to face up to some of his more damaging psychological problems. "You know how I respect struggle," she said, which seemed to sum up the history of her last ten years.

Miranda would never tell me the full story and I did not sit down and rehash the past with her as I had done with my other college friends, but I knew the outlines. Paige, Daisy, Eleanor, Tess and I had it easy compared to what Miranda had been through.

At first our information had come only from Miranda's mother. Ruth was upset because Miranda had cut off all ties to home. (Actually, her parents always knew where she was and even at the worst times they were in touch—by phone, not to mention the therapy bills, which they paid—but my information came from my mother, via Ruth, and the separation may have seemed more extreme to them.) Miranda was steadfast about her plan, as she could be when she made up her mind about something. My mother could not understand it. "Isn't it odd? And the strange thing is Ruth was so happy raising her children. She told me after the first, she enjoyed it so much she didn't want to stop and had Miranda's youngest brother because she couldn't bear to put the baby clothes away." I tried to explain to my mother Miranda's point of view about what had gone on in that cozily disheveled house. Miranda and I would argue about it many times over the years, whether the kind of life you perceived your parents as having, as revealed in the confines of your psychotherapist's office, was "true" or merely your truth, useful only to a limited extent. I sided with my mother, always hesitant to be too fully on Miranda's side, and said it was only a partial truth, a distortion at best. Miranda, fully immersed in the analytical process by then, said it was your truth, and what else mattered?

She was stubborn in those days, but it seemed she had to be. She had seized on psychotherapy as the answer, and so she had to blind herself to other truths. The process was long and painful, and over the years I often heard Miranda say ridiculous things, but therapy worked for her as completely and certainly as it had not worked for me.

At first, of course, she refused even to come up to Cambridge, and I was reluctant to see her when I visited New York, still eager to push away all thoughts of our terrible freshman year. But usually I called her, if only out of guilt. Once she came to my parents' house. Ruth had not seen her in months, so my mother spent more time looking at Miranda than she did at me; she wanted to give Ruth a full report. And although it got to the point where she could give Ruth good news—"She looks lovely, yes, and seems to be doing fine"—I knew monitoring the details of Miranda's life scared her. Secretly, my mother viewed Miranda as my other half, the part that had yielded to the disturbing impulses inside. My mother was relieved when I made it through freshman year. But I always felt that in leaving, Miranda had done the more courageous thing.

Therapy was the reason she had moved to New York in the first place. She had a name that the psychiatrist up at Harvard had given her and she clung to it as if it could save her. Her analyst specialized in treating young people with "separation anxiety," his fancy term for people who had trouble leaving home. At first she did nothing but see him, fifty-five minutes a day, five days a week. The rest of the time she stayed at home with her parents, but very quickly saw the need to get out. Anything that reminded her of her past—her mother, her father, the room where she had spent so much of her childhood, in anger it now seemed—upset her. She soon moved in with an aunt, a strong indomitable person and a successful literary agent. Miranda had always admired her, but now that she was in therapy she saw everything in psychoanalytical terms. Aunt Jane no longer represented warmth, love and financial independence, but only accounted for Ruth's unwillingness to promote herself.

As soon as she was able to get a job and earn some money, Miranda moved into a room at the YWCA. It was one of the nicer midtown branches where a lot of troubled women stayed (we called it the Radcliffe Club of New York), but the stories I heard about it made me cringe. I imagined Miranda eating supper off a hot plate and looking out on Madison Avenue from her cold cheerless room. But it wasn't so bad, she said. Besides, she didn't have the money to live anywhere else. Her parents were paying for her therapy, but in all other ways Miranda was stubbornly independent. For years she lived like a pauper, never indulging in a taxi or an evening out. She believed that getting well rested upon her cutting her ties from home, financially and otherwise; she paid for everything, including school, and refused all other help. And I had to admire her when I saw the circumstances in which she lived. While I was handed winter coats and birthday money from home, Miranda received and accepted nothing. For eight winters she wore the same flimsy coat. She bought her pocketbook at Woolworth's. I heard her complain only once. A cousin had brought her an expensive vase for her birthday. "Doesn't she know how desperately I could use a blouse?"

Sex was the issue that troubled her most. She was convinced that because of her mother's strict intellectual upbringing (her mother had been typecast as the "intelligent" child, not the "pretty one"), both she and her mother lacked confidence in their womanhood. "That's ridiculous," my mother said. Ruth, more than any woman she knew, loved having children. But according to Miranda, her mother sacrificed too much of herself in the process. The result was that Miranda had problems growing up and as a teenager, was anxious about sex. There were men, and even a few real relationships, but none that lasted for very long.

For sustenance, she did typing and filing for a small manufacturer. I thought it was very funny to get letters from her with the return address, "Ladies' Foundation Undergarments." Miranda viewed this as progress. When she had first moved to New York, she could do nothing but drag herself to Dr. Bernhardt's office. Now she had a job and was making friends.

After her second year in analysis, she decided to go back to school. She never considered going back to Radcliffe, which she would always see as her undoing. Nor did she wish to apply to any other regular four-year school—she wasn't quite ready for a dining hall full of eighteen-year-olds. Instead, she attended night school at a large university in New York, where she met older divorcées, sixties dropouts and retreads like herself. At Radcliffe, Miranda had planned to be an anthropologist or a sculptor. But after years of analysis, she decided to become an architect. She wanted something she could measure and touch. Her own therapy plunged her too frequently into the unknown, and even though it was almost a religion with her, she needed relief from it.

One day I started to feel safer around her. I began to believe she was making progress that before I had not. I had to admire the stubborn fierce way in which she had picked herself up and built herself anew. While we attended our Fifth Year Reunion, Miranda got her B.A.

By the time she entered graduate school, we were much better friends. She had a wonderful way with me. She would listen to my meanderings about what was happening in my own life and then, gently, offer advice. Actually, advice would be too harsh a word to convey what Miranda did; she seemed to reach into my mind and pull out what I really thought. Miranda suggested graduate school, which I saw as the perfect cocoon, a way to avoid making decisions and a reasonable excuse for moving back to New York. When I was in high school I had applied to Harvard, Princeton, Yale, Cornell, Smith, Jackson, Barnard and then only as a last resort, and I'd probably have preferred death, City College as my safety school. Now, for some perverse reason, it was my first and only choice.

I also saw Miranda as a connection to home. On the trips I made to New York in my newly "abstinent" state, I slept on her couch and had breakfast at her messy dining-room table. She was a terror in the kitchen. She broke dishes, cooked mushroom omelets that somehow came out green and ruined recipes with the cheerful alacrity of Julia Child. Yet she had the things I wanted now, not simply a home and a life in New York City, but a new self. As powerfully as we had been drawn to each other in weakness during the early days of our friendship at Radcliffe, we were drawn to each other now in our new strength.

I moved to New York in the summer of 1979. It was a miserable day in August, the rain beating down so hard on the windshield of my yellow Plymouth Duster that I could hardly see. I had misgivings about coming back to New York even then. I drove my car to the garage in the back of my parents' house, and as soon as we started discussing the best way to unload my car, my older brother, who was there to greet me, made a suggestion and we started to fight. I wanted to go back to Boston immediately.

How I got through that day and others like it, I don't know. The first week I got so angry at something my mother said that I threw an ashtray at the wall. But that was as bad as it got. Afterwards, I began to settle into the idea of living in the city and felt happier than I had in a long, long while.

The first year I simply adjusted to being back in New York and staying abstinent, which I now viewed as the major focus of my life. I joined a group for women with eating disorders, similar to the one I had belonged to in Cambridge. I continued to draw support and practical wisdom from those meetings, always bearing in mind the psychiatrist's words: "Now that you've taken care of your mouth, there's only your mind, your heart and your genitals left." Gingerly, I approached the typewriter again. I was still haunted by the piece I hadn't finished in Charlotte so I altered my approach. Instead of reaching for the best schools, the best newspapers, the best subjects I could find, I started with publications that were so bad I wouldn't mind if I failed. Much of my rent in those days was paid by the *National Enquirer,* which, for "mind-boggling" stories, paid mind-boggling fees. Eventually, I graduated to better publications and smaller fees.

I moved from my parents' house to Miranda's couch to a large airy apartment on the Upper West Side. I lived with three other women ("the Gang of Four," my older brother called us), typical New York career girls: one worked in a bakery that harbored Weathermen (of the Bernadine Dohrn type), one followed the guru Meher Baba and the third described her employer as Jesus. If I had made progress in most areas of my life, cooperating with roommates was not one. Tess would have sympathized with them. In addition to not believing in meat, cigarettes, happiness or success, they didn't believe in bug spray. ("I think roaches are less harmful than the DDT or whatever that capitalistic sauce has in it.") But I could not bear the sight of baby cockroaches crawling between the bristles of my toothbrush, so I called my father, who came and sprayed. The roaches were banished from the apartment and so was I.

It was about this time that Paige came to New York. She was clerking for a judge in Michigan. I was working on an article for *The New York Times,* which unnerved me as articles for the *National Enquirer* couldn't do, and Paige gave me her "workmanlike" advice. It was a nice way for us to see each other. Each of us felt we had overcome the worst of our troubles and were on our way to building better lives, hers with Alex in Montana, and mine with whatever new opportunities I could seize in New York. When I told her about my eating disorder and my new normality in regard to weight, she nodded. "It's about time."

I moved then to my first real New York home, a garret in the sky on the Upper West Side. It was so small I could touch all four walls by standing in the center. But I was so happy to be able to afford my own place on the basis of my writing that I got used to being cramped. My landlord, Mr. Perlstein, an Eastern European who had survived a concentration camp, gave me encouragement: "A nice girl. Such a waste!" It was such an ordeal to climb up the five stories that most people who got up there stayed. After dropping enough cigarette ash on my floor, Mr. Perlstein settled in to tell me stories about his life. After the war he went back to the village where he and his wife used to live. A strange family who spoke a language he didn't understand was living in his house. On the finger of the woman, he saw his wife's wedding ring (she had been killed in the camps). The woman saw him looking at her finger and without saying a word, took it off and gave it to him.

When Mr. Perlstein wasn't around to keep me company, I climbed across the roof and visited Buddy. He was a graduate student in physics who, like me, lived in a one-room cell on the top floor. When the writing business got too wearisome, or nuclear fusion was clouding Buddy's brain, we'd abandon our work and set up a table, chairs and bottle of wine and dine under the stars.

I was very methodical: heart, mind, let's see, what next? I decided to try to have a social life, which I had abandoned during my last two monkish years. (When I gave up cigarettes, coffee and sweets, I also gave up men for fear that they might drive me back to the other three.) I knew that my tendency was to date men who were either unavailable or inappropriate (my ideal date was a convicted felon twice my age). So just as I had done with my food, I developed certain rules: I could date only men who were (a) between twenty-five and forty; (b) without being snobby, basically of my background and social class (no bikers); and (c), I must confess, smart. The point was to stick to my peers with whom there was the potential for a serious relationship. These boundaries led me to Philip (thirty-eight, free and single and he used the word "exegesis," which made me place him in the 730-to-750 verbal SAT range). Naturally, we met at the Harvard Club. I wasn't a member but occasionally used the ladies' room, one of the nicest in midtown, and helped myself to the free club stationery. It was slow going until Philip told me the name of his former wife, whom I remembered from freshman year. "You were married to Cassandra?" I then did my imitation of Cassandra (I have a gift for imitating people with nose jobs), which caused Philip to laugh and me to relax. Cassandra, when I knew her, was an ex-model with expensive taste. I did not see how anyone who had been married to her could be interested in me.

Our courtship proceeded slowly. I was not used to dating without bingeing or trying to pretend I was something other than I was, but Philip made it easy for me. On our fourth date he made me an offer. "I have to go to Oklahoma on a little deal," he told me one day over lunch, "and thought perhaps you'd care to join me afterwards for a little vacation in Palm Beach." In the past I would have immediately said yes. But I was a little less reckless now. "You don't have to worry," he said, reading my mind. "You can have your own room." For a week I worried whether I should go. "You should go if you're interested in him, but not if you're just looking for a free trip," said my mother, whose morals had loosened considerably with her daughter's advancing age. And since I was pretty sure it wouldn't work with Philip, I decided it wouldn't be right to go. But the next week it snowed, and since I was never very good at being virtuous anyway, I went.

Had it not been for that vacation, I'm sure we would never have fallen in love. The trip was largely at Philip's expense (although in a grudging concession to feminism, I forced myself to pay as much as I could afford and rationalized the rest with Marx—from each according to his ability, to each according to his need). Therefore, I was forced to practice gratitude and restraint, as was not my custom.

As it turned out, we shared a room but not a bed. But by the fourth night, I started to wonder if something was wrong. Maybe I was too skinny for Philip. Or too pale. Maybe he was spoiled and used to beautiful women like Cassandra. But Philip had a sixth sense in dealing with women like me. He knew first that stalling was maddening but effective, and second, that there was a Cassandra in each of us, and that the inside of a Howard Johnson's motel room was not the best setting for a seduction scene. The next night, in a much splashier resort in Key West, he made his move. It was just what it should have been but never was—warm, familiar, friendly and nice.

For four days we lingered in the sun and I marveled that like any fool, I, too, could fall in love. David and time had caused me to doubt my abilities. Not since my old boyfriend Willie had I felt happily in love. I assumed I would never again live a normal life.

But now I actually woke up and decided I'd rather be here with Philip than anyplace else in the world.

On the way to the airport, my old anxiety returned. I developed a sudden aversion to Philip, which did not surprise me as I had experienced it before: Often when a man liked me, I started seeing his failings in exaggerated form. I wanted to rush from the car and never see Philip again. On impulse, I grabbed his arm. I thought that since what I wanted to do was run, perhaps I should try the opposite tactic. I asked Philip if he would kiss me every half hour or so until we got back to New York. By the time we got to the airport I felt better and had nearly forgotten about our plan but at ten minutes to five, in front of a whole crowd of passengers waiting to check their bags, Philip pointed to his watch and gave me my kiss.

The day I moved into his apartment in SoHo, he led me into a small room with a wobbly table and a typewriter on it. "You can do your work in here," he said. I worked harder and better than I ever had in the past. Each time one of my articles appeared, he covered the coffee table with copies of the magazine it was in and invited friends over for champagne. People came to our house for dinner, and instead of feeling like the outsider looking in, I felt like the center of a vast and loving world. It was during this period that I received the call from Daisy after she had broken up with Ben. My life seemed so safe and settled in contrast to hers. For the first time since leaving Brooklyn for college, I felt that I had a home.

Not long after we started living together, Philip wrote up a "Franny Worry List":

FICTION

Will never write.
If write, will never finish.
If finish, will never publish.

If publish, critics will pan.
If don't pan, still just a one-book author.

US

We won't get along.
We will get along, which is even worse because we're not right for each other.

Mother will die some day.
Book Review section will never let me write again.
Times Travel section will take out a full-page ad denouncing Fran as terrible person in bold print.
Hers section will read Travel section and never let Fran write.
Mysterious disease, spawned on South Pacific island, carried to mainland by spore, wipes out the winter cantaloupe harvest and threatens summer harvest. (I loved cantaloupes.)
Harvard discovers several mistakes in one of Franny's old Soc Stud papers and after duly giving legal notice by publication in requisite local newspapers of record, revokes Fran's degree.
Reagan appoints Phyllis Schlafly to Supreme Court.
Someone three years younger scoops Fran, publishes autobiography of Fran Schumer first; S.L. (my agent) is her agent.

But if he understood my fears, his humor and tolerance did not ward them off. After a year of living together, the question of our future arose. People were dropping like flies. Girlfriends I was sure would never meet Mr. Right gave up and married Mr. Notwrong. Even men got married. But I didn't feel ready. I had just learned how to eat like a normal person; anything else was asking too much. Besides, Philip and I had our differences. I wanted him to do fifty percent of the housework. He wondered why he should do fifty percent of the housework when he earned ninety percent of the income. I didn't think it was fair to expect me to earn as much as a capitalist pig. Philip wanted to know how come it didn't bother me to live like one.

But our arguments were the sign that something deeper was wrong. While he brooded about oil wells, I stayed in my room. After a year of freelancing, I decided to write a novel. I wrote for three months but nothing exciting happened. Every time I read a review of a novel written by someone my age or younger, I felt ill. Philip used to hand me the paper with at first, the author's age cut out, and then, when things were really bad, the Book Review section deleted altogether, unless the review was bad.

That winter we took a vacation in the Caribbean. One night I went for a walk on the beach. I thought of how wonderful it was to get away from Philip and walk on the beach alone. But when I returned I thought how wonderful it was to have Philip waiting for me. Not long after we got back to New York, Philip suggested we get engaged. I said "Yes," but the next morning changed my mind.

I didn't want to leave Philip and yet I knew I couldn't stay. There was something else I wanted but I didn't know exactly what. I kept going back and forth in my head, changing my mind, driving Philip and everyone else crazy. "It's your fear of intimacy," *Vogue* magazine said. Maybe you're just "profoundly immature" *(Psychology Today)*. "You're crazy and Lillian Potashnik thinks you're crazy, too" (my mother and her Scrabble partner, whose daughter was happily married and living in Teaneck). And what a miserable time it was to break up. People were talking about the return of romance and love and marriage and the oncoming baby boom (at least according to the freelance dreck I wrote). And there I was, once again, out of whack with the rest of the world.

After a few more months of this, I finally moved out. It was the worst time to return to the Upper West Side. My once seedy neighborhood had sprouted awnings and condominiums. No more bodegas that sold cigarettes by the one. Instead of the usual riffraff who made me feel relatively well off, the neighborhood was invaded by relatively normal people who actually got up every day and went to work. At noon a flotilla of Caribbean housekeepers wheeling baby carriages sailed down Broadway.

The day I moved back to New York, my mother and her cleaning woman, Louise, trooped up the five flights to my dilapidated apartment to help clean up the mess my subletter had made. At the top of the landing, my mother looked at me and said, "Franny, I'm getting too old for this." Another fifty-seven-year-old woman might have been referring to the ordeal of climbing up the stairs, but tennis and cottage cheese kept my mother relatively fit. What she meant was, I'm getting too old to watch my daughter keep screwing up her life. My mother and Louise took me out to lunch to cheer me up. They consoled me with the thought that I could always go back to Philip, but that was the worst thing they could have said.

Every time I read a wedding announcement of a friend, I called Philip and begged him to change his mind. Just when he was about to, I changed mine back. I was so desperate I sought the help of psychiatrist number three. "Dr. Young, I know I'm going to leave your office, get into a taxi and haul Philip out of his business meeting and ask him to take me back again. Stop me from doing this. Please. Help." Dr. Young only looked sad and distressed, which he often did. Frankly, I don't think he believed in psychoanalysis any more than I did, which is why I liked him. He encouraged me to continue with the eating program, which was the only thing that seemed to help. They did not psychoanalyze my paralysis but counseled me in more practical terms: "Make a decision and stick to it." Finally, I made a promise to one of my friends in the program that I would not call and ask Philip to marry me again unless I was sure. And this time I kept my word. Philip and I saw each other only once after that. We had previously gotten tickets to see *Death of a Salesman* a week after my final vow. I had brought with me to the theater some of his laundry to return. We cried all through the performance, but Philip did not have a handkerchief so we dried our eyes in his laundered B.V.D.'s.

I spent several miserable months getting over Philip, but after that I no longer regretted my choice. I didn't approve of it either; I just didn't think about it. I went to dozens of meetings of my eating disorder group. All I was told was not to starve or binge and everything would work out, which it did, although not right away.

Not long after I broke up with Philip, David returned. He had called me from Miami, where his plane had just arrived. He said something in Spanish, knowing I didn't understand Spanish, and immediately I remembered what a pain David could be *(¡Que dolor!).* The revolution was always more important to David than any individual he was with. "Okay," he said, lapsing into Imperialist English. "I'll be in your city in a couple of days. I'll call you then."

We sat at McSorley's Ale House in Greenwich Village, as I had recounted to Paige, and I watched David wash down sixteen beers. It was then that he asked me to marry him and I said no.

He shuttled back and forth between New York and Chicago, where he was finishing his book about his travels in southern Africa. The following fall it was published to favorable reviews. Some days I would flick on the TV set and there was David with Phil. Or David with Merv. But he met his match in William Buckley on *Firing Line.* Buckley, after their debate, had the grace to concede that David had won.

We were friends now and although in the past I might have been tempted to make it something more, I wasn't anymore. Still, when my thirty-second birthday came and went and there was no card from David, I felt more than a twinge. It arrived a month later from Swaziland, where he was working on a postscript to his book.

"What woman who I respected would want to give up her life and follow me around the globe?" he asked. His next book required that he spend at least the next two years abroad. Perhaps after that he would think about settling down and joining the bourgeoisie. But I was happy for David. He had not "sold out" as my brother predicted, and had been true to his ideals, which were worth being true to.

I did not see Miranda as frequently as I had when I moved back to New York. Our friendship had suffered a few minor upheavals. She was angry at me for my indecisiveness about Philip. She felt I was "running away." Miranda always did have a fidelity to the unadulterated truth, which is what had put her on such a difficult path. She had to face everything head on and solve each problem without letting any slide. At times I grew weary of her purity. I was angry at her for "projecting her own maladies" on me. In May her father died. They had reconciled in recent years, and she was terribly upset and troubled by his death. It made her somewhat less tolerant of her friends and for a while we did not speak.

In June she was scheduled to get her degree in architecture. I made her tell me one hundred times when and where the ceremony would be. I could have skipped my own graduation and never batted an eye, but I knew I would not miss this. It mattered to me almost more than anything else. "Just look at what that woman has accomplished," my mother said. "You girls got your diploma but Miranda had to fight for hers."

Just about that time, we received our Tenth Year Reunion book from Harvard. It listed Miranda's name and address, but the space for any other details about her achievements was blank.

ONE rainy morning in January, I was sitting in a coffee shop with my father, who now made a point of seeing me after what Johanna had said. "Don't worry, Fran. Life is like streetcars. You miss one, another comes along."

One did. He made me much more miserable than Philip ever had and I worried about him even more than I had worried about my work or getting into Radcliffe, so I knew this was right.

For weeks I was certain something would go wrong but as the

months wore on, I felt more calm. Good fortune makes you look back on your life and see only the good. I felt, perhaps inaccurately, that maybe the worst had passed. All I had to do was get up in the morning and take my chances, like everyone else. I was eating abstinently, which put me on solid ground. I felt ready to send a letter to that psychiatrist in Cambridge who told me now that I had learned how to deal with my mouth, there was only my heart, my mind and my genitals left. I wanted to tell him the basic repair work is finally done.

Epilogue

I did not enjoy my Tenth Year Reunion. Few of the women I cared about were there. Eleanor was working. Tess had no intention of coming. Paige stayed away, frightened that someone might ask her what she was up to. Felicity was listed in the In Memoriam section of the Tenth Year Reunion Report, and David, who was in Nicaragua at the time, sent a message that said, "To quote the Reverend Jesse Jackson, 'God is not finished with me yet.' "

I thought it would all be different, coming back at age thirty instead of sixteen. But I still was not happy wandering in and out of what now looked like the Rouse Corporation version of Harvard Square. The dark and dingy Pewter Pot had been transformed into a cheerful monstrosity called The Greenhouse, and the innards of office buildings had been scooped out and replaced by indoor shopping malls with names like Galleria or Garage. The place looked not like a university town but a utopia for readers of the Living (that is, "Having") section of *The New York Times.* At least Tommy's Lunch had survived, still serving cheese-steak subs made with real processed cheese.

My classmates danced to dinner party music, and if the truth be told, most had dinner party lives: doctors, lawyers and business executives. The typical returnee was married, had a child and a career, and was renovating a house. When I graduated from college, education was the most popular field for women and business the least, but now, according to the career counselors on campus, it was just the reverse.

Only a quarter of the class returned for the reunion, which made the rest of us feel as if everyone else had more important things to do. I bumped into one woman who complained that after twenty years of working as a lawyer, her mother was having an "identity crisis" and wanted to "find herself." "My mother did the eighties in the sixties and is now doing the reverse," she said. I spoke to another I recognized vaguely from my *Crimson* days. You noticed her because she wore a shocking pink silk dress to the dinner dance that night and black patterned stockings with stiletto black heels. I liked her for being flashy, oblivious to the prevailing more professional style. "Let me guess, Agatha," I said, happily remembering her name. "And you're—." "Fran," I replied. "Oh I remember now." And I wondered just what she remembered about me, who had been so disoriented freshman year. We talked about our work on our way to the dinner dance. She, too, was a lawyer. She wanted very much to be married but felt her work was making her "hard." She had read somewhere that women get tough at their professions and lose their romantic allure. There was a lot of talk about that among the single women in our group. A graduate from the Class of '64 told me that within a year, seventy-four percent of the members of her class had been married, whereas in the Class of '74 it seemed that almost no one was.

The entire weekend all I wanted to do was sit down and talk to Daisy, but we were interrupted by events I had no desire to attend: tiresome lunches, fund-raising pitches by an earnest but unctuous Harvard dean whose excessive devotion to the college was cloying. He told us it was mandatory that we all send money to the college to help make it number one in the computer science field. Another deserving cause, he said, was the problem of the "sinking" of Harvard Yard under the weight of the books in

Widener Library. Unless something was done, the books might have to be placed in cold storage in Waltham. One of my more cantankerous classmates asked if it was true that the university was cutting back on its scholarship fund. "I'm afraid so," he said, looking excessively dismayed. It was that earnest look that impelled me, I suppose, to go up to him and tell him that I had been a scholarship student at Harvard, which was pretty much a lie, and that I felt there were more important things in life than being number one.

At a breakfast the following morning, Radcliffe College President Matina Horner talked with us. It had been ten years for her, too; she had become president of Radcliffe College during our junior year. Now she sported a little gray in her raven black hair. It was nice to see her, chatty and much more at ease than she had been when she was first given the job, ethnic and Greek amid Harvard's generally Puritan crowd.

According to Dr. Horner, the women's liberation movement (misnamed, as it was now a social phenomenon broad enough to include men) was entering its more difficult stage. "Women in their thirties are having a very rough time," she said. "It used to be that you had problems getting in the door. Now women are finding there are problems once they get inside. It's one thing when you're dealing with sex ratios," Dr. Horner continued. "It's more difficult when you're dealing with people's hearts."

Her name had made headlines during the spring of our junior year with her theories about women and the fear of success. She said she had not had reason to revise her original position, but I had. In looking back on my progress and that of my friends, I do not think it was our fear of success that hindered us so much as our wanting it so badly.

I thought about success and what it means now to the women I knew. To Daisy it would mean a reason to come home at night. To Paige it would mean being satisfied with a "workmanlike job." To Tess and Eleanor success wouldn't be too different from what they have now: Tess might like to graduate from security to fulfillment in Maslow's hierarchy of needs; Eleanor might like simply more time to do research. And to Miranda success would be building, seeing fanciful plans poured in concrete. To some extent, she has already achieved that.

Not that any of us has tired of chasing the bitch goddess; we've just learned not to let her destroy us. When I first came into my eating program, I was told that eating abstinently was enough. It isn't, but believing it is takes some of the pressure off and perhaps that's all that was required.

There was only one thing I wanted to do at the reunion, which was the real reason I had come back. Just once, I wanted to walk through my freshman dormitory and make it down the hall without having my knees start to shake. I hated that room, 302 Holmes Hall. I never wanted to see it again, which was why I went to the trouble of getting the janitor to find the key and open it up. Bang, he opened the door and I shut my eyes, as if I expected a hundred goblins to come rushing out. All those goblins of growing up—fear, envy, insecurity and sloth. And all that I saw in that room, in which I began my most difficult years, were two opened windows and the loop of a shade fluttering in the breeze.

ABOUT THE AUTHOR

FRAN SCHUMER graduated Phi Beta Kappa from Harvard in 1974. She has been a reporter for various newspapers, an editor at the *Boston Globe,* and a teacher of literature at City College in New York. Her fiction has been published in the *North American Review* and her articles in *New York Magazine,* the *New York Times, The New York Times Book Review, The Nation, Barron's* and *Vogue.* She won a Goodman Loan Award for fiction and is the coauthor of Mary Cunningham's best seller, *Powerplay.* Ms. Schumer lives in New York.